DYLAN

Born in Manchester in 1950, Jonathan Fryer spent his childhood summers in Wales fighting asthma and boredom, becoming an avid reader and collector of books in the process. After ten years of travelling around the world, he settled in London in 1982 and became a regular contributor to BBC radio. His books include a biography of Christopher Isherwood and an edited selection of the writings of George Fox, the founder of the Quakers.

DYLAN

The Nine Lives of Dylan Thomas

Jonathan Fryer

KYLE CATHIE LIMITED

for my dear
Bernice Rubens
fy hoff awdures gymreig

First published 1993 in Great Britain by
Kyle Cathie Limited
7/8 Hatherley Street, London SW1P 2QT

Paperback edition 1994
ISBN 1 85626 158 1

A Cataloguing in Publication record for this title is available from
the British Library.

Typeset by York House Typographic Ltd
Printed in Great Britain by
Cox & Wyman Ltd., Reading, Berks.

CONTENTS

ACKNOWLEDGEMENTS

The author would like to thank Bruce Hunter of David Higham Associates (on behalf of the Dylan Thomas Trustees) for permission to quote from Dylan Thomas's published work.

He is also most grateful to Lady Avebury (daughter of Pamela Hansford Johnson), the late Rupert Shephard (widower of Nicolette Devas) and Rollie McKenna for help with the photographs.

Individual photo credits are as follows:

1, 2: origin unknown; 3, 14, 15, 16, 17, 18, 21: Rollie McKenna; 4, 5: courtesy Lady Avebury; 6, 7, 9: Shephard-Devas collection; 8: Nora Summers; 10: Bill Brandt estate; 11, 12: BBC; 13: Jack Lane; 19: Bunny Adler; 20: Elizabeth Reitell; 22: courtesy Paul Ferris. Sincere thanks to all.

Every possible care has been taken to acknowledge the correct source for the photographs reproduced in this book. The author wishes to apologise to anyone whose copyright may none the less have been unknowingly infringed.

J.F.

FOREWORD

I doubt whether Dylan Thomas and I would have got on. He had a lofty contempt for Oxbridge intellectuals, not to mention globe-trotting aesthetes. And I loathe pubs, drunks and people who wander around with a smouldering cigarette hanging from a corner of their mouth. However, as I was only three when he died, the chances of our meeting were slight.

Yet Dylan did impinge on my consciousness from a very early age. His name was uttered with a mixture of reverence and knowing winks by Welsh landladies, farm-wives and others with whom I was parked as a child. For Dylan was quite a boy, and what could you expect, being a poet and all that? 'That's how you'll probably end up!' one memorable dragon in Rhyll added with a snort, propelling me and my asthmatic wheezing away from the bedroom table with its miniature Snowdon of books, out into the rain for a bracing walk. I shuddered and muttered, 'Not on your nellie!' No martyr me.

Then I'm sure that the second poem I learned off by heart was 'And Death Shall Have No Dominion' (the first was that Words-worth thing about daffodils). I don't think I really grasped exactly what it meant at the time, but I knew that it sounded bloody marvellous. Well, perhaps on that level Thomas and I *would* have understood each other, because the young Dylan felt the same way about words and meaning. He was seduced by the force of his father reading Shakespeare out loud, and words – robust, English words – were his favourite playthings.

Then by one of those very strange coincidences that have punctuated my life, my first nights in London were spent on a friend's sofa in his rather grotty lodgings in Redcliffe Street, Earls Court, where Thomas and his Swansea friends Mervyn Levy and Alfred Janes had taken rooms forty years before. I can't claim the poet's spirit haunted the area, but the aura of bohemianism and sexual licence was almost palpable.

It has been very odd working on someone whose relatively short life has been so well documented; to my knowledge, there are getting on for fifty books about Dylan and his work, some of them shamelessly flimsy. Yet as his fellow Swansea poet Vernon Watkins noted perceptively,[1] Dylan was so responsive a person where he found affinity in others that the number of biographies that might be written about him would almost equal the number of people he seriously and adequately met. This does not, of course, take into account those people like me who have come along afterwards, trying to make sense of it all.

Among all the memoirs and the critiques and the studies, there are two previous full-length biographies of Dylan Thomas: Constantine FitzGibbon's authorized *The Life of Dylan Thomas* (1965), and Paul Ferris's *Dylan Thomas* (1977). Both are fine and fascinating in their way, particularly the Ferris, which discreetly corrects a number of errors in the FitzGibbon. Yet as I have been so painfully made aware in writing about Dylan Thomas, it is not always easy to *know* what is fact. Dylan was a compulsive liar and a good many of the accounts left of him by those closest to him are highly subjective. At times it is easy to see why Dylan lied, especially when he was on the scrounge. But at others, it seems like a gratuitous act, which could only be explained away by perversity or a wish to make life more interesting. This presents great problems for any biographer.

Since 1977 a great deal of new material about the poet has come into the public domain, not least the *Collected Letters* (edited by Paul Ferris) and the memoirs of a number of Dylan's friends and contemporaries. Each offers new insights into Dylan's multifaceted character with its many contradictions. He was chameleon-like, adapting to his surroundings and his current needs – though he did not always remain in control of his changes of camouflage. This has become glaringly obvious to me in the many conversations I have had with people who encountered him professionally and personally.

The new material alone makes a thorough reappraisal of Dylan Thomas overdue. But this biography also differs in a very fundamental way from its predecessors. I was not a personal friend of Thomas and I don't come from Swansea; I have no cherished memory or home territory to protect. But there is another crucial altered perspective. The two earlier biographies seemed to start from the premise that Dylan Thomas was a wonderful poet who had certain glaring character defects which were none the less excusable in the name of Art. I have viewed my subject from the other end of the telescope. Right from the very beginning of the project, I have been asking myself: how could someone who was such a shit (to borrow his widow Caitlin's blunt description) produce such magnificent work at his best?

I use the phrase 'at his best' advisedly. Dylan Thomas's greatest poems – over a dozen, but probably fewer than twenty – are, in my view, among the finest in the English language. One thinks of 'Fern Hill', 'And Death Shall Have No Dominion' and 'Do Not Go Gentle Into That Good Night'. On them rests his reputation. But he did write a lot of less worthy stuff, some of it quite disgracefully opaque. Mellifluous, certainly, but not necessarily very meaningful.

In fact, I believe Thomas was consistently far better as a prose writer than as a poet. I suppose this largely reflects the fact that one cannot get away with quite as much obscurity and stylish word-juggling in prose (unless one is James Joyce) because it is designed to be read at greater speed. For me one of the great ironies of the Thomas reputation is that he actually deserves greater renown as a prose writer than he has been accorded. The best stories in *Portrait of the Artist as a Young Dog*, for example, to my mind rate among the most remarkable English-language short stories of this century, powerfully evocative and deceptively simple. Even some of his many radio broadcasts – assumed at the time to be ephemeral, and mainly produced simply to earn money – manifest an innate sensibility and a skill at handling words of which most scriptwriters can only dream.

Of course, in the popular imagination, poets are far more romantic than prose-writers, and Dylan *is* an extremely romantic figure; this despite his bloated adult physique, his pawing hands and his accidents on the way to the loo. I believe he was not just aware of this romantic image: he played up to it, indeed he created it, as a determined act, at a very tender age. Therein lies what for me is the greatest paradox of all in the complex personality of Dylan Thomas: the calculated, artificial, public persona cohabiting uneasily with an intuitive being of immense sensitivity. The resultant tension could never have been comfortable, and I suspect that in the end, that is what really killed him.

I remember being nearly lynched in Brussels in 1975, at a critics' forum hastily arranged in homage to the Italian film director Pier Paolo Pasolini after his brutal murder, when I said I thought he had got the death he was looking for: violent, slightly mysterious, and with a supporting cast of rough, sexy youths. But I think something similar could be said of Dylan Thomas, equally fairly. As a vital young teenage poet, self-consciously modelling himself on Arthur Rimbaud, he would have found the idea of living beyond the age of forty grotesque. Denied the supremely romantic end of tuberculosis (about which the young Dylan seems to have fantasized repeatedly), he achieved the next best thing: gross abuse of the body through too much drink, rounded off with a probably fatal dose of morphine. I suspect he was ready for death. For all the genius of his last major work, *Under Milk Wood*, he knew that his creative golden era had long since passed. Moreover, he had enjoyed the great good fortune of having loved, and been loved by, a quite remarkable woman, but that relationship was turning sour.

Anyone who visits the Dylan Thomas museum at The Boat House in Laugharne must be struck by the large number of fans, not least from the United States, who still make the pilgrimage there. Even those not normally 'into' poetry seem susceptible to the Dylan magic. Their devotion reflects the passionate loyalty so many people who were close to him felt, even when he had treated them appallingly. Some of them had to pay the price of this friendship long after Dylan's death. The composer Daniel Jones (who died while I was completing this book) became so exasperated by Thomas devotees turning up on his Swansea doorstep uninvited that he routinely turned them all away. The painter

Alfred Janes told me he too was beginning to feel he could no longer have a life of his own because he had been 'marked' as one of Dylan's pals.

I am therefore particularly grateful to Dylan's in-laws and friends like Mervyn Levy and Kay Stahl, who could not have been more welcoming to my questions about their memories and impressions; individual acknowledgements are made in the notes and the photograph credits. It took me a long time to understand the reason for that personal loyalty to Dylan, which could not just be explained by admiration for his poetry. Yet now here I am, at the end of my task, feeling considerable affection for the bugger myself.

1

THE MIDDLE ROOM

1914–1925

Dylan's mam was fiercely protective of her boy right from the moment he was born, on 27 October 1914, in the Thomas family's newly built home at 5 Cwmdonkin Drive, Uplands, in Swansea, South Wales. Local rumour has it that ten years before she had lost a child, probably a boy, who was conceived before her marriage, but was stillborn. As was normal practice at that time, there is no written record of this. A daughter, Nancy, had followed in 1906. Dylan's arrival was like a form of belated blessing for Mrs Thomas, and nothing was going to be allowed to snatch this precious son away from her.

Florence Thomas may have been a simple woman in the eyes of her in-laws and neighbours, but she was doggedly determined. She was also a survivor. She outlived not only her husband but both her children as well. And to the end of her days, her proudest achievement was being the mother of Dylan Thomas.

A later occupant of 5 Cwmdonkin Drive told the author George Tremlett[1] that when he took up the original lino in what had been Dylan's parents' bedroom, he found sheets of Welsh prayers laid out neatly underneath where the bed would have stood. Presumably this was Mrs Thomas's work, because her husband did not hold with such things. Many people today would consider this act an example of almost peasant superstition. But Florence may well have felt that she needed what divine help she could get to preserve both her marriage and her children.

Florence Hannah Williams, to give her her full maiden name, was Dylan's strongest link with the very particular world of rural, Welsh-speaking West Wales, with its myths and its passions and its curious mixture of Celtic romanticism and Christian Nonconformity. It was her family that provided the uncles and aunts and farms and chapels which feature in so many of Dylan's poems, stories and broadcasts.

Born in 1882, Florence was the seventh and last surviving child of a railwayman, George, and his wife Anna; an eighth child, a boy, died while still in his teens. George and Anna, who shared the surname Williams, may well have been cousins; matrimony between close relatives was not uncommon in that part of South Wales. Indeed, Florence herself sometimes made jokes about how incestuous the region was, with occasionally disastrous results for the sanity of the progeny. Her parents grew up on farms in the Llanstephan Peninsula in Carmarthenshire (as that part of Dyfed was then known), barely a mile apart. But George's job on the railways took him to anglicized Swansea, then a town of about 100,000 souls.

Even a century ago, Swansea bore little resemblance to the outsider's preconception of South Wales: the land of pits and miners, slag-heaps and factories belching out smoke. Despite its industrial importance, it was, and is, a rather prim town in parts, with a nice shopping district, though most of the original centre was destroyed during the Second World War. Much of Swansea is distinctly suburban in character. There is, of course, the rougher area of the port. And the Williamses settled in a rather grim little house in Delhi Street, in the working-class area of St Thomas. That was where Florence was born.

Florence was fussed over by her parents and older brothers and sisters, just as she in turn fussed over her own children. Far from stifling her, this seems to have helped make her into a confident and happy girl. Small in stature, with big bright eyes, she had a bubbling personality and a chattering tongue, as well as a highly inventive imagination. In fact, Florence had a fairly elastic interpretation of truth, a characteristic she passed on to her daughter Nancy and – more spectacularly – to her son Dylan. Yet there was no real malice in Florence. She could hold her own in the indiscreet speculations that spiced the women's gossip she so much enjoyed, first while she was a seamstress in a Swansea drapery store, prior to her marriage, then in the kitchen of her marital home. But her little inventions and flights of fancy rarely seem to have had any motivation other than her own or her listeners' amusement, except when there was a member of her family to shelter from attack.

The Williams children often visited their farming relations, and one of Florence's sisters, Ann, herself married a farmer, Jim Jones. He was the Uncle Jim of Dylan's story 'The Peaches', who was more interested in stopping off at pubs to drink the proceeds of the sale of a piglet than in taking care of his nephew or making a success of his farm. That was left to Aunt Annie, whose determination ensured the Joneses' modest well-being in a series of properties; they ended up as tenants of the rather large but dilapidated farm, Fernhill (written as two words in one of Dylan's most substantial and best-known poems).

One of Florence's brothers, Thomas, was a minister of religion, and another of her sisters, Theodosia (Aunt Dosie to Dylan and Nancy), married the bright new minister, David Rees ('Uncle Dai'), who came to preach at the Canaan Chapel in Swansea, where she played the organ. The Reverend Rees was a classical scholar and something of a righteous puritan – a veritable pillar of his local community. The boy Dylan got to know him when he was transferred to the Paraclete Church at Newton, just along the coast from Swansea, on the way to the Mumbles. Dylan didn't think much of this uncle or his brand of religion, later writing uncompromisingly that he hated him from his dandruff to his corns. In return, David Rees was the first, but not the last, to express the opinion that Dylan belonged in a madhouse.

There are conflicting accounts of how and when Florence Williams met her own husband-to-be, David John ('D. J.') Thomas. The most demure one was that D. J. had spotted her in the congregation of the very church where they were to marry on 30 December 1903: the rather smart Congregational Church in Castle Street, Swansea. But another version placed their first encounter at a fair in Johnstown (on the outskirts of Carmarthen), where D. J. was born and his parents still lived. An apparently deliberate vagueness about just how many months before the marriage this meeting took place, and the fact that the wedding was unusually scheduled for the week between Christmas and New Year, give weight to the story whispered around town that the couple had had to get married; the fruit of their supposedly illicit liaison was said to be the stillborn child.

Certainly, for all her giggling, girlish charms, Florence Williams was not the most obvious choice of wife for D. J. Thomas, despite the fact that both their fathers worked for the railways. 'Jack' to his parents Evan and Ann, D. J. was an exceptionally brainy and ambitious child for someone from such a relatively humble background. Born in 1876, he won a scholarship to the University College of Wales at Aberystwyth, emerging in 1899 with a first-class honours degree in English. He would have liked to have gone on to study further, and ideally to have become a university professor. It is not quite clear why he did not, though the most plausible explanation would have been a need to start earning some money. Dylan claimed that his father had also confessed to a ruinous passion when young for the demon drink (whisky to be precise), before weening himself off spirits on to less harmful stout. But it is far from certain that that was true, let alone whether it might have stood in the way of his achieving higher things.

Whatever the reason, D. J. Thomas became a schoolteacher instead. After a few months at Pontypridd County School, he got a job as English master at Swansea Grammar. He disgruntledly stayed in that rut for the rest of his working life. Yet he cannot have found the routine entirely unpleasant, as he seems to have made no serious effort to move elsewhere.

D. J. was twenty-seven when he married the twenty-one-year-old Florence and he had already started to go bald. He was a neat man, correctly if not exactly elegantly dressed, and he was highly sensitive about his receding hair. He tended to keep his hat on, even in the house, to hide it. All in all, he felt that God had dealt him a pretty poor hand. This largely explains why he had little time for organized religion, or indeed God. In contrast to Florence's more traditional and largely unquestioning piety, D. J.'s cynicism towards the Lord of Creation verged on blasphemy at times. A good example was provided many years later when, to Dylan's delight, D. J. went to the window and declared bitterly: 'It's raining, blast Him!'

4

None the less, D. J. had considerable admiration for the legacy of a preacher uncle of his, William Thomas, who is better known in Wales by his bardic name, Gwilym Marles or Marlais (taken from the River Marlais, near his Carmarthenshire birthplace of Llanybydder). Born in 1834, Gwilym Marles started out as a cobbler, before going to study theology in the town of Carmarthen, and then winning a scholarship to Glasgow University. He returned home a Unitarian Minister, and got involved in some heated confrontations over social reform, using the eloquence he had acquired through his education to defend the interests of the sort of humble folk from whom he had sprung. Gwilym was a radical Liberal, who sided with tenants against local landowners. When he was evicted by his own landlord from his chapel of Llwynrhydowen, as a reprisal against his political activities, his loyal congregation followed him. He also had a deep interest in children's education and founded a popular school at Llandysul in Cardiganshire.

However, what made Gwilym Marles's reputation really special for D. J. was that he was a published writer. His first volume of verse came out while he was still at university. Although he only lived to the age of forty-five, he acquired considerable local renown as a Welsh-language poet and polemicist (these days his work is hardly read). D. J. would have liked to have been a writer too, and there is evidence that he wrote some rather undistinguished English verses in his youth. Unable to emulate his uncle's talent, however, D. J. compensated by giving both his own children Gwilym's bardic name: 'Marles', in the case of Nancy, and 'Marlais' in the case of Dylan.

The name 'Dylan' was also a respectful nod to literature. For Dylan is a minor character in that great Welsh classic prose romance the *Mabinogion*: a sea-child of the waves, with rich yellow hair, who supposedly dropped from a virgin's womb when she stepped over a wand held by Math, the son of Mathonwy, the magician king. In the story, the child then headed straight for the sea, where he swam like a fish. It was a most unusual name to give a boy in 1914, though it had had an airing in July of that year, when a now-forgotten opera by Josef Holbrook, *Dylan, Son of the Wave*, was staged at Covent Garden.

The choice of the name seems to have been the cause of a row between Florence and D. J.[2] The normal Welsh pronunciation of

'Dylan' would be 'dullun', and Florence was sure that future schoolmates would tease her golden boy mercilessly as 'the dull one'. Accordingly, she preferred the very English pronunciation 'dillun'. That is how Dylan himself told his first girlfriend, Pamela Hansford Johnson, his name should be pronounced, to rhyme with 'chillun', the 'children' of Negro spirituals.[3] This is still a matter of raging controversy for some purists.

The issue is all the more sensitive for champions of Welsh culture because Dylan Thomas is, in the eyes of the world, Wales's most famous literary son. Yet he turned his back firmly on the Welsh language from an early age. This was despite the fact that both his parents were bilingual: Welsh was actually Florence's preferred tongue; D. J. was far more ambivalent. He seems to have taught some Welsh at one time early in his marriage, at evening classes, to supplement his schoolmaster's pay. He certainly often spoke Welsh with his wife and her relatives, though Nancy's first husband, Haydn Taylor, recalls D. J. laughing at his wife for using it when other English-speaking people were present.[4] Yet D. J. apparently took pleasure in teaching Pamela Hansford Johnson some very basic Welsh on one of her visits to Wales. This makes it all the odder that Dylan never made any serious attempt to learn it. True, Swansea was and is an overwhelmingly English-speaking town. But the reason for Dylan's shunning the Welsh language was more personal: even more than his father, he saw *English* literature as the paragon, though he made copious use of Celtic mood and imagery.

The house in Cwmdonkin Drive the Thomases had moved into only a few months before Dylan's birth was considerably more substantial than their former home in the more downmarket community of Sketty. Dylan himself, who spent half his life at 5 Cwmdonkin Drive, often referred to it as a Glamorgan suburban villa. It still exists and now boasts an incongruous blue memorial plaque to Dylan on its front wall. A semi-detached property, it has its entrance at the side, which Dylan's parents confusingly referred to as 'The Front'. This was a cause of infant mystery to Dylan, as neighbours would talk in hushed tones about how many local men had failed to return from The Front, and the little boy wondered how they had fitted in there in the first place (this seems to have been about the only instance of the First World War impinging on his consciousness). The house is larger than it looks, stretching far back into the rather poky garden. The stark symmetry of its facade, with its large bay-windows, makes it look anonymously respectable – just the sort of house to appeal to a provincial, professional middle class.

The Thomases had not been there very long when, around the time that war broke out, they took on a young live-in maid, Addie, to help with the household chores and look after the forthcoming baby. She was the first in a line of usually non-resident domestic servants and part-time help. This was made possible because Florence, who was in charge of the household accounts, was assisted financially by more affluent members of her family. But she was also expert at juggling bills, often settling accounts with tradesmen only when they started to get really pressing. She also economized on the shopping budget by baking her own bread and bottling her own jams, though she doubtless felt that that was a normal part of being a conscientious housewife and mother anyway.

For D. J., one of the greatest joys of moving into Cwmdonkin Drive was the fact that there was now enough space for him to have a study. This was the middle room downstairs, between the 'best' front room – kept for Sundays and the most important visitors – and the breakfast room and kitchen for everyday use behind. The middle room, with its puttering gas fire, was crammed with books. It was a sanctuary into which D. J. was only too happy to retire, to escape the chatter of his wife and her friends. He would snatch his slippers, which Florence had warmed by the fire, and settle down with one of his beloved tomes. D. J.'s library was substantial, including not only the predictable classics of English literature and a large collection of nineteenth-century poetry, but a fair amount of modern literature as well. D. J. also belonged to the Boots lending library, so he could keep abreast of interesting new English and American novels. The books in the middle room were far more than just texts that he taught at Swansea Grammar School. They were his companions and his inspiration – almost his consolation for living an otherwise humdrum life.

A good many of the boys whom D. J. taught at Swansea Grammar found him an intimidating man. He had a quick temper with those he felt were not giving his chosen subject enough attention or respect. Sometimes he would scream at the boys and grab them by the ears, or rap their knuckles with a ruler and call them worthless guttersnipes. When really riled, he had been known to knock a boy right across the classroom, to his classmates' horrified fascination. D. J. could also be woundingly sarcastic, informing one class that he had already forgotten more than all of them would ever learn in their lifetimes. Yet many of his pupils were enchanted when D. J. read aloud in his wonderfully deep, sonorous voice, which Dylan was fortunate enough to inherit. D. J. genuinely wanted to communicate his love for and knowledge of English literature. As Daniel Jones recorded, for those who showed a genuine interest, he was a master in a million. For the rest, he was a pain.

D. J. was equally selective in his attitude towards his fellow-teachers. There was really only one with whom he got on well, a classics master called W. S. ('Soapy') Davies. D. J. felt that Soapy was more or less on an intellectual par with himself, and therefore someone with whom it was worth having a conversation. They had something else in common as well: a taste for a convivial pint or three. On the Wednesday school half-holidays in particular they would often go off together to the pub. Then D. J. would make his way briskly but carefully up the steep hill that is Cwmdonkin Drive, trying hard not to betray the slightest signs of inebriation. That part of Uplands was full of twitching curtains, and D. J. was a stickler for keeping up appearances. None the less, he could hardly keep his drinking a secret. Of an evening, he would go down to the Uplands Hotel for a few pints; his family could gauge how many by his temper and the redness of his face on his return. Regulars at the pub christened him 'The Professor' and would consult him about his views. He seems to have been more tolerant of untutored pub-goers than he was of apathetic boys. But he almost never invited anyone home.

Before going out to the pub, though, D. J. would often read or tell stories to his children. As Nancy was so much older than Dylan, this meant that the boy heard some relatively advanced things at a very early age, as well as the more usual nursery rhymes and his father's own impromptu doggerel verse. Florence once chided 'Daddy' (as she tended to call D. J., to his irritation) for reading Shakespeare to Dylan when the boy was only four. D. J. maintained that it didn't matter if the lad didn't understand all the words – let alone the psychological complexity of the plays themselves – as he should be able to sense their power. According to Dylan's nostalgic recollections in pubs years later, that is exactly what happened. He relished these sessions with his father, despite the fact that he did not really appreciate the man himself until much later. And he fell in love with words.

Similarly, Dylan lapped up the magnificent language and poetry of the Bible that he heard at Sunday School, and the cadences of the best preachers who came to the Walter Road Congregational Church where Florence took him. As the pubs in Wales were closed on Sundays in those days, D. J. stayed behind at home while the rest of the family was out at church, savouring the peace and quiet. Sometimes one of his own family (so much more aloof from Dylan's childhood world than the Williams clan) would come over on a visit and stay for Sunday lunch.

Florence was quite convinced that Nancy and Dylan were both sickly children and should therefore be treated accordingly. She was a physically affectionate person, who loved to cuddle and kiss her offspring. But she also bustled round making sure little Dylan was properly wrapped up; from an early age he showed signs of being chesty. Florence was particularly nervous about her children's lungs: tuberculosis was her special dread. It was still a major killer at the time in South Wales and she used to claim her father had died of the disease (though actually his death certificate gave the cause of death as pneumonia) and she talked about TB so often that her little boy acquired a morbid fascination with it. Florence was alert to Dylan's every wheezing or shortness of breath. He cried a lot as a baby, and as his cot was in his parents' bedroom, D. J. would rage and invite the maid to 'put the little bugger through the window'.[5] Instead, Addie took the screaming bundle with her to the boxroom at the back of the house where she slept, and which later became Dylan's own room.

Nancy wasn't very impressed with the infant either. Before Dylan came on the scene, she had rather enjoyed being the sole focus of her mother's attention while D. J. was out of the house, and she was not quite old enough to enjoy play-acting at being a sort of surrogate mother herself. She did end up babysitting sometimes, though, when D. J. and Florence went out together. On those occasions, Nancy's best friend Gwevril Dawkins kept her company. Gwevril later remembered Dylan as a ghastly little boy: noisy, undisciplined and used to grabbing things without asking permission. This was the other side to the Dylan-cherub with angelic features and golden curls, who elicited cooing appreciation from the women in church.

The age-gap between Nancy and Dylan was such that they probably never stood a chance of being close friends. Just as he was getting over infancy, she was starting to take an interest in the big world outside. Despite childhood asthma and a weak liver, Nancy was an outgoing child who became theatrical in both the literal and metaphorical sense. She occurs as only a marginal figure in Dylan's adult reminiscences, yet her influence on him was much stronger than he chose to admit. As she didn't leave home until she was twenty-seven, she was a constant presence throughout Dylan's childhood and adolescence. It is difficult to say exactly when brother and sister decided they rather disliked each other, but over the years they both accumulated a number of understandable reasons why they should. From the start, Nancy was hurt that their mother always seemed to side with Dylan in any dispute. She felt Florence was blind to Dylan's faults and was spoiling him rotten.

Mother and daughter did not get on very well in any case. Nancy ridiculed the idea of becoming a busy, devoted housewife like Florence, feeling she was destined for much more exciting things. And Florence thought her daughter was becoming a right little madam. So there was considerable tension in the Thomas household behind its placid exterior.

D. J. may have given Dylan his entrée to literature, but it was Nancy who gave her young brother intimations of a wider world of people beyond the confines of home and relations. Watching her, he also learned how one could make oneself popular by keeping people in stitches of laughter, even if this meant telling whopping lies or employing the sort of language not normally associated with genteel Uplands. Precisely because Nancy was such a good actress, she could see through the infant Dylan's guiles and the way he could wheedle what he wanted from his mother and other gullible individuals. It seems as if, from an early age, Dylan knew Nancy knew what he was up to, and he didn't like it.

Other signals of a world far beyond the closed environment of the Thomas household came from the view of the sea from the upstairs windows at 5 Cwmdonkin Drive. On a clear day, one could see the whole glorious sweep of the bay round to the Mumbles lighthouse. The sea was a permanent near neighbour, forever changing according to the light and the seasons, and it occurs again and again as an image in Dylan's writing. Beyond the water lay Devon, and beyond that a whole wide world. Yet oddly for a child who grew up in a port town, and who enjoyed the sound of exotic names, Dylan did not have recurrent childhood fantasies of distant travel. Instead, the little boy discovered a marvellous mystery-land almost on his own doorstep, which could be turned into the four corners of the earth in his mind.

There were houses on only one side of Cwmdonkin Drive; on the other was a grassy patch that doubled as a grazing area for sheep and a rather inadequate school playing-field – 'cap-sized', as Dylan himself described it, with deliberate and typical ambiguity. But beyond that was the wonderland of Cwmdonkin Park, which Dylan later called (in his radio broadcast, 'Reminiscences of Childhood') a world within the world of Swansea sea-town. The park comprised several acres of gardens and recreational facilities, full of terrors and secret treasures, fit to fire his burgeoning imagination. The young maid Addie was the first to take him there, in his pram, for airings when the weather was fine. But the park really took on special significance for Dylan when he was old enough to run around and explore it with other boys from the neighbourhood, while his big sister Nancy, with what he called her braying 'hockey-voice', went off in her black-and-white gymslip with her own friends from school. Once Dylan's mother had ensured he was sufficiently wrapped up in vests and pullovers, he was free.

The park had been laid out across a steep hillside by what had been an old reservoir that also ran beneath the adjoining playing-field. There was a scenic lake, whose water, forbidden to bathers, was protected by angry swans. In Dylan's time, Cwmdonkin Park still boasted a bandstand, as well as notices telling people to keep off the grass. Rather than go into the park through the gates, like ordinary, unadventurous human beings, little Dylan and his closest mates would scramble under a piece of broken wire fence, then make their way up the curving moss-covered alleyways and steps that ran between the evergreens, the alpine firs, the monkey-puzzle trees and the more exotic palmettos and yuccas. As Dylan grew older, so the inner secrets of the park were revealed: its numerous hiding-places and dens, where cowboys and indians could plot ambushes, and pirates and robbers set scaring dares and devise awful punishments for those who failed the tests and challenges of the moment. The boys organized beetle races under the bushes, and lit fires for roasting potatoes.

In Dylan's mind, the trees and the bushes were also the territory of nightmare creatures who had made the park their home. On summer nights, as he lay in bed listening to the cries of older children still out playing in the park, he would wait for the shadows of the twilight to come, savouring the thought that the hour was approaching when those dreadful creatures and monsters would come into their own.

The real-life human inhabitants of the park were another constant source of fascination. There was the old man who sat on the same bench, summer and winter, staring out over the lake. The frightening ex-policeman who arrived regularly as clockwork, to check how the dahlias were doing. The old woman in a bath-chair, accompanied by six snuffling Pekinese dogs and a chillingly pale girl, who read to her from a newspaper. And the hunchback man, who became the subject of one of Dylan's most haunting poems,[6] who stayed in the park from the moment the gates opened in the morning till the closing bell sounded. He ate bread from a newspaper and drank water from the little metal cup on a chain that hung from the water fountain. Naughty local boys sometimes filled the cup with gravel and jeered at the hunchback until he shook his paper at them, sending them skipping away, laughing, past the rockery and the flower-beds and the surly park-keeper with his spiked stick for picking up litter. When these pleasures palled, they could always go and see who were making fools of themselves on the tennis courts or the bowling-green, or creep up on couples smooching in the rose-garden.

The young Dylan (as the poet remembered himself in both poems and radio broadcasts) was as wild but strawberry-innocent as his companions in the park, as they schemed and invented and founded secret societies. Dylan was small and semi-officially sickly, but out with the other lads he could cast aside these handicaps and be swift and tough. As curious as a kitten, he was mindless of many of the risks of play. He repeatedly fell off walls and out of trees. Once he plummeted down over the stair-banister in a friend's house, breaking his nose. The result became one of Dylan's distinguishing features, and his life turned into a saga of fractures and breaks of what his wife Caitlin called his 'chicken bones'.

There were friends outside Uplands, too. Often Dylan went away to stay for weekends with Aunt Dosie and Uncle Dai Rees, the preacher at the Paraclete Church at Newton. Guests there were expected to attend chapel three times on a Sunday: morning service at eleven, Sunday School at two-thirty and evening service at six-thirty. No wonder Dylan had little trouble winning his Swansea Sunday School certificate, which he proudly displayed on his bedroom wall. But he made up for all this enforced juvenile piety by playing in the streets of Newton with a lad who went on to become the local grocer. This grocer told Constantine FitzGibbon[7] that Dylan and he used to make simple paper boats and race them in the swift-flowing open gutter that ran from a pump at the centre of the steep-streeted village.

At Fernhill, Aunt Annie and Uncle John's isolated farm at Llangain, there were no children of Dylan's age. But Dylan looked on his much older male cousin Idris with a degree of wonderment. Idris is the 'Gwilym' of Dylan's story 'The Peaches' – the trainee preacher who practises his hellfire oratory from the back of a farm-cart on an appreciative audience of two small boys. In the story, 'Gwilym' asks the boys to confess their sins, and little Dylan mentally runs through a catalogue of his own offences, such as beating a dog to make it lick his hand, and dropping his trousers to give a friend of his a look. More momentously, the real-life Dylan claimed he once caught sight of Idris himself sitting on the outdoor loo at Fernhill, masturbating, while studying a magazine in his other hand.

Long before Dylan felt his own sexual awakening, his fertile mind was filled with terrible imaginings and fantasies about the farm. Fernhill was a dank, dark house, built round three sides of a small farmyard. Only the kitchen was bright and cosy, with its roaring fire sending reflections off the polished brass on to the sides of cured bacon hanging from the rafters. Aunt Annie kept a few pigs and dairy cows, out of which she tried to make enough money to support the family.

The front sitting-room at Fernhill was dusty and neglected, its poor furnishings including a wilting fern and a forlorn stuffed fox. There was a smell of animals and damp and rotten wood about the house, and the stairs creaked. There was no electricity, of course, only oil-lamps, and the boy would take a candle with him up to bed. Its flame would quiver in the draughts and the curtains at his window waved menacingly in front of the night sky. In the boy's imagination, ghostly visitors moved about the house, passing through walls and over people's beds. He imagined some of these to be vampires, but others were reportedly the souls of the victims of a public hangman at Carmarthen jail, who was supposed to have once lived in the house, and even to have hanged himself there. This was as the result of his inconsolable grief at the escape and elopement of a lovely daughter whom he had tried to keep prisoner in a tiny room without windows. Whatever the truth of this particularly gruesome local legend, the bars on the downstairs windows certainly helped give Fernhill a sinister atmosphere.

According to Dylan's broadcast recollections, the ramshackle outbuildings at the farm had tumbling roofs, broken shutters and great jagged holes in their sides. Inside was a mess of rubbish and broken bottles. The lean farm cat and some scraggly hens would make their way through the mud and piles of useless rotten wood in the farmyard, surviving as best they could. But there was another side to the generally deprived nature of the place, especially in summer. Then Dylan would muck in with everyone else and help bring in the hay from the meadow that ran up the hillside, or sit under the boughs of the apple trees in the orchard. So in its own dirty, chaotic way, Fernhill was a child's paradise, and it won an important place in the firmament of the poet's remembrance of things past.

Back in Swansea, Florence Thomas would react to her boy's occasional coughing up blood by packing him off to bed. The blood probably resulted from some form of temporary haemorrhaging in Dylan's lungs, though he once tried to frighten his mother by telling her that the blood in his handkerchief had come out of his ears. Once in bed, propped up with pillows and swathed in blankets, Dylan would be fed bowls of milk and salted bread cut into neat little squares. This dish became a reliable comforter for Dylan for the rest of his life – the simple recipe was passed on by his mother to his wife, to be prepared and lovingly served whenever he was ill, depressed or struck down by a particularly vicious hangover. In the eyes of some of his friends and in-laws, those little milk-sodden squares of bread were symptomatic of a side of Dylan's character that never really grew out of infancy.

The boy's illnesses persuaded Florence that it would be most unsafe to send him to school until he was seven. Surprisingly, D. J. – who readily put his foot down with his wife in other matters – seems to have accepted her decision on Dylan's schooling with equanimity. Though he did not try to give his son much formal schooling at home, D. J. was none the less delighted that the boy had taken to reading like a duck to water. And if Dylan was lying in bed, devouring books from D. J.'s library for hours on end, what did it matter that he wasn't getting a more conventional primary education?

In fact, when the time came when even Florence accepted that her son ought to go to school, the choice was certainly not made on the grounds of academic excellence. Rather than going to the local (free) primary school, where at least the 'three Rs' were adequately taught, Dylan was sent to the more socially desirable, but educationally inferior, fee-paying dame-school in nearby Mirador Crescent. The painter Mervyn Levy, who was Dylan's contemporary at the school, claims that they learned nothing whatsoever there. Although that is undoubtedly an exaggeration, the institution run by the memorably named Mrs Hole seems to have been little more than a glorified child-minding centre. There were only a couple of dozen children, both girls and boys, and once the daily hymn and prayer were out of the way, the emphasis seems to have been on keeping them amused. In 'Reminiscences of Childhood' Dylan affectionately recalled Mrs Hole's school as 'firm and kind and smelling of galoshes'. When the children were good, one of the teachers would read fairy stories to them, a little girl standing behind her and massaging her neck as she did so. The children's book which most stuck in Dylan's mind was *Struwwelpeter*, with its graphic portrayal of the scissor-handed tailor who cuts off the thumbs of boys who suck them. The image of having his fingers chopped off (and later, a more intimate part of his anatomy) became one of the adult Dylan's set-piece nightmare horrors.

Mrs Hole was already quite elderly by the time Dylan went to her school, and he seems to have looked on her as a kind of honorary grandmother. There was a Mr Hole too, a middle-aged son who lived on the premises. He was a red-faced man, who was said to go through life semi-permanently drunk. He allegedly thrilled Dylan and his more ghoulish little classmates by informing them that the curious string with shrivelled things hanging down from it, which decorated the mantelpiece of his room, was in fact a chain of puppy-dogs' tails that he had bitten off with his own teeth.

Mrs Hole's daughter, who helped with the teaching, was a very different character, gentle and patient and apparently enchanted by the curly-haired devil–angel Dylan. He would clamber up on her knee whenever he had the opportunity, and if he was asked to do anything he didn't want to do, he would put on the wheedling voice that Nancy loathed so much and complain that he had a pain in his tummy.

It is hardly surprising that the adult Dylan looked back on Mrs Hole's little school with so much affection, as he seems to have been able to get away with almost anything there. Naughty children were usually sent tearfully upstairs, to the room where unharmonious piano lessons were given. But Dylan generally seems to have managed to pass on the blame when he did wrong. When he knocked a little girl off her chair, upsetting an aspidistra in the process, Dylan was happy for the girl herself to be held responsible. And when he fell down in the lane at the back of the school and cut his knee on a piece of broken glass, he ran home and said that the same little girl had pushed him. This brought Florence round to the school in a rage of protective fury.

The narrow lane behind the school was the scene of much mischief and shared secrets. A lively barter market operated there, as the children swopped marbles for old knives, kite strings for foreign stamps, and 'gob-stoppers' for slings. Gob-stoppers were one of Dylan's favourite things, along with hard-boiled sweets, toffee, fudge and marzipan bought from Mrs Ferguson's sweetshop ('Fergy's') on his way home.

The lane behind the school was also where the kids showed off. The bigger boys would throw pebbles up at windows, while the smaller ones vied with each other to establish a pecking-order, more often than not based on sheer bluff. One would claim – falsely – that his father was a policeman, while another said his father had a chauffeur. Finding little he could brag about, true or false, the child Dylan (in his partly fictionalized adult recollections for radio) stuns everyone by announcing that he can fly. He starts flapping his arms, and in his imagination, he takes off over the grey tile roofs and the bay below. But Dylan really did impress some of his classmates one day, when he undid his fly and started peeing against a wall, declaring, 'Look! I can write *God Save the*

King!' In later life, Dylan also claimed that as a child he drank some of his own urine, to see what it tasted like.

As Mervyn Levy recalls, Dylan was certainly an unusual little boy. So childish in some ways, he would startle Mrs Hole by suddenly quoting chunks of Shakespeare's *Richard II* off by heart. But the thing which really struck Levy, and was a major reason for their becoming close friends, was the intensity of Dylan's emotions when confronted with something that genuinely interested him. On one particularly memorable occasion, Dylan was visiting Mervyn at his home. Mervyn's mother had died when he was only eight, and his father employed a succession of nursemaids to look after him. One of these was a particularly buxom lass and Mervyn speculated with Dylan that she probably washed her breasts in the handbasin.[8] The glass panels of the bathroom door in the Levys' house were masked by thin coloured paper, designed to imitate the effect of stained glass. One day, during the school holidays, the two friends made two tiny peepholes in the coloured paper, and after waiting for the maid to go into the bathroom, had their suspicions confirmed. Dylan was nearly beside himself with excitement, not out of any precocious sexual desire, but for the sheer daringness of it all. Mervyn was almost as fascinated by Dylan's reaction as he was by the ablutions they had just witnessed. It was almost as if part of Dylan was standing outside his body, enjoying his own excitement and egging himself on.

More conventional boyhood experience-gathering included picking cigarette-butts up off the street and smoking them in secret. Although the first such occasion left Dylan feeling green and distinctly off his tea, he persevered, and effectively became a chain-smoker from the age of fifteen, doing nothing to enhance the state of his lungs or diminish his asthma.

The initiation into the temptations of the weed seems to have started more or less simultaneously with an even more exciting new pastime: deception and theft. In one of its more harmless forms, this would manifest itself in sneaking into the local Uplands cinema without paying. Films became a serious passion with Dylan, who would roar with the other boys when there were boring bits in a film, but the rest of the time he was watching and learning. The pictures were all the more satisfying when spiced with the knowledge that one had got in free. And as little Dylan grew older and more street-wise, he became an adept filcher of money from his mother's handbag, sweets from Fergy's shop and small items which caught his eye.

Yet in Florence's eyes, Dylan could do virtually no wrong. In one cringe-making episode at the Mirador Crescent school, he appeared in a Yuletide end-of-term entertainment. He had been assigned a rather low-key role as an army officer, who was meant to walk around looking serious, carrying a cane and reading a newspaper. But the showman in Dylan took over, as he made a hole in the newspaper and started shooting orange pips through it at the audience. Then he leaped around the stage, slashing the air with his cane and frightening the other characters away, until the show ended in pandemonium. Far from reprimanding her show-off son, Florence is said to have been delighted with the spectacle.

She was pleased, but rather non-plussed, when Dylan began writing poetry. This seems to have started quite soon after he went to the dame-school, by the time he was eight or nine at the latest. Florence discovered that the only way of stopping her boy running out in the rain was to give him some paper and a pencil. He would then go meekly up to his room and write and write. From the beginning he was writing poems. He quickly understood that his mother wasn't exactly a born literary critic, and as D. J. tended to be out at work, or at the pub, or holed up in the middle room, it was Nancy who found herself constantly pestered for instant judgements of his efforts. This was not a role she relished. In fact, Dylan's recurrent appearances, bearing his latest childish creation, exasperated her so much that she would send him away, telling him to write a poem about an onion or the kitchen sink. Undeterred, he would take this as a challenge and do precisely that.

Florence passed some of Dylan's juvenile poems on to a friend of hers, but seems to have burned the rest. The ones that do survive suggest a mind still coming to terms with the power of words as a means of expressing reality and emotion. Yet the boy already commanded an unusually extensive vocabulary. Some of those surviving examples of juvenilia have clearly been annotated by D. J., who must therefore have started to take an interest in what his son was producing once it became clear that this was something more than just child's play.

Much of the style and the language of those early verses is imitative, and one could hardly expect otherwise. But unlike many child poets who practise in the well-trodden fields of romanticism and lyricism, before moving on to something more abstract and intellectual, Dylan was laying the foundations of a new evolution of those very qualities of lyricism and romanticism, in stark contrast to most of the contemporary verse being produced.

2

THE RIMBAUD OF CWMDONKIN DRIVE

1925–1932

Dylan was nearly eleven when he entered Swansea Grammar School at Mount Pleasant, in September 1925. It was a fairly forbidding institution, standing tall and stark on the top of a hill (which made it an easy casualty of German bombing raids over Swansea in the Second World War). But in many ways it was the obvious place for Dylan to go, as a respectable fee-paying school designed to encourage the best talents of the sons of Swansea's middle class. The fact that D. J. Thomas was by now the senior English master there doubtless helped his son's placing in class 3A – the top stream for the brighter and better-educated lads – despite the fact that Dylan was younger than most of his classmates and considerably less well versed in almost every academic area except English. This was a situation that lasted for the boy's entire secondary school career, as he regularly came bottom of the class in every subject except the only one he thought worth his attention. This meant that there would be very little chance of Dylan's achieving D. J.'s ambition for him to go on to university, preferably Oxford.

Yet D. J. seems to have been remarkably indulgent about his son's scholastic indolence, presumably because Dylan's all-consuming passion for literature mirrored his own. Moreover, for all its severe exterior, Swansea Grammar was a notably progressive institution, which sought to help boys discover and realize their potential in whichever field it lay, rather than forcing everyone to conform and become competent all-rounders. This was largely thanks to the headmaster, Trevor Owen, a large, kind-natured man who did not believe in either regular corporal punishment or compulsory games. Mr Owen had been at the school since 1901 and had been responsible for getting D. J. on to the staff. He had a high regard for D. J.'s teaching, which meant that Dylan was doubly protected from the wrath of other masters that might well have fallen on any other boy at the school who was as persistently lazy and mischievous, but who didn't have the senior English master as his father.

Not that all the teachers at Swansea Grammar let Dylan get away with murder. The Latin master who taught 3A, J. Morgan Williams, used to start every lesson by asking those boys who had failed to do their homework to put up their hands. One day, when Dylan did not have his hand up, and hadn't done his homework either, Mr Williams gave him a sharp clip around the ear. Few of his colleagues would have dared to do the same, in case D. J. complained. Besides, as they quickly discovered, when Dylan felt cornered, under threat or merely about to be forced to do something he didn't want to do, he would often bring on an asthma attack. These could turn quite nasty and keep him off school for a week. So for everybody's peace of mind, many of the teachers decided it was best to leave him alone. As he progressed through the school, Dylan responded to this liberal attitude with insolence. When one of the maths teachers accused him (correctly) of cribbing, Dylan stood up and said that if that was what he thought, he would not come to any more of his classes – and didn't.

Many of the 400 or so boys at Swansea Grammar also learned to deal cautiously with Dylan. Initially, he was picked on because of his small size and rather girlish looks. As a newcomer at school, he got tossed into the bushes round the lower playground by the bigger boys. One group of classroom bullies used regularly to stuff him into the waste-paper bin, bum first, so he couldn't get out. This caused one of the masters to incant ritually on entering the room: 'Take Dylan out of the basket!' But Dylan soon learned how to fight back. Inside the little angel-faced, tousled-haired creature lurked a pugnacious demon who realized that unfettered aggression and surprise could overcome mere brawn. Once some of the larger lads had been bitten, scratched and kicked in the goolies by Dylan, they thought it wiser to give him a wide berth. Sometimes Dylan didn't even have to show his claws. By this time he had acquired a formidable vocabulary of graphic swearwords (largely picked up from D. J.), which he could use to stun some of his classroom adversaries into grudging respect.

One of Dylan's most memorable schoolboy brawls is recorded in his story 'The Fight', published in the collection *Portrait of the Artist as a Young Dog*. His opponent on this occasion was a rabbit-faced boy, Daniel Jones, later to become a polymath composer. Jones was nearly two years older than Dylan, but was a contemporary in 3A. According to the story – which Dan Jones says sticks fairly closely to the truth[1] – Dylan was standing down on the lower playground at the beginning of the lunch-break, staring through the railings at a man who was sitting in his garden in a deckchair, reading a newspaper. Dylan was determined to continue staring at the man until he made him lose his temper. All of a sudden, however, he was pushed hard from behind by Dan Jones, which made him fall down a bank. Dylan then threw a stone at Dan, who calmly took off his spectacles, hung his blazer on the railings and launched an attack.

The man in the deckchair, who had stopped pretending he hadn't noticed what was going on, folded up his newspaper and stood up to watch. Momentarily distracted, Dylan received two sharp punches from Dan, and fell against the railings. By now the man was jumping about with excitement at the fight. Dylan picked himself up and butted Dan Jones hard, sending them both rolling about in a heap. The man then made the mistake of cheering them on, at which point the two boys turned on him instead, throwing gravel over the railings at him as he tried to beat a dignified retreat to his deckchair. The earlier hostility between the two boys melted into instant comradeship. As they walked home together, Dylan admired Dan's bleeding nose, while Dan assessed the finer points of Dylan's black eye. When Dylan returned to school after dinner at home, he was sporting an eye-patch.

At the beginning of their friendship, Dylan and Dan often went to 5 Cwmdonkin Drive, where they would settle down in the middle room and discuss the merits of various books around them.

Literature was their strongest common bond; the precocious Dan had already written several childhood 'novels'. But soon the invitations to the Thomas home stopped. When Mrs Thomas ran into Mrs Jones in the street one day, she explained in embarrassment that D. J. had enough of seeing boys at school without having them around during his free time. Besides, the atmosphere in the Thomas household was not good during Dylan's time at school. D. J. often lost his temper with Florence and shouted at her. And Dylan's relations with Nancy had hit a new low. This seems partly to have been because one day – it's not exactly certain when – he raided her wardrobe, dressed himself up in her clothes and stood in the street, flirting outrageously with the boys who walked past. Nancy was not amused.

None the less, Dylan did try to communicate with his sister at times, if only because there was really no one else around. One childhood letter from Dylan to Nancy survives, sadly undated but presumably written when one or other of them was away on a short holiday, probably with relatives. In it, young Dylan is experimenting with words, punning and joking. One gets the impression that this was as much for his own benefit as for the enjoyment of his sister. In the letter,[2] Dylan wonders in rhyme why it is that if a drummer is a man who plays drums, a plumber has nothing to do with plums. And if a cheerful man who sells one hats can be a cheerful hatter, why is it that a serious man who sells one mats is hardly a serious matter? What Nancy made of these adolescent musings is not on record.

D. J., meanwhile, was delighted that Dylan was still writing poems. In his very first term at Swansea Grammar, Dylan got one into the school magazine (for which D. J. was the editorial overseer, ultimately responsible for the contents, even though schoolboy editors selected the pieces themselves). It is a jolly little verse, entitled 'Song of the Mischievous Dog', written from the point of view of a dog that likes to take a bite at a plump calf or other well-padded piece of exposed flesh. This was an imagined situation that became a positive obsession with Dylan.

In Dylan's memory, it always snowed at Christmas. As he recalled in a 1945 BBC broadcast, 'Memories of Christmas' (a precursor of the immensely popular *A Child's Christmas in Wales*), this brought new japes and joys. Cwmdonkin Park was deserted, making the old swans tempting targets for well-aimed stones. Cats foolish enough to show themselves on fences would be pelted with snowballs between the eyes. The best tea-tray from home was turned into a makeshift toboggan. On one glorious occasion, when the local grocer went out skating, he disappeared through a hole in the ice. Dylan and his pals would go down to the sea and wander along the deserted white shore, wondering if the fish could see that it was snowing. Back at home, Dylan would warm his chilled hands in front of the fire and wince with the pain as they thawed.

Over Christmas, the house was full of uncles and aunts, hitting the sherry and the elderberry wine and cracking awful jokes. Every year 'Uncle Arnold' would pull a nut out of the glass bowl on the cluttered table in the front parlour and say ponderously, 'I've got a shoe-nut here. Fetch me a shoe-horn to open it, boy.'[3] It was 'Uncle Arnold' who always seemed to find the silver threepenny piece in the Christmas pudding. 'Auntie Hannah', who had a little seasonal weakness for port, would stand in the snowbound back-yard and sing like a thrush. Mistletoe hung from the gas brackets and chestnuts roasted in the fire. Dylan would sit among the paper festoons, nibbling dates and playing with his presents, or blowing up balloons until they burst and made his snoozing uncles jump.

Winter and summer, the sea-shore was a favourite place for Dylan and his schoolfriends to linger, especially on the Wednesday half-holidays. He would scour the ground, hoping to find a gold watch, or a corpse, or even a message in a bottle, thrown into the sea by some shipwrecked sailor and washed up on Swansea shore. Emboldened by the company of other boys, Dylan started to explore the seamier parts of town around the gasworks and the slaughterhouse. Well away from the eyes of family and neigh-bours, they would whistle in the streets or make rude remarks to strangers, and wink at older girls who walked along the promen-ade near the cindery recreation ground where the boys played an improvised version of cricket. Sometimes they would ride the splendid double-decker tram that clattered along the coast to the Mumbles, where they would clamber down below the pier, hang-ing from the girders and swinging their legs.

Although Dylan showed no real interest in sport other than cricket, he gave the lie to his status of a semi-invalid by winning a number of athletic events in his early years at school. In June 1926, for example, he won the one-mile race for the under-fifteens. True, he seems to have been given a 100-yard handicap start, because of his small size, but he was inordinately proud of the achievement. He got his picture in the local paper, looking spindly-armed and rather dazed; he still had the newspaper cutting in his wallet when he died twenty-seven years later.

Shortly after Dylan's running triumph, disaster struck when he had a serious road accident. He was a dare-devil cyclist, who loved to pelt down steep hills. But one day, while heading for the Mumbles, he collided with a van. He broke his right wrist and was in hospital for a month. Although only eleven, he was put into the grown men's ward. He was fascinated by one of his fellow patients who had fallen down inside a ship's hold, and he asked D. J. to bring the man cigarettes. Dylan's arm was still in plaster when he got home, so the doctor told Florence to make him practise writing left-handed. As she told Paul Ferris years later,[4] she sat Dylan out by a table in the garden, with a lot of paper and pencils. But when she looked out of the window shortly afterwards, he was just sitting there with his feet up on the table, smoking a cigarette.

It wasn't until nearly the end of 1926 that Dylan got another poem into the school magazine. But by then he had started to set his sights higher. He sent off a poem entitled 'His Requiem' to the *Western Mail* newspaper in Cardiff, which paid him for it and printed it, in the 'Wales Day by Day' column, over the signature D. M. Thomas, on 14 January 1927. The poem is romantically sad, involving a bird's mourning for an unloved old man. Dylan cut it out and stuck it on the mirror in his bedroom, having scrawled across it 'Homer Nods!' In his story 'The Fight', he writes that he was always waiting for the opportunity to take someone into his room, so they would see the poem accidentally, but only his mother ever did so. He comments in the story that he had also displayed the poem to make himself blush, but that after a while 'the shame of the poem had died'. It was nearly twenty years after Dylan's death that the true meaning of this phrase became clear. In 1971, the *Sunday Telegraph* reprinted 'His Requiem', which appeared in a new collection of Dylan Thomas's poems, edited by Daniel Jones. A sharp-eyed *Telegraph* reader identified it as the work of a popular children's writer, Lillian Gard, who had published it in the *Boys' Own Paper* in November 1923. Dylan's version differs only very slightly from Miss Gard's original. In a nutshell, this was blatant plagiarism.

Given that Dylan was writing so much of his own poetry, it is at first hard to understand why he felt it necessary to steal someone else's. Perhaps he was just desperate to see his name in print and thought he might have a better chance with the proven work of a professional. But I suspect he also saw the whole episode as a challenge, to see if he could get away with it. He doesn't seem to have let anyone in on the scheme, not even Dan Jones. Moreover, this is not the only example of the young Dylan's literary theft. In 1929, E. F. McInerny, who was at that time editing the Swansea Grammar School magazine, received a short poem from Dylan called 'Sometimes'. He planned to publish it until a colleague said it sounded familiar; sure enough, it was the work of the American poet Thomas S. Jones, and had appeared in Arthur Mee's *The Children's Encyclopaedia*. McInerny felt obliged to report this matter to D. J., who was most distressed.

Otherwise, Dylan's poems in his schooldays were imitative, rather than outright steals. The influence of Walter de la Mare and John Keats is particularly noticeable. There is nothing reprehensible in that; many poets only develop their own voice after practising using the style of others. Most have literary heroes, who act consciously or unconsciously as models. The walls of Dylan's bedroom acted as his pantheon of heroes, as they were decorated with pictures of a wide range of writers, many of them cut out of D. J.'s literary magazines. Apart from Walter de la Mare, they included William Shakespeare, Robert Browning, Rupert Brooke and the American Quaker poet John Greenleaf Whittier.

Dylan was delighted to acquire a new potential critic on whom to try out his poems when Nancy started seeing a regular boyfriend. This was Haydn Taylor, a handsome young English insurance salesman, who was sent to Swansea by his firm in February 1926. Haydn, like Nancy, had a great passion for amateur dramatics, and that was how they met. As he had two aunts called Nancy, both of whom he loathed, Haydn tended to call Dylan's Nancy 'Thomas'. After a while, 'Thomas' started to invite him home, and they would be allowed to sit in the front parlour. As Haydn had gentle canoodling in mind, he was more than a little irritated by the frequent interruptions there by 'this wretched boy with his exercise book, forever wanting to read me his poems, which I didn't understand – not then or now.'[5] To make matters worse, Nancy had to warn her suitor not to leave his wallet in an unattended jacket. At least one of her girlfriends had already had money pinched from her purse when she called at Cwmdonkin Drive.

There is little wonder, therefore, that when Dan Jones visited the Thomas household, he had the impression that Nancy behaved as if her brother and he did not exist. By now a strikingly attractive young lady, she would swirl out in her perfume and furs for dates with Haydn, barely giving the two boys a glance. Dan thought her tremendously attractive and elegant, and had to remind himself that she was his friend's sister.[6]

By the beginning of 1927, though, Dan and Dylan would usually meet at Dan's home in Sketty, about ten minutes' walk away, rather than at Cwmdonkin Drive. 'Warmley', as the Joneses' house at 38 Eversley Road was called, was a larger and much more artistic home than the Thomases', boasting three sitting-rooms and a sizable attic, as well as a back garden big enough to play a kind of cricket in. Dan lived there with his father and mother, an elder brother called Jim, and a cousin of his mother's who was always referred to as Aunt Alice.

Mr Jones was a man of considerable culture but few academic pretensions (unlike his younger son). He had very wide-ranging interests covering music and the arts, literature in the broadest sense, and the natural sciences. He was an adjudicator at *eisteddfodau* – the Welsh bardic gatherings and musical competitions – at both local and national level. He had a rich sense of humour and a well-endowed fund of stories about Welsh folklore and the odd characters he had come across in rural Wales. These kept Dylan enthralled. Mrs Jones had been a singer, and still played the piano with gusto. By the time Dylan entered the Jones household as a kind of honorary third son, however, she was concentrating more on elaborate tapestries and needlework, which were of exhibition standard.

But it was Aunt Alice who had done most to educate Daniel Jones, teaching him at home from the age of five until he went to Swansea Grammar. He began piano lessons with her while still an infant, and claimed to have composed his first piano piece when he was four. He had carried on writing music, though at school he was thought of more as a poet. This in itself would have been reason enough for Daniel and Dylan to be friends – or fierce rivals. Dan's seniority, and the easy, semi-bohemian atmosphere of the 'Warmley' household, meant that Dylan looked on him, at least in the beginning, with a degree of admiration and respect. Not to be outdone, however, Dylan made his own impression, on both Dan and his parents, with his attractively cheeky sense of fun and the superficially careless display of a half-convincing worldliness.

For example, Dylan claimed (doubtless falsely) to have played strip poker with the maids at Mervyn Levy's house. And when Mrs Jones brought in a plate of figs one day, he bit into one and declared to Daniel's gratifying awe that it was just like sucking a woman's cunt. Soon it dawned on Dan, however, that Dylan's precocious sensuality was something he had acquired not by direct experience, but rather through reading, or observing Nancy clandestinely, or listening to the stories told by older youths who gathered under Swansea's railway bridges, or simply by his hyperactive imagination. If anything, Dan observed, Dylan seemed to have even less interest in actually getting to know any girls than most schoolboys of his age.

So while Jim Jones went off to the cinema with his latest 'date', or to play real cricket with other sporty young men, Dan and Dylan burned up much of their juvenile energy in violent horseplay. They would engage in bouts of a kind of karate, or lively cushion-fights – the sort of activity that was quite unimaginable in the less liberal atmosphere of Cwmdonkin Drive. Dylan would throw himself with vigour into such childish occupations, then all of a sudden decide he wanted to do something else, like going into the garden to play cricket, or discussing a book. Usually he was the one who dictated what the two boys did.

More often than not, though, the arts beckoned. The fact that Dylan had no musical talent or knowledge was no bar to his being willingly recruited into the riotous 'concerts' put on at 'Warmley' either just by the boys or with the assistance of everyone else present. While Daniel and those who could actually play a musical instrument did so, Dylan accompanied on percussion. This included a collection of biscuit tins and a rubber motor horn that had been doctored to make extremely rude noises. The suggestive cacophony the ensemble then produced may well have helped Dan and Dylan choose the name they adopted for a fictitious joint literary persona: Walter Bram. In his book of memoirs of Dylan, Daniel Jones decorously claims that he imagines they chose the name 'Bram' in deference to Bram Stoker.[7] But he surely would not have been unaware that 'bram' in Welsh means 'fart'.

'Walter Bram' was a prolific poet of bewildering obscurity. This was largely attributable to the fact that the Jones–Thomas creative process was often a spontaneous form of literary Consequences. The two friends would write alternate lines – Dan the odd ones, Dylan the even – to poems in inspirational mode, producing word and thought patterns that ranged from the serene to the surreal. On occasions, they would take this exercise to an extreme, and draw lines written on strips of paper out of two hats. The results were at times a relatively clean precursor of the 'cut-up' works of the American experimental novelist William Burroughs.

However, the closest literary parallel to Dan and Dylan's fantastic output is provided by the Gothic conversations and unpublished stories produced by Christopher Isherwood and Edward Upward at Repton School and Cambridge University earlier in the 1920s. There is no way that Dan and Dylan could have known about these, as Dylan's link to Isherwood – through the Swansea poet Vernon Watkins – had not yet been established. Yet one character in the Jones–Thomas repertoire, a composer and pianist called the Reverend Alexander Percy, would have been perfectly at home in the Isherwood–Upward imaginary world of 'Mortmere'. According to the programme notes produced for one 'Warmley' concert, the Rev. Percy performed three pieces: 'Buzzards at Dinner', 'Salute to Admiral Beatty' and 'Badgers Beneath My Vest'.

The boys even began to write Alexander Percy's biography. This revealed that he had been found wandering at an early age with his negro mother on an iceberg north of King Edward VII Land, before being rescued by Redskins. The biography fizzled out after a few pages, as their imaginations took them ever further from reality. A joint play got no further than the opening stage directions, which decreed that the audience should be blinded by a magnesium flare at the curtain's rise. When Dylan took over the editorship of the Swansea Grammar School magazine towards the end of his school career, however, he managed to get past D. J.'s sceptical eye a learned article about the work of the Croatian composer Dslepp – who was, of course, a figment of the Jones–Thomas collective imagination.

Some of the exotic names the boys gave their characters and locations were not just funny inventions, but 'palingrams', as Dan

Jones dubbed them. He says that as a toddler, he had an unconscious habit of saying words back to front, such as 'ananab' for 'banana'. The same principle, in adolescent collaborations with Dylan, brought forth composers such as 'Zoilreb' and 'Ffeifokorp'. And very soon afterwards – long before he worked out how to capitalize on it – Dylan came up with the name of the ultimate Welsh village: 'Llareggub' ('Bugger-all').

More seriously, though not necessarily more importantly, Dylan was also making use of his countless afternoons and evenings at 'Warmley' to familiarize himself with modern poetry. Mr and Mrs Jones's tastes were fairly avant-garde, and Daniel himself was beginning very gently to acquire a passion for books that before long would turn into rampant bibliomania. The fruits of Dylan's new reading and literary conversations can be seen in a remarkably competent essay entitled 'Modern Poetry',[8] which he published in a 1929 edition of the school magazine. In it, he expounds at length on the new element of freedom that characterizes modern verse: freedom of form, of structure, of imagery, and ideas. One of the most interesting aspects of this early critical piece is the attention Dylan gives to the Sitwells, notably Edith. He judges that she achieves a narrowness of poetical effect within wide psychological and natural fields, and that her poems show a shrewd grasp of detail as well as sudden illuminations and an intensity of emotion. Whether or not some or all of these opinions were assimilated from elsewhere, they undoubtedly reflect some of the thoughts that Dylan was mulling over and that would affect the development of his own poetry.

Writing poetry – and his pieces for the school magazine – had by now become far more important than attending classes at school. In his final two years there, Dylan increasingly played truant. If one story popular among his schoolmates of the time is true, then this was with a certain degree of compliance by the school authorities. The headmaster, Trevor Owen, reportedly stopped him as he was sneaking out of the building one day and asked where he was going. Dylan replied that he was going off to write for a few hours, to which Mr Owen retorted, 'Well, don't get caught!'

It had become a standing joke in the staff-room at Swansea Grammar that whenever examination time came round, Dylan would be ill and away from school. Yet even he couldn't miss every exam. Once, in the Central Welsh Board Examination for English, he scored a magnificent 98 per cent. But this couldn't make up for the fact that he failed everything else. Florence Thomas decided to tackle her son about this. She pointed out that at this rate he would never be able to go on to further study, which at this time of growing economic depression in Wales was one of the few keys to virtually guaranteed employment. She recalled after his death that she said, 'Anybody'd think you were a Keats or something,' to which he replied, 'I'll be as good as Keats, if not better.'[9] It was then that Florence decided there was no point ever remonstrating with him again.

John Keats (1795–1821) was indeed one of Dylan's models. The fact that he had died at the age of twenty-six made him especially attractive. As Dylan developed the concept of his own destiny as a poet, he became convinced that he, too, must die young. Moreover, John Keats's short life was full of the sort of romantic detail which appealed to Dylan's growing sense of poetic doom. Keats's younger brother Tom had died of consumption, and his own love affair with Fanny Brawne was full of anguish. Fittingly, Keats himself also contracted TB, and died in Rome in a house at the foot of the Spanish Steps.

Before long, however, Keats ceded pride of place in Dylan's mythology to the French poet Jean Arthur Rimbaud (1854–1891). Rimbaud, who early displayed a sullen and violent temperament, started writing at the age of ten. His most prolific poetic output was in his fifteenth year. In 1870, after a blazing row with his mother, he ran away from his stifling provincial home to Paris, and published his first book of poems. After a series of adventures, he assumed a life of hedonism in Paris, and became noted for his drinking and bawdy conversation. He had a tortuous homosexual affair with the poet Paul Verlaine, ten years his senior, who shot and wounded him in Brussels in 1873. Though Rimbaud lived to be thirty-six, he stopped writing verse at the age of nineteen, disillusioned with both literature and France. Rimbaud's major work, *Les Illuminations*, makes considerable use of his memories of childhood, dreams and mystical images to underline his distaste for the material world and his longing for things spiritual. Dylan had no particular wish to get involved sexually with an older man, but apart from that, Rimbaud's life and work were a source of immense inspiration and hope. From about the age of fifteen, therefore, Dylan started referring to himself, half-seriously, half-jokingly, as the 'Rimbaud of Cwmdonkin Drive'.

One school activity Dylan did deign to take part in was the amateur dramatics society. The school magazine recorded his performances in a number of plays and repeatedly dwelt on the splendour of his voice, even when his physical presence wasn't up to the part. He once appeared as Oliver Cromwell, and was described by the magazine's reviewer as 'looking as young and fresh and clean as if he had just come off the cover of a chocolate box'. This seems to be as much a heavy-handed jibe at Dylan's often grubby and dishevelled appearance as a critique of his acting ability. Equally mischievously, the reviewer of his performance in John Galsworthy's *Strife* said that his interpretation of the strike leader Roberts suffered somewhat because 'his vowels were occasionally too genteel'.

The genteel vowels and the 'cut-glass voice' (as Dylan himself called it) were D. J.'s fault. That was how *he* spoke, and he had sent both Nancy and Dylan to elocution lessons to make sure they did the same. As a teenager, therefore, Dylan enunciated as precisely as an English public schoolboy. As Pamela Hansford Johnson tartly noted in her memoirs,[10] he only recovered a Welsh lilt later in life, when it came in useful.

Dylan had ample opportunity to test the effectiveness of his voice at 'Warmley', thanks largely to the mechanical skills of a musician friend of Daniel Jones's, Tom Warner. Warner helped devise a system of internal transmission in the house which Dan grandiosely christened the Warmley Broadcasting Corporation, or WBC. According to Daniel Jones, three strategically placed loud-speakers in the upstairs sitting-room were converted into micro-phones linked by wires to the radiogram in one of the parlours downstairs. Performances of music or recitation upstairs therefore came out of the radiogram speaker exactly as if they were being broadcast. The inauguration of the WBC was a memorable occasion. While Mr Jones was sitting downstairs near the radiogram, Dylan asked if he would mind if he tuned in to some foreign radio station. He played with the dial until he got the WBC 'broadcast' of Dan Jones upstairs, playing Beethoven's Waldstein Sonata on the piano. After a few seconds, Daniel starting introducing false notes, and indulging in such musical contortions that the piece was soon no longer recognizable as Beethoven. His father ran to the door and called his wife to come and listen, saying that the world had gone mad. She replied that she could hear it too – and that it was coming from upstairs. Mr Jones thought this a most wonderful wheeze and became an avid WBC listener and 'broadcaster'.

When it was Dylan's turn to be upstairs, he would recite poetry, often his own. Dan Jones noted how he dropped his normally rather high-pitched voice several tones, to give the performance more resonance and weight. As there was no recording equipment in the house, there was no way that Dylan could listen to his own readings. But Dan would give him detailed criticisms of these, just as he did of the poems themselves. One of Dan's principal attractions in Dylan's eyes was that he was such a marvellous listener. Dylan liked people who were useful.

Dan was not Dylan's only friend, nor did Dylan spend all his time among those who shared his passion for literature. The autobiographical story 'Extraordinary Little Cough', for example, portrays him going off with three other schoolfriends one August on a two-week camping holiday at Rhossilli, at the far end of the Gower Peninsula. Rhossilli, with its magnificent, 5-mile sweeping arc of a beach, and spectacular cliffs, was one of Dylan's special places. He probably first saw it on a day outing from his Uncle Dai and Auntie Dosie's at Newton. For Dylan the beach and the mile-long rocky promontory of Worm's Head at its end, the latter accessible only at low tide, were part of a magic, isolated landscape where at times he could imagine himself living. In the story, he and his mates fix a ride out to Rhossilli on a truck, and Dylan drapes his coat over his suitcase so that his friends won't see the initials 'N. T.' stamped on the leather and realize it's his sister's. The wimp of the story, however, nicknamed 'Little Cough', is George Hooping, who decides to prove himself by running right along the beach at night. Other figures in the story include the two main Swansea Grammar bullies who happen to be there, Brazell and Skully. (They were the ones who had stuffed Dylan into the waste-paper bin when he was smaller.) More exciting for Dylan and his companions, though, is a group of girls. Dylan braces himself to approach one, by devising something witty or unusual to say, like 'Sorry we couldn't arrange to have the sea in when you came.' But he loses his nerve, and only manages to say 'Hello', dropping his cap at the girl's feet. Sugar-lumps fall out of his pockets when he stoops to pick it up: 'For horses,' he mumbles. Crushingly, she asks him who Brazell is, as she thinks the bully is awfully handsome.

Under Dan Jones's tutelage, however, Dylan did pluck up another kind of courage, to try alcoholic drink. When he was about fifteen or sixteen, he accompanied Dan to the pub nearest to 'Warmley', where they sipped slowly from half pints of mild, making each glass last as long as possible. Within months, though, the two pals had accelerated their intake. By the time Dan had started attending Swansea University College in the autumn of 1931, they would embark on pub-crawls. Haydn Taylor, whose protracted courtship of Nancy Thomas was still going on in the front parlour of 5 Cwmdonkin Drive, remembers the sound of an obviously paralytic Dylan being ushered bumpily upstairs by his parents, with much whispering and shushing, in the vain hope that their daughter's suitor wouldn't notice. Dylan had a very poor head for drink throughout his short life, which meant that it took comparatively little to get him drunk.

Pocket-money alone could obviously not have paid for these outings to pubs before Dylan got a job. But he was a past master at raising funds by other means. Apart from raiding his mother's handbag with the same nonchalance he displayed when filching wine gums from Fergy's shop while Mrs Ferguson's back was turned, Dylan had once shown a certain brand of initiative by going from house to house in Uplands with a box collecting for orphans in Dr Barnardo's Homes. Once he thought he had collected enough money, he broke open the box and bought cinema tickets and other treats for himself and his friends. He also acquired a reputation at school as the boy with the largest collection of filed-down farthings for using in sixpenny slot-machines. For those with few moral scruples or an adolescent sense of adventure, Dylan was a boon companion.

During his last summer term at school, in 1931, Dylan came up with the idea of starting his own literary magazine, which presumably was intended as much as an outlet for his own writing as a potential means of raising cash. Since at least April 1930, Dylan had been filling his exercise books with poems, at the rate of about one a week. In general they were not the sort of thing he could publish in the school magazine (even though he was now the editor-in-chief), or submit to the conservative editors of local papers, so it would have been useful to have somewhere for them to appear, preferably before an audience of proven literary aficianados.

Each of Dylan's poems had been meticulously worked on. Establishing a technique that he maintained for the rest of his life, he would write down on a piece of paper a line or just a phrase that came into his head, then revise and add to it. Every time he made an alteration, he would write out the new version completely, on a fresh piece of paper. There would be dozens – or in some cases even hundreds – of these so-called 'work-sheets' before the poem finally reached the stage of being copied into the exercise book. Even then, it would be subject to revision. Thus every line was the product of many hours' work and individual words would be the subject of minute searching and reflection. To help him in that task, Dylan kept word and rhyming lists, eventually making his own little working 'dictionary'. The notebooks themselves, over the period 1930 to 1933, represented not only the most fertile period of Dylan's poetic output, but also the raw material for over half of his total published poems. Four of the notebooks were later acquired by the University of Buffalo, in New York State.

The magazine which Dylan hoped to launch in 1931 was to be called *Prose and Verse*. The only qualification for publication in it was originality of expression and outlook. He even got the *South Wales Daily Post* newspaper – on which D. J. had friends – to publish a paragraph about it, inviting contributions to be sent to Cwmdonkin Drive. One such contribution was a story entitled 'Freedom' sent by a twenty-six-year-old Swansea railway clerk called Trevor Hughes. Dylan acknowledged receipt of this on 10 June, and informed Trevor Hughes that he was accepting it for publication without reservation. Unfortunately, though, as the letter went on to reveal, Dylan had so far attracted only twenty orders for the magazine at two shillings each, and he had worked out that he needed 200 for the venture to be viable. He therefore invited Trevor Hughes to go out and try to sign up some subscribers to *Prose and Verse* himself.

Far from being put off by this unmasking of the shaky nature of the sixteen-year-old Dylan's enterprise, Trevor Hughes became a regular correspondent and a close friend. He had a rather melancholy disposition, which stemmed partly from his grief over his brother's distressingly bloody death from TB, and the burden of having to look after an invalid mother. Trevor Hughes is the model for the character Ray Price in the story 'Who Do You Wish Was With Us?', which recounts a day-trip the two made to Rhossilli. In this story, Dylan's friend becomes unbearably maudlin about his brother, spoiling what would otherwise have been a beautiful day. The portrait is not a fair one (hence, presumably, the pseudonym); far from finding Trevor's accounts of his family's illnesses a bore, Dylan revelled in them. He was also delighted that he now had someone else with whom he could discuss poetry seriously. This continued by letter after Trevor Hughes moved to London in 1932, and it is clear from the correspondence that instead of the older Trevor being Dylan's poetic mentor, it was usually the other way round.

Rather than find himself among the swelling ranks of the young unemployed when school ended in July 1931, Dylan took up an offer (arranged by his father) to go to work as a trainee reporter on the *South Wales Daily Post*, which soon afterwards changed its name to the *South Wales Evening Post*. The paper's editor, J. D. Williams, had seen Dylan performing as Cromwell in the school pageant mentioned earlier, and realized immediately from the boy's voice and bearing that this was someone special. It seems likely, in fact, that Dylan had already started doing some part-time work for the paper weeks if not months before he officially left school. To begin with, this was the routine trainee copy-boy procedure of reading out agency copy and other material aloud to reporters and similar rather menial tasks. But after a couple of months or so at this, Dylan was given what were considered 'safe' reporting assignments.

The first of these was an interview with the then famous music-hall star Nellie Wallace, who was appearing in a variety show at the Swansea Empire Theatre. The resultant article was published anonymously in the paper on 15 July 1931, a fortnight before the end of the grammar school term. Feeling in need of a little moral support on this first assignment, Dylan invited along his friend Wynford Vaughan-Thomas, the future broadcaster. According to Vaughan-Thomas,[11] they held their breath as they knocked on Miss Wallace's dressing-room door. Once inside, Dylan majestically intoned his well-rehearsed greeting: 'Miss Wallace, we bring you the homage of the artists of the future for the artists of the past.' Seemingly unoffended by his ungallant allusion to her age, the sexagenarian Miss Wallace asked the youths if they were variety or 'legit'. A bit unsure of the difference, they plumped for 'legit'. 'In that case, boys,' Miss Wallace declared, 'you've got a hell of a road to travel! Have some gin!' It was the first time Dylan had tasted spirits, and the gin burned his throat. Miss Wallace laughed at his discomfort and downed her glass in one gulp. Then she tidied up the hunting costume she was wearing for her next number, stuck a feather in her hair and pranced out of the dressing-room on to the stage for a stirring rendition of 'I was after the fox, me boys, but he was after me!'

After this, other journalistic forays were an anti-climax. Like all trainees, Dylan was expected to do the rounds of police-stations, fire-stations, hospitals, morgues, garden fêtes, concerts, sports events and charity functions in the hope of flushing out a story. But just as he abandoned a study of shorthand after a few fruitless weeks, so his heart was not in the pedestrian business of digging up news or human-interest stories that could be turned into column inches in the paper. Very quickly, therefore, he took to sloping off when he was meant to be out on the job. He would join up with pals at the YMCA to play billiards, or sit for hours over coffee at the Kardomah with more culturally minded friends like Dan Jones and the budding painter Alfred Janes – who stood out from the others, being tall, dark and handsome – discussing how the three of them, from their Swansea base, were going to conquer the world with their poetry, music and art. As Dylan later recalled in a radio broadcast called 'Return Journey', their conversation would range over communism, symbolism, Braque, free love, free beer, murder, Michelangelo, pingpong, Sibelius and girls. Dylan would have a word with the cashier at the Kardomah when he came in, to find out if one of the newspaper's senior employees was there, and if so, whether upstairs or down. That way he could be sure of avoiding him.

Inevitably, though, some of Dylan's absences were discovered. He once wrote up a lacrosse match that had actually been cancelled. More seriously, he failed to make a routine call at Swansea Hospital one day in February 1932, thereby missing the news that the matron had dropped dead. But even when he did report on events he had attended, the end result wasn't always what the editor had in mind. Dylan showed himself to be an incurable iconoclast, who attacked many of the functions and artistic performances he was covering, to the intense annoyance of the people involved. His review of an amateur production of *Hiawatha* failed to mention the performers at all, instead providing him with the opportunity for a blistering attack on Longfellow.

J. D. Williams indulgently decided to give Dylan's literary leanings full rein, and commissioned him to do a series of articles on local literary figures of the past, which appeared in the *Evening Post*'s weekly sister-paper, the *Herald of Wales*. Articles such as 'The Poets of Swansea: Walter Savage Landor to James Chapman Woods' show an entirely different side to the more usual portrait of Dylan at this stage in his life as the careless, idle reporter. They are obviously the fruit of considerable research and are written with perceptive understanding. It is true that he did seem particularly in his element when dealing with the more eccentric members of the South Wales literary fraternity, because he obviously found it easier to identify with such people. In his piece on the nineteenth-century poet and actor Llewellyn Prichard, who drank too much and died when his bed caught fire, he observes that the most attractive figures in literature are always those around whom a world of lies and legends has been woven: half-mythical creatures whose real characters are cloaked in a veil of the bizarre. Read with hindsight, this seems like a defiant declaration of intent.

But even if Dylan's short series of literary features is testimony to the precocious knowledge and industry of its seventeen-year-old author, he was quite incapable of showing such zeal and stamina when it came to straight reporting. He would spend the hours when he was meant to be correcting galley proofs doodling or writing doggerel on the back. His closest friend among his colleagues on the *Evening Post*, Eric Hughes, recalled that Dylan was quite the worst trainee journalist he had ever met. Even if this made Dylan the butt of affectionate jokes, it was a situation which could not last.

Dylan was generally popular with the rest of the staff at the newspaper offices. Florence had made sure he was well turned out, in a clean white shirt and neatly pressed trousers, which endeared him to the ladies. And he would usually be quiet and polite around the office. His wilder side only became evident when he went out to the pubs for a pint with older male colleagues. There he learned how to make people laugh. He also self-consciously modelled himself on some of the mannerisms of one of the senior reporters, Fred Farr. Farr – who appears under his own name in Dylan's story 'Old Garbo' – was a chain-smoker with nicotine-stained fingers, who kept a cigarette hanging from a corner of his mouth. Dylan duly adopted the pose. Farr was round-faced and round-bellied, and in the story takes Dylan on a pub-crawl to some of Swansea's seedier dives. Dylan envies the miners there who flirt boldly with the barmaid, and wishes he could do and say things that would make her call him 'saucy' too. In the Fishguard pub, down by the rocks, where sailors could be found knitting, Mr Farr gives Dylan his first taste of rum. This makes him lose control of his legs, and his trilby hat falls off.

Dylan's main escape from his short working life as a reporter was in amateur dramatics. He took part in some entertainments at the YMCA, but most of his acting was with a group called the Swansea Little Theatre, which he joined in 1932. This had premises in an old church hall in the Mumbles. Both Dylan's sister Nancy and Haydn Taylor were prominent members, and in February 1932, all three of them, together with Eric Hughes, appeared in Noël Coward's comedy, *Hay Fever*. Nancy, who had developed into a very fine amateur actress, was seriously considering trying for a professional acting career. She had not gone on to further education after finishing at high school, and had shown little inclination to look for any other sort of job, to her parents' evident displeasure. She got glowing reviews for her interpretation of the empty-headed and maddeningly well-brought-up Jackie Corynton in *Hay Fever*. For all his feel for language, and his fine voice, Dylan, who played the arty Simon Bliss, couldn't even begin to match her on the stage.

Besides, once he had discovered the delights of Mumbles pubs like the Antelope and the Mermaid, he preferred to spend time there rather than with the rest of the cast. Wynford Vaughan-Thomas recalls playing Lorenzo in Shakespeare's *The Merchant of Venice*, in which Dylan had the minuscule part of a messenger from Belmont. Wynford cued him in, but no Dylan appeared, as he was still making his way up from the Mermaid tavern. In despair, Wynford ad-libbed a little, then once again cued Dylan who this time rushed on stage, to be greeted by Wynford's exasperated 'And about time too!'

The other interest which Dylan shared with his future brother-in-law Haydn Taylor was cricket. Haydn would sometimes take him to matches in Swansea and the surrounding area. Unlike

Nancy, Haydn thought Dylan could be an amusing companion when sober. But these outings ended when Haydn was transferred to London in the summer of 1932, much to Nancy's disgust: Haydn and his car had been her regular means of escape from the increasingly stifling atmosphere at 5 Cwmdonkin Drive. The only way out now would be to agree to marry him and move away. They got engaged that Christmas.

Just how unbearable Nancy was finding home life comes over clearly in the letters she wrote to Haydn in the six months beginning September 1932. D. J. was perpetually starting rows, which sent Florence into floods of tears and Nancy running up to her room. Dylan would often turn up after midnight, rolling drunk; he boasted to Trevor Hughes that he got drunk four nights a week. His late arrivals and dishevelled state provoked D. J. to yet more angry scenes. In fact, D. J. – whose own temper was fired by too much booze – was becoming increasingly unreasonable. When he found Nancy entertaining some friends over coffee in the kitchen at the beginning of October, he ranted at her about the cost of feeding half of Swansea, and ordered her to send them home. He swore at Nancy repeatedly and on one occasion in October told her it was a pity she was alive. He moaned that all that she and her 'beautiful brother' did was take money off him. As Nancy complained to Haydn, being classified alongside Dylan was the ultimate insult.

Nancy took to eating on her own, to avoid seeing the rest of the family. In her worst moments, she wished she was dead. She also had to warn Haydn Taylor to seal his letters with wax, as she realized that Florence was steaming them open. This provoked a showdown with Florence herself, who said that having one's boyfriend send sealed letters so one's mother couldn't read them was the most deceitful thing she had ever heard. Florence constantly nagged at Nancy, and when Nancy told her mother to shut up one day, D. J. threw a book at her.

By mid-December, things were coming to a head. On the last day of the school term, Nancy had cooked a special pie for her father's lunch and gently chided him when he sat down grumpily and whingeing. 'Now, Daddy . . . ' she said, which for some reason triggered an explosion. He said he'd screw her bloody head off, and who the hell did she think she was anyway? She ran upstairs to pack a bag, but when she came down again to say she was leaving,

D. J. sneered, 'No such luck! You'll come cringing back again, I know.' She had no money to go off anywhere anyway, as they were both aware.

D. J.'s bitterness may well have been exacerbated by the fact that Dylan had been such a disaster at the *South Wales Evening Post* that his employment there had been terminated. The official reason was his failure to master shorthand, but kindly J. D. Williams had had a heart-to-heart talk with Dylan and they had both agreed he wasn't cut out for a career in journalism. Dylan claimed in a letter to Trevor Hughes that the paper had offered him a five-year contract which he had turned down, but this was just one of his lies. He left the newspaper offices without rancour on either side, however, and it was agreed that he could submit freelance articles and poems.

Mr Williams had reason to rue this offer within a matter of days. Dylan produced a light-hearted piece headlined 'Genius and Madness Akin in World of Art'. In it he referred to the Bohemian artist Nina Hamnett, who had lived in Paris and was now regaling London with her accounts of fascinating friends and lovers. Miss Hamnett had written an autobiography, *Laughing Torso*, which Dylan incorrectly claimed had been banned. This brought a threat of a libel suit from Nina Hamnett's lawyers, and a grovelling apology in the paper the following week, saying her book had enjoyed wide circulation. Typically, Dylan later embellished this story, telling Pamela Hansford Johnson that he had alleged that Nina Hamnett was insane.

He seems to have treated the whole incident as a lark. After all, while the other three residents of 5 Cwmdonkin Drive had their reasons to be miserable, he had cause to be happy. Within a period of about sixteen months, he had proved to himself and everybody else that he was quite unsuited for gainful employment. Therefore he could drop the pretence of conventionality and follow his vocation of being a full-time poet.

3

THIRTIES' WRITER

(1933–1934)

Dylan's new status as a poet merited a new image. While playing at journalism, he had acquired a pork-pie hat, which he now dangled jauntily from one finger; he dyed his cricket shirt green, and stole one of his sister Nancy's loudest silk scarves, tailoring it into a most satisfyingly artistic tie. Given his small size, cute curls and pouting mouth, some people thought this new pose made him look like a screaming queen. He wasn't, but he quite enjoyed the idea that people might think so. One of the pub stories Dylan most relished telling in his Soho days was how one day he went into a gents' toilet and a big navvy standing at the urinals looked at him and growled, 'Now, you wouldn't think I was a pansy, would you?' to which Dylan allegedly retorted, 'Now you wouldn't think I *wasn't*, would you?'

Dylan maintained that Nancy never knew where her scarf had gone. More likely, she was past caring. By early 1933, she was counting the days until she could get away from Swansea. Her letters to her fiancé Haydn Taylor were one long scream for help. On 13 January she wrote that Dylan now lay in bed most mornings, and then got up and wrote. In the evenings he would trot off to see 'Danny' Jones, unless he had got his thieving hands on some money, in which case he would go to the pub and drink. Nancy was getting quite paranoid about leaving money anywhere, as even tiny amounts always seemed to disappear – and Mr and Mrs Thomas would then say it was her fault.

Florence even chided Nancy for using the ink-pot for writing letters to Haydn, when she ought to have known that Dylan needed it for his work. Florence had obviously decided that she did indeed have a unique creative force under her roof and that everything must be done to assist him in his art. She would lay out two or three pieces of fruit and a Woodbine cigarette on his bedside table, so that his 'breakfast' would be waiting for him when he woke. Nancy would have to wait until May for her escape into marriage, and she had already come to realize that that event was of only marginal interest to the rest of the family. D. J. had informed her that she could not expect him to pay for any fancy 'do'.

Of far more impact on Florence was the death from cancer of her elder sister Ann Jones, on 7 February at the age of seventy. Florence had gone to Carmarthen to be with her during her final days in the infirmary. Given the affectionate nostalgia that pervades the poem 'Fern Hill' and other pieces relating to Aunt Annie and her farm, Dylan's reaction to her terminal illness seems astoundingly callous. In the first week of February, he wrote to Trevor Hughes (who, as we know, was hyper-sensitive to the suffering of members of his own family), saying that he was utterly unmoved by the fact that Aunt Annie lay in hospital dying, 'save for the pleasant death-reek at my negroid nostrils'.[1] He recalled that Aunt Annie had loved him inordinately and had spoiled him, often giving him sweets and money which she could ill afford. But now Dylan was saying that it was the same to him whether she lived or died; he would miss her bi-annual postal orders, that was all. He claimed that he didn't feel worried about other people, and that he didn't care about others' emotions; what interested him was his own reaction to emotions. Did that mean, he asked Trevor Hughes in the letter, that he lacked a soul?

It certainly sounds like it. Or is this Dylan experimenting with another disguise or act: the hard-bitten cynic who has determined to let his most selfish impulses hold sway? It is interesting to compare the two versions of the poem 'After the Funeral' which he wrote in memory of Ann Jones. The first, written in his notebook shortly after she was buried, emphasizes the pointlessness of death and the hypocrisy of the mourners. But the much better-known second version, written five or six years later and published in his 1939 collection *The Map of Love*, has a completely different tone, infused with love, reaching out to the lost aunt, not pushing her away. Had Dylan really changed so much in the intervening years?

Certainly, in 1933 the young Dylan was beginning to think he needed to get away from Wales. In his letter of early February to Trevor Hughes, he threatens to go and stay with Nancy sometimes, once she gets married and moves to London. Whereas by 1938 he had gone to live in Laugharne, a short crow's-flight from Fernhill, and he was rediscovering his roots. Yet I don't think the passage of time is the only explanation of his changeable attitude to his homeland. Daniel Jones once said that Dylan was six or eight different people, not one; it is a telling remark. Most people have moods, whereas Dylan seemed to have a myriad personalities, all existing simultaneously within the same human being. Sometimes he would deliberately let one of these personalities take over, even making it into a caricature. But he was a bundle of contradictions, which was uncomfortable both for himself and for the people who had to live with him.

While Florence was still mourning Ann Jones, Dylan and Eric Hughes had strengthened their position within the pecking-order at the Swansea Little Theatre at the Mumbles. They had managed to persuade the company's management committee, under the guidance of an English lecturer called Thomas Taig, to put on H. F. Rubenstein's *Peter and Paul*, in which they would be the stars. J. D. Williams, no less, reviewed the play in the *South Wales Evening Post*, when it opened in March 1933. He mischievously stressed in the review how obvious it was that the 'young lions' of the Little Theatre had wanted this play because it gave them two such plum parts: Dylan as Peter, the would-be writer, who has to run the family business instead; and Eric as Paul, whose only dream had been to enjoy bourgeois comforts in peace, but who finds himself driven into the painful role of persecuted writer. Mr Williams ended his review by saying that Dylan might with advantage tone down his acting in the first act.

Some of the more strait-laced customers of the Antelope and Mermaid public houses in the Mumbles were probably wondering if Dylan might not with advantage tone down his acting there too. He had become keen on a game called Cats and Dogs, which tended to disintegrate into him running around on all fours snarling and taking a playful bite at any fanciable leg. He even broke one of his front teeth at Cats and Dogs by biting a lamppost. The more boisterous customers of the pubs joined in the spirit of the thing, while others thought it embarrassingly infantile.

It is hard to reconcile this oafish young man with the timid, serious, rather bookish youth who one evening, probably around this period, called at the shop run by a grocer, Bert Trick, at 69 Glanbrydan Avenue, Uplands, not very far from Cwmdonkin Drive. Thomas Taig of the Little Theatre had suggested to Dylan that Grocer Trick was someone to whom it was worth showing his poems for critical comment. Bert Trick had been an engineering apprentice in the drab nearby town of Neath, then a clerk with the Inland Revenue, before borrowing the money from members of his family to set himself up in business in Swansea. By the time Dylan met him, he had written quite a lot of verse, much of it imbued with socialist ideology and outrage at the world's injustices. He also contributed articles on literary and political themes to publications like the *Christian Agitator*. Bert claimed to be an agnostic, yet he loved to talk about religion deep into the night. His poems are full of references to Christ and God. Sixteen years Dylan's senior, he was a member of the General Management Committee of the Swansea Labour Party, and was deeply influenced by Marxist theory.

Bert was busy when Dylan first called, but invited him to come round again at seven the following evening, which he did. The two of them went into the sitting-room behind the shop where they had a general discussion for about an hour, before Bert asked whether Dylan would like him to read some of Dylan's poems. Dylan retorted that poems should be spoken, not read. He then pulled a school exercise book from his pocket, draped one of his legs over the arm of an easy-chair and began to declaim some of his work.[2] Bert was astounded and realized immediately that this was a poet singing in an entirely new voice. Dylan stopped reading after three poems, and asked Bert what he thought of them. Bert was so excited that he went into the kitchen to fetch his wife Nell, telling her, 'I've found a genius!'

This was the beginning of an intense literary friendship that helped to get Dylan Thomas, poet, launched. The timing was perfect, as Daniel Jones's family had moved away from Swansea to

Harrow, on the outskirts of London, which meant that 'Warmley' was no longer available for heady discussions mixed with play. Instead, Dylan, Bert and Nell fell into a pattern of seeing each other twice a week, often with old 'Warmley' friends like Fred Janes and Tom Warner. Although Dan Jones was still in Swansea, studying, he apparently did not get on with Bert Trick, so stayed away. On Wednesday evenings, the group would often meet at 5 Cwmdonkin Drive (with D. J. safely out of the way in the pub), while on Sunday evenings they would gather at the Tricks'. Gradually other people were drawn into the circle, which swelled to a dozen or more. This proved to be the perfect forum for Dylan to try out his poems and fine-tune his growing repertoire of bawdy anecdotes. He had become a successful mimic of people and accents, which led to some riotous sessions. Bert Trick shared Dylan's taste for salacious puns and other word-games. He particularly savoured Dylan's perverted proverb, 'Too many cocks spoil the breath'.

Bert was dazzled by Dylan's talent and his ability to entertain, but found it impossible to raise the young man's political consciousness as he would have liked. Bert's opposition to the capitalist system and the rise of Fascism was total, whereas Dylan had only the woolliest political notions, albeit emotionally anti-Establishment. He was far more interested in people and the physical world than in politics. His poetry library at home included works by the highly politicized Auden generation, but his own subject matter and style were diametrically opposed to theirs, given their angry opposition to oppressive authority. Because Auden, Spender, Day-Lewis and the rest have been so forcefully projected as the Voice of the Thirties, it has escaped many people's attention that Dylan Thomas was equally a Thirties' writer, despite being their junior by several years. The vast majority of his poetic output was produced between 1930 and the outbreak of the Second World War. It is true that his work was in many ways a literary counter-revolution to what the Auden generation was doing, but that counter-revolution was taking place simultaneously.

Of course Dylan was not totally blind to the misery of the Depression; in South Wales that would have been difficult. In his story 'Old Garbo', he notes the men lining the street trying to make a few pennies out of selling shoelaces and the like. And when he and Fred Janes had been out walking one evening, they had overheard one young unemployed man standing in the shadows say to another, 'Nothing to do here. Let's joint the Fascists.' No sensitive being could remain immune to such things around him, yet the ogres and horrors that Dylan was seeing in 1933 were not Adolf Hitler and his colleagues, but gothic demons, corpses, worms, fearful insects, diseases and unfulfilled sexual lust: in short, the terrors of the flesh, alive and dead. These images burned in his mind far more fiercely than more abstract fears about alien political ideologies, although largely out of respect for Bert Trick, whom he recognized as a kind of mentor, Dylan did at times give the impression of at least half-assimilating some of the principles of socialism. Besides, concepts such as the State taking care of poets and artists so that they could write without financial worries or dependency on family and friends had an obvious appeal. But in reality, consciously or subconsciously, Dylan was too wedded to a number of the petty-bourgeois ideals of his upbring-ing ever to have made a convincing socialist.

The local Labour Party's attempts to draw him into its orbit received a setback that highlighted Dylan's ability to avoid getting into situations where he thought he might not be at ease. One of the Swansea Labour councillors, a friend of Bert Trick's, had a wife with literary interests, and Bert thought it would be nice for her to meet Dylan. Accordingly, he invited her to one of his Sunday evenings. Unfortunately, Bert told Dylan she would be coming when he saw him the Wednesday before. When Sunday came, Dylan did not turn up. But around midnight, after all the other guests had left, there was a timid knock on the door. It was Dylan, who said he had not been able to face the thought of meeting the stranger, and apologized for any embarrassment caused. Bert invited him in and they talked into the early hours. This was only the first of many occasions when Dylan would back out of an engagement – and one of the few times that he said he was sorry.

Bert Trick claims to have been the person who bullied Dylan into trying to get some of his exercise-book poetry known to a wider audience. That is not quite true, as Dylan seems at his own initiative to have submitted a poem, 'The Romantic Isle', to a BBC radio poetry competition, which closed at the end of February 1933. The winners would not be known for several months, but in the meantime, Bert Trick did manage to persuade Dylan to submit some of his work to the *New English Weekly*, whose editor, A. R. Orage, made a point of encouraging new young talent. Orage responded enthusiastically to the work that Dylan sent, and asked to see more. Dylan, however, was disgusted that the publication offered no payment. Winning a reputation as a poet was not much use, he told Bert Trick, if it didn't pay for one's Woodbines and beers. But Trick persisted and in April 1933 Dylan sent off 'And Death Shall Have No Dominion', which duly appeared in the *New English Weekly* on 18 May 1933.

It was a stunningly mature debut for an eighteen-year-old poet. Apparently the poem was prompted by a suggestion from Bert Trick that spring that the two of them each write something about immortality. Trick's poem (which was published in a local newspaper) was almost Victorian, with its conventional central image of the soul going up to God like a bird. But Dylan's 'And Death Shall Have No Dominion' burns with defiance and rings with the chimes of a craftsman perfectly in control of his tools. Unlike many of Dylan's other notebook poems, it doesn't even contain obscure lines.

Dylan then heard that out of the thousands that had been sent in to its competition, the BBC had chosen 'The Romantic Isle' to be one of eight poems that would be broadcast. The poem went out on what was then called the National Programme at the end of June. But the real breakthrough for Dylan came a little later in 1933, largely thanks to Dan Jones.

In April, the *Sunday Referee* newspaper had announced that it was starting a Poet's Corner, to be run by a literary journalist called Victor Neuburg. Contributions were invited. Neuburg, who was fifty at this time, was an extraordinary character, of German–Jewish parentage and omnivorous sexual tastes. While at Cambridge, he had fallen under the spell of the third-rate poet and Master of the Occult Aleister Crowley, whose abused acolyte he became. As such he was a party to the orgies and devilish machinations that Crowley contrived. Together they had reputedly summoned up spirits, and Crowley put a curse on Victor Neuburg when they split up: certainly, Neuburg subsequently had a nervous breakdown, and twenty years on, his behaviour was still pretty bizarre. He divided his time between a house in St John's Wood, London, and a cottage in Steyning in West Sussex, where he ran a small private publishing enterprise, The Vine Press, with the aid of a lady partner called Sheila Macleod, who preferred to be known by the curious pseudonym of Runia Tharp. Known to all and sundry as the 'Vicky-bird', Victor Neuburg was looked on with a mixture of amusement and alarm by the villagers of Steyning. He washed and shaved only intermittently, dressed in a weird collection of peasant smocks, plus-fours and kilts, and had a tendency to go off at the slightest provocation into long, rambling exposés of esoteric claptrap. As he was prepared to work for a tiny salary, however, and had a 'nose' for fresh talent, the *Sunday Referee* could hardly complain.

Daniel Jones went to a literary gathering at the cottage in Steyning in July 1933. He didn't think much of the people he met there, especially Victor Neuburg's new protégée, Pamela Hansford Johnson, as he considered them full of metropolitan pretensions. But the outing made good material for an amusing report-back to Dylan. Moreover, Dan recommended that Dylan send something for possible publication in Poet's Corner, which he did.

In August, Dylan came up to London himself. Nancy and Haydn had got married in a church outside Swansea in May, and had then moved on to a houseboat near Chertsey in Surrey, within commuting distance of London. Dylan said he wanted to come to stay, and apparently Haydn drove him from South Wales. It was the first of several visits, which were usually meant to last only a couple of days, but could go on for a fortnight or more, first on the houseboat, and later at a house called Wisteria Cottage that the Taylors found for the winter. According to Paul Ferris,[3] Nancy's friend Gwevril Dawkins came to stay on the houseboat just a few days after Dylan's first visit, and was told by Nancy that Dylan had done a bunk not only with some of Haydn's money, but also with her engagement ring. She said that Haydn had gone chasing after Dylan in the car and had tracked him down at Reading, where he retrieved the ring. This story appears to be a complete fabrication on Nancy's part, as Haydn Taylor has no recollection of it. Nancy and Dylan seem to have taken a perverse delight in spreading the most poisonous untrue rumours about each other. Yet, oddly, Nancy's fantasy was an uncanny premonition of things to come.

While he was in London on this first visit, Dylan went to see A. R. Orage at the *New English Weekly*, which published several of his poems the following year. He also called on Sir Richard Rees, who edited the *Adelphi* magazine. This Left-leaning monthly literary journal had been founded by John Middleton Murry and had an impressive list of contributors, including T. S. Eliot, D. H. Lawrence, Katherine Mansfield and Herbert Read, as well as a few up-and-coming new writers like John Lehmann. Sir Richard accepted one of Dylan's poems, 'No Man Believes', which appeared in the *Adelphi* a few weeks later. Dylan's pilgrimage to two of the crucibles of contemporary literary thinking had turned out to be most worthwhile. Otherwise, there is no record of what he got up to in London. In contrast to later visits, and the time when he lived in the capital, there are no accounts of winning admirers in pubs with his wisdom or wit, nor any details of drunken binges. Even his unfinished novel *Adventures in the Skin Trade* (published posthumously in 1955) is no help, as the scene in which the young hero, Samuel Bennet, arrives at Paddington Station from Wales for his first taste of metropolitan life is clearly one of the least autobiographical parts of that book.

Back in Swansea, and encouraged by his success in placing poems, Dylan wrote to Geoffrey Grigson, the poet and irascible critic who had recently launched a new magazine, *New Verse*, which was to become a highly influential publication. Dylan had read about it in *John O'London's Weekly*. He enclosed half a dozen poems, allegedly selected at random from his exercise books, with his letter to Geoffrey Grigson. In this he explained rather plaintively that if Grigson were to publish any of the poems, he would be doing Dylan a great favour, as 'grinding out poetry' in the smug darkness of a provincial town like Swansea was both depressing and disheartening. Unmoved and unimpressed, Grigson returned them.

A far bigger blow for Dylan came with the discovery that his father was seriously ill. At the end of August, D. J. had gone to the dentist, who noticed an ulcer in his mouth. The dentist recommended that he see his doctor, who in turn referred him to a specialist. The specialist diagnosed cancer, and gave him less than five years to live. Nancy and Haydn were summoned to Swansea, and from there they drove D. J. back to London in their car. On 10 September he was admitted to University College Hospital, where he began a course of unpleasant treatment with radium needles. This was repeated in October, temporarily affecting his voice. The treatment did nothing to improve D. J.'s temper, as Haydn Taylor discovered when he had the unenviable task of ferrying him back and forth between Swansea and London. But when it eventually became clear that the cancer had been caught in time, D. J. began to accept that he had had a lucky escape. Colleagues from Swansea Grammar School (not one of whom, incidentally, visited him while he was convalescing at home) noticed when he got back to work in the New Year that he had mellowed a little. The rows with Florence became less frequent as well.

Ever ready to dramatize, Dylan told his friends that his father had got cancer of the throat, implying that death might be only round the corner. But Dylan seems to have been genuinely upset at the prospect of losing D. J., unlike his reaction to Ann Jones's demise. What is more, the nature of D. J.'s illness appears to have triggered what Ralph Maud has so aptly described as Dylan's 'deeply organic imagery'.[4] The notebook poems that he wrote in the autumn of 1933 are full of bared nerves, foul blood and maggot-infested stool. Dylan could even sense the awesome power of life and death – the flux of the creative and the destructive – in plants. He had acquired an almost religious awareness of God the Father or Mother Nature pumping energy into the world around him, as witnessed in the poem that begins: 'The force that through the green fuse drives the flower'. As he says in the poem, this is the same force that is his destroyer, driving on relentlessly to the shroud. Characteristically, at the moment when his father's life was threatened, Dylan's consciousness was overwhelmed with his own mortality.

'The Force that through the Green Fuse' was the second poem of Dylan's published by Victor Neuburg, in October 1933. The first was 'That Sanity Be Kept', which had appeared on 3 September, and was declared by Neuburg to be a major prize-winner. The Vicky-bird showered the very best contributions to the *Sunday Referee*'s Poet's Corner with 'prizes' and 'honourable mentions', making the whole business sound like something out of school. This was just one of the reasons why Dylan held the man in a certain contempt. But the recognition and the encouragement provided by this first-prize mention in the *Sunday Referee* were useful.

Even more importantly for Dylan's development, 'That Sanity Be Kept' attracted a fan letter from Pamela Hansford Johnson. She recognized how much the poem owed to the influence of T. S. Eliot, but thought it very fine all the same. Her side of what evolved into a short-lived but most intense correspondence appears to have been destroyed. Dylan had a habit of casually dropping incoming letters into the waste-paper basket once he'd read them: it is obvious that he did not expect those at the receiving end of his correspondence to do the same. Many of his letters, like his poems, were meticulously worked and reworked, often going through several drafts before being neatly copied out and sent off. The correspondence with Pamela Hanford Johnson allowed Dylan to examine and expose himself. This was supposedly for her benefit and entertainment, but it served as a useful exercise for his own growing self-awareness.

Pamela, then twenty-one, lived in a respectable part of Battersea, south London, with her widowed mother. She was petite and serious-featured, and worked in a bank. Though later to become a distinguished novelist, she was concentrating on poetry at this time. Victor Neuburg had extravagantly described her as 'one of the few exquisite word-artists of our day'. That was not a phrase that Dylan would have used, although he did agree that the best of Pamela's verse was very good. He was quite merciless in his criticism of the rest, however, and Pamela rather revelled in the directness and rudeness of his comments, which struck her as being terribly 'modern'.

In his second letter, written sometime in mid-September 1933, Dylan claimed to be the same age as Pamela, whereas in fact he was not yet nineteen: he doubtless thought that she would never take him seriously if she knew he was still a teenager. In a later letter, he also lied about his height. He liked to think he was about five feet six, whereas he was probably nearer five feet three, a fact which he disguised in later years by buying shoes with discreetly raised heels. What was true, though, in his early descriptions of himself to his new correspondent, was that he weighed hardly anything at all – only about eight stones, anyway. Dylan also told Pamela that his unusual name meant 'Prince of Darkness'; which he presumably thought sounded more poetic than just plain 'sea'. More accurate was the description of himself as a 'thin, curly little person', smoking too many cigarettes despite a crocked lung and a wicked, phlegm-pulling cough, and spending his afternoons writing in the back bedroom of his family's provincial villa.

Several of Dylan's letters to Pamela Hansford Johnson in September and October were in fact written at Blaen Cwm, a pair of cottages at Llangain, not far from Fernhill, that belonged to his mother's relatives. The picture he paints of his existence there is touchingly bleak, as he says he finds himself 100 miles from anyone who is prepared to talk about anything other than the weather. But the rainsodden fields of the Llanstephan Peninsula are preferable to the industrial towns of South Wales, which are like festering sores on the body of a dead country. Dylan claims that all Wales is like that, and reveals that he desperately wants to get away from its narrowness and dirtiness, and out of 'the eternal ugliness of the Welsh people'. The one Welshman about whom he has anything really pleasant to say is his father, probably because he was feeling rather maudlin about D. J.'s cancerous state. He describes D. J. as the most broadminded man he has ever met. Florence, in contrast, is damned for her pettiness, along with her giggling relations. To summarize, 'this bloody country's killing me'.[5]

In November, Dylan and Pamela exchanged photographs, as their correspondence took on a more intimate tone. The snap of herself Pamela sent was so formal and severe that Dylan rechristened her Wilhelmina, after the much-loved but matronly Queen of the Netherlands. He maintained the deception about his age by pretending that the photograph he had sent Pamela was two-and-a-half years old, though he prepared her for the shock of any eventual meeting by saying that in real life he looked about fourteen. Furthermore, he claimed in an immensely long letter acknowledging receipt of her picture that a doctor had told him he had only four years to live. The jocularity with which Dylan repeatedly returned to this subject suggests that he didn't really expect Pamela to believe him. But she confided to her diary that she was really quite worried about his health, which he would have found most gratifying.

Meanwhile, Pamela had been given Victor Neuburg's ultimate accolade: the opportunity of having a book of her poetry published by his press. Initially, she wanted to call the book *Dayspring*, though it was to appear under the title *Symphony for Full Orchestra*. Dylan, by now clearly very taken with the young lady he had never met, was generous in his congratulations. But he also teased her in his letters about what an accomplished person she was. This was seemingly in response to details from her about her busy recreational life, playing the piano and taking part in amateur dramatics.

In a letter written in the second week of November, he tells her about his own experiences at the Swansea Little Theatre, claiming that he tends to get parts that he can play 'straight', like madmen, neurotics, nasty 'modern' young men and low comedians.

Dylan was currently rehearsing a play by Rodney Ackland called *Strange Orchestra*, which was directed by Eric Hughes and put on in December. Dylan played the part of Val, who was described in a review in the *South Wales Evening Post* (once again written by the editor, J. D. Williams) as 'an amoral cad: a young novelist . . . so absorbed in himself [and] in dramatizing his friends for his novels that he cannot see the greatness of [the young heroine's] realization of life's cruelties'.

The notice which appeared in the more conservative *Mumbles Press* highlighted the contrast between Swansea respectability and the lure of London for one such as Dylan. It declares ominously that *Strange Orchestra* comes perilously close to being a 'problem play'. The reviewer moralizes:

> Its people were all stamped with the fear and the 'artificiality' of the post-War 'artistic' London, and their emotions which were shown to be as real as those of the rest of us burst out into startling expression. This is not shallowness on the part of these neurotics – but the fact is that Chelsea and theatreland are a powerful forcing house which brings into public view those things which we normally think most decent to hide.

No wonder Dylan was so keen to move to 'Chelsea and theatreland' as soon as possible.

Dylan's creed, as expressed in one of his letters to Pamela,[6] was that everything that forbids the freedom of the individual is wrong. He lambasts governments because they are 'committees of prohibitors', publishing houses because they feed people what they want to feed them, and the churches because they standardize people's gods and label their morals. 'If only for one moment the Western world could drop the veils that, ever since the Reformation, have clung around it like the films of a disease,' he writes. A fortnight or so later,[7] he expounds the theory that the medieval laws of the Western hemisphere have dictated virginity before marriage (itself effectively barred before one's twenties), which means that young people are condemned to sexual abstinence at the very time of their lives when virginity should be seen as a crime against the dictates of their bodies. He believes that both boys and girls should be allowed to know and use their bodies from the age of puberty.

The passion with which Dylan sets out these ideas suggests a considerable amount of personal pent-up sexual frustration and implies (to me at least) that he was still a virgin. He later boasted that he had lost his innocence in the back of a vehicle at the age of fifteen, but I suspect that was wishful thinking. As the letters to Pamela become increasingly intimate, they bear all the hallmarks of a young man who senses that the forbidden fruit of carnal knowledge may at long last be within reach.

Pamela was obviously also keen to set eyes on her impassioned correspondent. She boldly invited Dylan to come to Battersea to spend Christmas with her and her mother. He was flattered and surprised, but felt he had to spend Christmas once again with his own family, given D. J.'s illness. But Dylan took time off on Christmas Day, sprawled out in an armchair, and smoking one of the fifty cigarettes Pamela had sent him as a present, to write her another vast missive. After a long résumé of the books to be found in his father's and his own personal libraries, Dylan launches into a rambling dissertation on the nature of existence and his own aspirations for what little time on this earth he has left: in particular, to *make* poetry, not just write it, and to open himself up to new perspectives on everything around. He signs off as a 'short, ambiguous person in a runcible hat, feeling very lost in a big and magic universe', and wishing Pamela love and a healthy New Year.

Dylan had committed himself to a busy winter season at the Little Theatre, which made any early visit to Pamela's unlikely. He appeared as Witwoud in William Congreve's *The Way of the World* in January 1934, including some performances in village halls in the Welsh valleys. He then went immediately into rehearsals for Jean-Jacques Bernard's *Martine*, in which he was to have played a Puritan journalist, Julian. *Martine* was directed by Doreen Goodridge, who was trying to stamp out the unsatisfactory practice of some of the young actors of disappearing off when they weren't needed to the bar of Cheese's hotel in the Mumbles. Given Dylan's bad reputation for missing cues and even appearing tiddly on stage, thanks to his fondness for the neighbourhood bars, she specifically warned him that if he went out for a quick one, he needn't bother to come back. Heedless of the risk, he slipped out of the dress rehearsal – and was promptly dismissed from the production. An understudy took his place. Although Dylan's link with the Little Theatre wasn't broken completely, it never resumed the same importance.

Suddenly finding himself at a loose end, Dylan rang Pamela in London, to see if he could take up her earlier offer of his coming to stay. It was the first time they had actually spoken, and she noted in her diary that he had 'such a rich, fruity old port wine of a voice'. The arrangements made, he took the train to London on about 1 March, and arrived palpably nervous at the Johnsons' house on Battersea Rise. As Pamela recalled in her collection of character portraits, *Important to Me* (published in 1974), he stood there in baggy trousers and a huge sweater, which exaggerated his boyish frame. He took off his pork-pie hat to reveal beautiful curling golden hair, freshly washed and parted down the middle. She thought his face curiously shaped: wide and strong at the top, tapering down to a weak mouth and chin. But it was his eyes that really caught her attention: 'dark brown, luminous, almost hypnotic'.[8] After exchanging courtesies, Dylan asked, 'Have you seen the Gauguins?'

Later he confessed to Pamela that he had been practising the remark on the train all the way from Swansea. It seemed an appropriate thing for one artist to inquire of another. There was a Gauguin exhibition on in London at the time, but whether Pamela had seen it or not was of minor importance; what was crucial for Dylan was the impression he made. He needn't have worried. Pamela was enchanted, as was her mother, who looked on him as a child. Used to being fussed over by Florence, Dylan didn't bat an eyelid when Mrs Johnson suggested, as he and Pamela were on the point of going out to visit some of her friends, that he might like to wash his neck.

Dylan stayed with Pamela and her mother for about three or four days. He and Pamela talked late into each night, about art and literature and music, exploring each other's minds and knowledge in a harmless game of one-upmanship. They drank a little beer together, which Dylan fetched from a nearby off-licence; he had arrived at the house with a quarter-bottle of brandy in his pocket, but that hadn't lasted long. Yet Pamela Hansford Johnson wrote that drinking wasn't a problem when he was with her then; in her company, he did not imbibe to excess. It is doubtful whether Pamela's mother would have endured his presence in the house if he had. Nor does he seem to have made a pass at Pamela on this first visit, though she could sense a certain tension in the air. When she saw him off at Paddington on the train back to Swansea, she was depressed at his departure. Three days later, her diary notes that she received a letter (now lost) from him telling her he loved her.

Pamela Hansford Johnson was not the only person who wrote to Dylan in appreciation of the verses that had been appearing in the *Adelphi*, the *Sunday Referee* and elsewhere. Glyn Jones, a Cardiff schoolmaster with his own literary ambitions, responded to the appearance in the *Adelphi* of a poem, 'The Woman Speaks'. Misled by the title, and Dylan's unusual name, Glyn Jones assumed the author was female. Once that misunderstanding had been cleared up, the two became good friends, and Glyn Jones went on to become one of Dylan's most sensitive critics and admirers.

On 14 March the BBC's magazine *The Listener* published Dylan's poem 'Light Breaks Where No Sun Shines'. It is a good example of a resounding, energetic Dylan piece that none the less defies definitive interpretation. As some prudish readers of *The Listener* groped for the poem's meaning, they recoiled from the lines 'A candle in the thighs/Warms youth and seed and burns the seeds of age', convinced that this was pornography posing as art. Some of the management staff at the magazine were concerned lest the poem harm its reputation, but the editor stuck to his guns.

Stephen Spender (who published two slim volumes of verse that year) liked Dylan's poem in *The Listener*, as well as those he had seen in the *Sunday Referee*, and wrote to tell him so. Dylan replied that he had been wanting to write to *him*, to say the same thing of Spender's verse. In his letter, Dylan mentioned that Geoffrey Grigson had been in touch, via *The Listener*, to see if Dylan would submit some work to *New Verse*. Obviously Grigson had lost Dylan's address – or else forgotten his earlier approach. Either way, his opinion of Dylan's poems had gone through a radical reappraisal. Dylan sent him some poems, and Grigson accepted two of them.

Not all of Dylan's literary advancement was by chance. There was also a strong element of self-promotion. For example, he had written to T. S. Eliot (then editor of *Criterion*) late in 1933, enclosing some poems. Having received no reply, Dylan wrote again in March 1934, this time enclosing a stamped self-addressed envelope. Suitably chastened, Eliot replied that there were indeed things that he liked in Dylan's verse, which prompted Dylan to ask whether he could call to see Eliot when he was next up in London, at Easter. He made the same request of Geoffrey Grigson. As Stephen Spender had suggested that Dylan come and have a meal with him in London as well, he left for the capital with a fairly full diary.

Once again, he stayed with Pamela and her mother in Battersea, arriving in time for tea on Saturday, 31 March and staying in London until 9 April. A lunch appointment with Geoffrey Grigson fell through, as Grigson cancelled because of illness. And Stephen Spender got nervous about the prospect of meeting this unknown young Welshman on his own, so he asked the South African novelist William Plomer to join them both for lunch at the Café Royal. It was not a success. Dylan struck Spender as being pale and intense, and altogether too subdued. The problem was that Spender and Plomer had too much to gossip about together, and Dylan felt completely left out. However, Stephen Spender did arrange some reviewing work for him, and although they never became friends, Spender was someone to whom Dylan could – and did – turn when he needed professional and even financial assistance.

Dylan's first encounter with T. S. Eliot was even more of a disaster. Eliot was not the most warm and communicative of men, especially with strangers, and Dylan interpreted his aloofness as condescension. He complained to his friend Trevor Hughes that Eliot had treated him like some curiosity from the Welsh valleys, 'from pitboy to poet'. However, Eliot was too important a person for the young Dylan to protest to his face, and his failure to publish Dylan's first book (for Faber and Faber, where he was a director) would be the result of Eliot's lack of certainty about Dylan's talent rather than of any unpleasantness between the two.

The book came about because Victor Neuburg decided in April that Dylan should follow Pamela Hansford Johnson as the second *Sunday Referee* poet to be enshrined in hard covers. For Pamela, the appearance of her book of poems proved to be the end of one road. The reviews were pretty awful, and she realized she would be better off turning to prose. For Dylan, though, the offer of sponsorship for his first book of poems was a major breakthrough.

In the meantime, there was the awkward question of how Dylan's relationship with Pamela should develop. Their letters were now full of 'loves' and 'darlings' as well as the more habitual critiques of each other's work and Dylan's complaints about life in Swansea. He had by now firmly decided that he wanted to come to London to live and he seemed keen on the idea of marriage. But the bourgeois side of both of them kept that possibility at a distance until Dylan was in a position to provide for Pamela. The prospect of one slim volume of verse was hardly sufficient collateral for marriage.

Dylan was back and forth between Swansea and London during the summer of 1934. Later Pamela Hansford Johnson recalled happy walks over Clapham Common and sitting by the little fountain in the garden of the Six Bells pub in Chelsea, listening to the sound of the water and of bowls clacking against each other on the nearby bowling-green. Dylan astonished her by informing her that apart from drinking and being tubercular, one of his three criteria for the life-style of a poet was that he should get fat. At least he managed two out of the three as he grew older.

Yet as the months went by, Pamela sensed that something was going wrong. In London she noticed that Dylan tried to keep her apart from his other friends. If he saw another young poet on the other side of the King's Road, for example, he would cross over alone for a chat, rather than offering to introduce them. Worse still, when he was back in Wales in May, he had a fling with another girl – or so he said. He had spent Whitsun with Glyn Jones in West Wales, visiting Llangain and Laugharne, amongst other places. He described Laugharne in a letter to Pamela as the strangest town in Wales, with a population of just 400, who spoke English with a marked English accent. The town had a striking town hall, a portreve and a ruined castle with a splendid house attached, where the novelist Richard Hughes (author of *A High Wind in Jamaica*), lived and wrote.

Dylan reported that he had drunk a lot in Laugharne, and had carried on boozing when he went to stay with another friend, Cliff (allegedly a colleague from his *South Wales Evening Post* days), at a bungalow in the Gower Peninsula. After a few days, Cliff's fiancée purportedly came down: a dark, tall, thin girl with 'a loose red mouth'. According to Dylan's letter to Pamela, the girl and Cliff had a row, so she left her boyfriend's bed and shacked up with Dylan for the next three nights instead. The letter goes on to say that the girl now loves Dylan, and he must get away from her and

Wales. He swears that he loves Pamela and is only telling her all this because he doesn't want to hide anything from her. He also declares that he is on the verge of delirium tremens.

The letter is a bravura performance of a sinner confessing his debauchery. Apart from the semi-incoherent tone of parts of the letter, so unlike his other well-honed communications, the content not unnaturally upset Pamela. She replied saying the relationship was over, but Dylan pleaded for a second chance. She relented and the relationship jogged on through the summer, though she would never view Dylan in quite the same way again. But did the three nights of abandon with the 'loose red mouth' really happen? When Paul Ferris made exhaustive investigations into the affair, he could find no convincing supporting evidence.[9] It is true that Dylan sent a letter to his friend Trevor Hughes in early June, claiming to be indulging in 'unrepeatable displays of carnality' with an erotic girl, but that sounds suspiciously like fantasy. The story may of course have been exactly as Dylan related it. Or it could be that he was trying to make Pamela jealous. Or that he wanted to shock her into sleeping with him, by indicating that if he was to be deprived of her body, he would seek solace elsewhere. Or that he actually wanted to terminate the relationship, realizing that nineteen was far too young to be seriously contemplating marriage. Or maybe he was just indulging in mischief. After all, throughout his life, Dylan did very hurtful things to everyone who was close to him: his parents, his sister, his wife, his in-laws and even good friends like Daniel Jones. So why should Pamela Hansford Johnson be an exception?

By mid-June, Dylan was back in London, making things up. But during this visit, and a subsequent one in August through to mid-September, Pamela became increasingly worried by his behaviour. One Sunday he went off for tea with Geoffrey Grigson and did not return until after one in the morning. Pamela started to wonder if she could believe all he was saying and realized that his drinking was increasing. None the less, she followed up a suggestion that he had first made in a letter in early July, to visit him on his home territory. Her mother came along as well, and the three of them travelled together from London. Dylan initially put them all on the wrong train, which would have taken them to Torquay had Mrs Johnson not realized the mistake. A number of Dylan's friends assumed that this was done deliberately.

To begin with, Mrs Johnson and Pamela stayed at 5 Cwmdonkin Drive. Pamela got on well with Florrie and Jack, as she called Dylan's parents, but Mrs Johnson found Florence deeply irritating. After a few days they moved out to stay at the Mermaid Hotel in the Mumbles. By then Pamela had discovered Dylan's true age, which came as something of a shock. They went to the Gower Peninsula, and explored Rhossilli Bay and Worm's Head and all the other childhood places Dylan had told Pamela about. Photographs of the visit show them larking about like any other young courting couple. But behind the jolly facade, things were cracking up. Pamela became increasingly hysterical and she and Dylan had a number of rows. Although the romance puttered on for a little while longer, by the time Pamela and Mrs Johnson left Swansea for home, it was doomed.

4

THE VAGABOND

(1934–1936)

The smouldering discontent that Dylan had been feeling about Wales had burst into flames in the summer of 1934. He sent an intemperate letter to the editor of the *Swansea and West Wales Guardian*, a somewhat less conservative-minded publication than his erstwhile employer, the *South Wales Evening Post*. Dated 4 June and headed 'Expose Humbug and Smug Respectability', the letter declared that the Philistines exercised an inevitable dictatorship in that 'ugly contradiction' of a town of theirs, that 'overpopulated breeding box', Swansea. The main purpose of the letter seems to have been to awaken people to the danger of the lure of Fascism to the poor and downtrodden of the world, but the message is almost lost in the stream of Dylan's invective.

The political influence of the socialist grocer Bert Trick is obvious. Indeed, four weeks later, Bert Trick took Dylan with him to heckle Sir Oswald Mosley, the founder of the British Union of Fascists, when Mosley came to Swansea to address a rally in the Plaza Cinema. Dylan – by now an inveterate fabulist – subsequently claimed in letters to Pamela Hansford Johnson and others that right-wing thugs at the meeting kicked him down the stairs. As Bert Trick recalled the incident, however, both he and Dylan got nervous when scuffles broke out and they fled like rabbits.[1] A few days later Dylan returned to the columns of the *Swansea and West Wales Guardian* with a longer and if anything even more incoherent contribution on the 'Peculiar Heavens Created by Little Orators'. The piece ended with the fine-sounding but largely impenetrable statement: 'Our symbol of faith must be a naked life'.

Such public utterances, complementing a growing body of published poems, were none the less helping to establish a reputation of sorts for Dylan amongst the more liberal intelligentsia of Swansea. About the time of Pamela's less than successful visit there with her mother, Dylan accepted an invitation to speak to a Swansea literary society called the John O'London's, at a soirée scheduled for the beginning of October. The curious origin of this engagement came from an approach to Bert Trick by a young man who had read some of Trick's newspaper articles promoting various socialist reforms. Trick's political writings must at times have been almost as opaque as Dylan's few foolish attempts at the genre, as the young man had so misinterpreted what he had read that he asked Bert Trick if he didn't think he had a useful role to play in the local branch of the British Union of Fascists.

That misunderstanding cleared up – to Dylan's intense amusement – the young man then asked if Dylan would speak to the John O'London's Literary Circle on a subject of his choice. Dylan accepted with alacrity and settled on the theme 'Pornography in Nineteenth-century Literature'. He had several weeks to prepare the topic, and according to Bert Trick[2], he regaled their own informal Wednesday literary group with extracts from the draft lecture as it came along. These were so outrageous that Bert thought Dylan would never have the nerve to deliver the text. He assumed Dylan's readings were merely an elaborate joke to amuse his friends.

When the evening of the lecture came, Bert Trick, Dylan and about four others (including Fred Janes) set out from Trick's home in riotously good spirits. The John O'London's met above Bates's ironmonger's in St Helen's Road; Mrs Bates was one of the group's leading lights. As the party passed the Westbourne Hotel in St Helen's Road, however, Dylan said he needed a drink to fortify himself. Several pints later the little band rolled out of the hotel bar and in the darkness failed to notice that council workmen had dug a trench in the road outside the hospital opposite. This the friends proceeded to fall into, one after another, in a heap. So by the time they reached Mrs Bates's, not only were they half-hysterical but their boots were covered in mud.

According to Trick, about five men and a dozen smart ladies were waiting for them in the sitting-room upstairs. In a letter to Pamela, Dylan inflated this audience to thirty-five, thirty of them women. He said the chairman introduced him as a Young Revolutionary; Dylan certainly looked the part, with his wild eyes and scarlet tie. He then gave his audience the works. At the beginning, as he recounted to Pamela, everyone sat frozen in horrified silence as he expounded on the interrelationship between Victorian creative writing and sexual perversion in its multiple forms. As his discourse progressed there were a few titters. After Dylan had ended on the triumphant battle-cry 'Let copulation thrive!', there were even some risqué questions. But the good literary ladies of Swansea – mostly virgins, Dylan surmised – had not exonerated themselves in his eyes. He was not surprised to hear that an urgent committee meeting of the John O'London's was called later, at which the view had been expressed that the society had better be more careful who it invited in future. But as Dylan told Pamela, 'The more I see of Wales, the more I think it's a land entirely peopled by perverts.'[3]

Glyn Jones (he who had initiated Dylan into Laugharne) thought this was an opportune moment to introduce Dylan to one of the great Welsh iconoclasts of the early part of this century, Caradoc Evans. Evans, whose real Christian name was actually common-or-garden David, was a former Carmarthen shop assistant who had become a journalist, and then won a scandalous name for himself during and immediately after the First World War as a writer, primarily of short stories. His collections *My People* (1915), *Capel Sion* (1916) and *My Neighbours* (1919) were a no-holds-barred exposé of the hypocrisy, lust and greed of the chapel-going people of West Wales. No aspect of the modern manifestations of the Celtic cultural tradition was safe from Evans's brutal analysis. His play *Taffy* (1923) only served to add salt to the wounded pride of an outraged Welsh public, many of whom regarded him as nothing less than a traitor.

Caradoc Evans was fifty-six and living in Aberystwyth when Glyn Jones and Dylan made their pilgrimage to see him in October 1934. Over tea, Dylan and Evans got on like a house on fire. In the evening, Dylan and Glyn Jones did the rounds of the local pubs, drinking to the eternal damnation of Almighty God and the destruction of the little Welsh chapels ('tin bethels'). Had the person who later unwisely asked Dylan about his attitude towards Welsh nationalism been present on that pub-crawl, he would not have been so surprised by Dylan's succinct response: 'Fuck Welsh Nationalism!'[4]

Dylan and Glyn stayed in Aberystwyth that night, and as they lay on their beds, Glyn recounted the story of an eccentric Welsh doctor who had christened his illegitimate son Jesus Christ. The infant died, and the doctor burned his body on a hillside. This was to be the inspiration for one of Dylan's most striking and controversial short stories, 'The Burning Baby'. When Dylan later dictated the story to Pamela Hansford Johnson's mother, who sometimes typed for him, she protested that one couldn't write things like that, but he told her not to worry and just carry on.

As an up-and-coming young poet, Dylan found himself interrogated about his attitudes to all sorts of things. Moreover, right up to the end of his life he replied to such queries thoughtfully and at length, if he believed they came from people or institutions with a serious interest, and especially if the questions were written down. In October 1934, the literary periodical *New Verse* printed Dylan's responses to a number of detailed questions about his beliefs and his work as a poet. It was in answer to that questionnaire that Dylan made his often-quoted political stand as a revolutionary who believed in the right of all men 'to share, equally and impartially, every production of man from man and from the sources of production at man's disposal'. This sounds suspiciously like a verbatim quote from a socialist pamphlet that Dylan may have got from Bert Trick.

Much more characteristic – and telling – is Dylan's reply to a question about the degree to which he had been influenced by the teachings of Sigmund Freud. He acknowledged that Freud had cast light on a little of the subconscious darkness that the great Viennese psychiatrist's writings had exposed. What is more, Dylan believed that poets could benefit from that light (and the knowledge of the darkness), and that they had a duty to drag into the light even more of the hidden causes that Freud had identified.

Dylan was certainly dragging a lot of sex and erotic word-play into his correspondence with Pamela Hansford Johnson in the latter half of 1934. His letters had graduated from rather prim analyses of the strengths and weaknesses of Pamela's own poems to great fanciful catalogues of anatomical explorations, sexual deviations and straightforward smut. In one letter (in which he recounts his lecture to the John O'London's ladies and the visit to Caradoc Evans), Dylan produces: an epitaph for himself, which says he doesn't care a damn if people trample on his balls; three lines of another epitaph that looks in danger of turning into a bawdy limerick about a girl with someone's teeth in her buttocks; a moan about why Pamela won't agree to go to bed with him; and references to abortion, lesbianism, brassières, sanitary towels and French letters. It was a strange way to woo a girl, especially in the 1930s. Even though Pamela could turn a few heads in Battersea with her own liberated range of conversational topics, Dylan was pushing her way beyond the limits of her fascination with the 'modern'. It was almost as if he was testing her, as well as letting his own imagination run free.

At the same time, Dylan was putting the finishing touches to his *18 Poems*, whose publication in book form Victor Neuburg was sponsoring. Neuburg's partner, Sheila Macleod (alias Runia Tharp), was enchanted with Dylan when she first saw him in the garden of Victor Neuburg's house in St John's Wood. As she recalled in typical gushing style nearly twenty years later:

> I saw his bronze head of curls against a summer delphinium sky, with its drifting snow of clouds behind him: the head, then, of a handsome cherubic youth, crowned with an aura of thunderous power and doom . . . To hear Victor Neuburg and Dylan conversing was like being present at the reunion of a young immature Jove, unaware of his powers, with the more remote fatherhood of older unknown Gods. Their play of trenchant wit and humour was like summer lightning, streaked with the forked incision of the older man.[5]

Given T. S. Eliot's continuing procrastinations, Neuburg and Macleod decided to withdraw the offer of Dylan's book to Faber and Faber, and instead arranged with the bookseller David Archer to co-finance the project. David Archer and his partner Ralph Abercrombie ran the Parton Bookshop in Parton Street, a small crescent of Georgian buildings off Red Lion Square near Holborn that no longer exists. The bookshop was not exactly run on commercial lines, but at the beginning, at least, David Archer had the private means to subsidize it. Since coming down from Cambridge, this tall, camp, willowy, rather Proustian figure had felt a mission to be of use to young poets. This included providing refuge to runaway schoolboys with literary ambitions, like Winston Churchill's nephew Esmond Romilly, who fled Wellington School in 1934 and started producing an anti-public school magazine called *Out of Bounds* from a room above the bookshop. The shop itself was a cheerful place, somewhat chaotic and decorated with colourful Soviet posters. Largely under Ralph Abercrombie's influence, it had taken on a markedly left-wing tone. Yet the atmosphere for browsers was not so much subversive as homely.

According to Sheila Macleod, she and Victor Neuburg stumbled on the Parton Bookshop quite by chance one foggy evening. Enchanted by its atmosphere and even more by its comprehensive avant-garde stock, Miss Macleod asked David Archer if Dylan Thomas had possibly discovered this haven on one of his visits to London. Archer replied solemnly, 'It is known to all poets.'

David Archer was in fact a natural publisher for Dylan's first book. He had already brought out two slim volumes of verse by promising youths: a collection of surrealist poems by the sixteen-year-old David Gascoyne, and the first collection of poems by the twenty-year-old George Barker. Accordingly, Archer agreed to put in £20 which, with £30 from Mark Goulden of the *Sunday Referee*, was enough to produce a first edition of 250 copies of Dylan's *18 Poems*, to be published on 18 December and sold at three shillings and sixpence a copy.

Dylan was determined to be installed in London by the time the book came out. In the second week of November, Fred Janes turned up at 5 Cwmdonkin Drive in his father's car, and Dylan piled in with his books and some clothes. He was dressed in an enormous check overcoat like a tent, in which his slight, small body seemed to disappear. Liberation had come; it was bye-bye Wales – 'the land of my fathers, and they can keep it', as he wrote.[6]

D. J. and Florence Thomas approved of Fred Janes, who was a couple of years Dylan's senior. The son of a Swansea greengrocer, Fred was studying at the Royal College of Art in London and had got to know his way around the city, though he tended to come back to Swansea for his vacations. He had found rooms in a lodging-house in Redcliffe Street in the southern part of Earls

Court, not far from Brompton Cemetery. Mervyn Levy, Dylan's former dame-school chum (who took to sporting a most arty beard) was in the same building. For most of the time, Dylan shared Fred Janes's large room, which was a mess of dirty dishes, half-eaten food, papers, artist's materials, discarded clothing and soiled ashtrays. Dylan's small library of books was spread out along the mantelpiece.

Each of the two young men had a camp-bed, but Dylan's collapsed when D. J. once came down on a visit and sat on it, after which Dylan tended to sleep on a mattress on the floor. Dylan was intrigued to discover that Fred actually cooked breakfast for himself, as well as doing workouts every morning. In contrast, Dylan would usually wake up in the clothes he had failed to take off before getting into bed the night before, nibble on an apple and a piece of cake, smoke a cigarette and drink warm, flat beer from a tea-cup. He also went through the alarming morning ritual of hawking in a fashion that would have embarrassed even the most uninhibited Chinese. He would cough and retch until he brought up some phlegm or, even more satisfyingly, the occasional drop of blood. A doctor Dan Jones once met in a pub told him that such traces of blood were probably merely the result of a burst blood vessel from Dylan's coughing and straining, but Dylan naturally saw it as evidence of his imminent tubercular end.

Sometimes, for a change, Dylan would flop down in Mervyn Levy's room, or stay out with friends if he had been to a party or boozing on the town. Fred Janes soon learned not to be surprised if Dylan didn't return at night, or even disappeared for days on end. On at least one occasion, he stayed in Wimbledon with a young gay writer friend, Oswell Blakeston, who claimed that the two of them shared a bed and made love in a rather desultory fashion. Given Dylan's keenness to experience life to the full, it would probably have been surprising if he hadn't gone along with Blakeston's pass, just to see what sex with another man was like, but he doesn't seem to have enjoyed it very much and he found the idea of buggery repulsive. The only other homosexual experience Dylan is supposed to have had was some heavy petting and French-kissing with the painter Max Chapman. In Oswell Blakeston's case, in particular, Dylan none the less kept up a curiously coy correspondence, in which he called himself a rat and Blakeston a mouse. This was rather odd, as Dylan had a mortal fear of small rodents, most notably bats.

Fred Janes painted a striking portrait of Dylan in 1934, which captures the full-lipped, wide-eyed cherub just waiting to tumble zestfully into debauchery. In fact, by the end of 1934, Dylan's mind – and maybe his body – was far more dissolute than his looks suggested. It would be nearly five years before he would start filling out like a balloon, and part of his intriguing charm at the beginning of his London rollicks was the fact that his outrageous stories and public behaviour were so out of keeping with his baby-face.

Even so, some of Dylan's earliest London exploits bordered on the infantile, especially when he went out with Mervyn Levy. The two of them would clamber up lamp-posts and shout at passers-by, or go to dances at the Royal College of Art and pretend to be rolling drunk, so that they had to be physically removed from the dance-floor. Cats and Dogs, with Dylan scampering around among the tables, was still a favourite pub pastime. Once he'd had a session of it in one pub, he would move on to another and start all over again.

The two areas which Dylan frequented most in his London escapades were Chelsea and Soho–Fitzrovia. The latter and Dylan were to become synonymous. Fitzrovia, to the north of Oxford Street, in and around Charlotte Street, took its name from the Fitzroy Tavern, then run by a huge, coarse and kind-hearted Russian called Kleinfeld. He had a soft spot for artists, as well as a firm hand when it came to expelling noisy drunks, and he put up with eccentrics and scroungers like Nina Hamnett, who would ask any likely man to buy her a drink – or merely rattle a tin in front of him in the hope that he might drop in a few coins. In return, the donor – whether a stranger or a regular – would be likely to get an embroidered extract from Nina Hamnett's autobiography (which Dylan had almost libellously reviewed). She had been born in Tenby on the western side of Carmarthen Bay, where she had been a childhood friend of the painter Augustus John. During her time in Paris she had had an affair with the brilliant young sculptor Henri Gaudier-Brzeska, and she counted Pablo Picasso, André Gide and Ernest Hemingway among her friends.

More subdued than the Fitzroy Tavern was the Wheatsheaf pub in Rathbone Place, which was still predominantly working-class, having been not quite so well colonized by the Bohemian set. Men played darts or bantered gently with the barmaids. Nina Hamnett's counterpart in the Wheatsheaf was Betty May, who was reputed to have grown up in a Paris brothel; certainly she had put her fine looks to good use in making the acquaintance of many famous men. Like Nina Hamnett, Betty May had written a racy autobiography (or perhaps had it written for her by a journalist) entitled *Tiger Woman* – she often wore a tigerskin coat. Dylan met Betty May within days of moving to London, and wrote to Bert Trick back in Swansea that he was going to write an article for her in her name, sell it to the *News of the World*, and then demand that she pay him with her body.

When Dylan's own book of poems came out in December, David Archer is said to have organized a launch party to which he forgot to invite the author. The story may well be apocryphal, like so many of Dylan's best tales; he would never let the truth get in the way of a good laugh. But little attention was likely to be paid to the book over Christmas, and although initially Dylan had not intended to go back to Swansea, his mother had taken to phoning and writing to Haydn Taylor and Nancy, asking if they had seen Dylan, and whether they knew if he had enough socks. The temptations of home cooking were all too much, and he succumbed. Besides, he could hold court amongst his cronies in the Kardomah café in Swansea, as the local boy who had made good. Friends like Bert Trick and Glyn Jones rallied round, making sure that *18 Poems* was written about in the local South Wales papers and talked about by those who cared about verse.

As Dylan had a store of over 200 poems in his notebooks, deciding which ones to polish and include had proven difficult. He seems to have changed his mind about a number of them during the long months of uncertainty over the book's publication. With the benefit of hindsight, the most curious omission was 'And Death Shall Have No Dominion', which had to wait another two years before appearing in a bound collection.

From the opening line of the opening poem in *18 Poems*, 'I See the Boys of Summer', the atmosphere is charged with sexuality, not erotic but troubling, hinting at forces both pagan and pantheistic. Even when Dylan is at his most obscure in these poems, however, he gives the impression of being in control. The contrast of style and content with the contemporaneous work of fashionable poets like Auden and Spender is breathtaking.

Back in London, Dylan, Fred Janes and Mervyn Levy had by the end of January 1935 moved round the corner from Redcliffe Street into new lodgings at 21 Coleherne Road, where they were joined by the painter William Scott. Their new landlady kept late hours herself and didn't really care very much what her lodgers got up to as long as they paid their rent. Dylan increasingly slept out. He had by now become much more wedded to 'Comrade Bottle', which Pamela Hansford Johnson realized was coming between the two of them. He still protested his love for her, but she found this increasingly unconvincing. She did, however, enlist Trevor Hughes's help in trying to curb Dylan's drinking – to little avail. Sometimes Dylan managed to get home, but often he did not. It was during 1935 that he acquired the habit of regularly accepting offers of a bed for the night from concerned or amused young women. Some of these got cuddles as thanks, and a few much more. But others seem to have realized that they had ended up with an outsize inebriated baby on their hands, and just watched him curl up and go to sleep.

One of Dylan's new-found drinking pals was the lively Yorkshire writer Rayner Heppenstall, who was two or three years his senior. Sir Richard Rees, editor of the *Adelphi*, had given Dylan Rayner Heppenstall's address in Chelsea, suggesting that he could be a useful contact. Dylan called round at Heppenstall's lodgings in December 1934, with a presentation copy of *18 Poems* under his arm. When Dylan returned to London in the New Year, the two of them went on a number of drunken sprees, in which more often than not it was Heppenstall, rather than Dylan, who disgraced himself. On one memorable evening, the two of them had met up at the Parton Bookshop and then gone on a pub-crawl, during which Heppenstall rapidly got the worse for wear. While he went to the loo in one pub, Dylan emptied the Yorkshireman's glass, which so enraged him when he got back that he swept all the glasses off the bar-counter with his arm. The next thing he knew, he was lying pinned down to the floor, with Dylan sitting on his chest.

Heppenstall was then carried out into the street where a small crowd gathered. A policeman had materialized and restrained Heppenstall with one hand while trying to get his police-whistle to his lips with the other, to summon assistance. According to Dylan,[7] a little man then detached himself from the other onlookers and meekly asked the policeman if he would let him blow his whistle. This was the sort of surreal detail Dylan relished. Heppenstall made one successful attempt to lurch into another pub on the way to the police-station, where his blasphemous rantings and ravings in the cell so annoyed his jailers that they opened the cell door and threw a bucket of cold water over him.

Heppenstall's review of Dylan's book of poems appeared in the February issue of the *Adelphi*. Dylan could hardly have asked for a more helpful critical debut. Although Heppenstall acknowledged some faults, which he put down to Dylan's 'overfertile imagination', he wrote that he saw in Dylan Thomas a poet 'so free from embarrassment, sore throat, sulks and stutters, that I must formally declare his *18 Poems* the most hopeful thing in poetry since Robert Graves' last volume . . . You ought to read this book.'

Desmond Hawkins in the magazine *Time and Tide* was equally enthusiastic:

> A verse-critic may review 500 books in a decade. He will be fortunate if, in the same period, he discovers two considerable poets . . . Mr Auden is already a landmark . . . . But the Audenesque convention is nearly ended; and I credit Dylan Thomas with being the first considerable poet to break through fashionable limitation and speak an unborrowed language . . . For a first book this is remarkably mature. Thomas's poetry is personal or universal, but not social . . . .This is not merely a book of unusual promise: it is more probably the sort of bomb that bursts not more than once in three years.[8]

Such acclaim brought Dylan invitations to some of the salons and parties of literary London, where people were beginning to express curiosity about the wild young man from Wales. One of his first sorties into such society – possibly shortly before *18 Poems* came out – was recorded by the twenty-year-old future novelist Rosalind Wade, who was a friend of both David Gascoyne and George Barker. She had been looking forward to meeting Dylan, following enthusiastic reports from David Archer of the Parton Bookshop. But at first she was put off by the young man's grubbiness. His fingernails were filthy, his raincoat shabby and his curly hair was tangled and unwashed. None the less, when Rosalind Wade found herself with David Gascoyne and Dylan in the Café Royal one day, she asked Dylan if he would like to accompany

David and her to a party being given by the literary critic Joseph Bard and his surrealist painter wife Eileen Agar.

The Bards' white drawing-room was artfully lit and furnished with low modern chairs. Most of the guests were in evening dress. Dylan, in contrast, had on a very grubby green jersey of the kind worn by Wolf Cubs, and he sat cross-legged on a small pouffe, all red in the face, looking like a 'malignant gnome'.[9] As if he were a child deliberately out to shock, Dylan attacked everything and everybody, employing every swearword in his vocabulary. If he had hoped to create a scene, however, he was disappointed, as the sophisticated company at the party merely laughed good-humouredly at his blasphemies and urged him to cheer up and grow up.

In his letters to Bert Trick, Dylan affected to despise such arty parties. Yet he did not behave badly at them all. In fact, a number of people, including the novelist Anthony Powell, recall his usually being polite, amusing and sober when they met him. It all seems to have been a matter of luck and Dylan's mood. What's more, Dylan would change the colour of his spots – often very rapidly – depending on who he was with, so that some people came away feeling he was really charming, while others thought he was a fiend.

Dylan developed a particular dislike for ex-public school Communists, who he believed knew nothing of the realities of the class struggle about which they so loved to pontificate. As he explained to Bert Trick, their antics and posturings helped him understand that he himself could never get involved in the political ramifications of pseudo-literary London. 'Honest writing does *not* mix with it,' he wrote.[10]

The strains of this multi-faceted existence seem to have got to Dylan, as by early March he was back home in Swansea for a few weeks' rest and recuperation, with the help of Florence Thomas's ever-gentle ministrations. She told him that a stranger had called to see him while he was away, to discuss his work. This was Vernon Watkins, an as yet unpublished Swansea Anglo-Welsh poet, who had seen a display of copies of Dylan's *18 Poems* in the window of Morgan and Higgs' bookshop in Union Street. He had gone inside and browsed through a copy – a performance he repeated on several occasions before eventually deciding to buy one. Not long afterwards, Vernon Watkins ran into Dylan's uncle David Rees, whom he had known as a child, and who had recently retired as

Minister at the Paraclete Church in Newton. David Rees gave him the Thomases' address in Uplands and urged him to make contact with Dylan. When Dylan got the message from his mother on his return to Swansea, he phoned Vernon Watkins to arrange a meeting.

Watkins was then a twenty-nine-year-old bank clerk working at Lloyd's Bank in St Helen's Road. His quiet, rather austere exterior belied the true nature of the complex and at times tormented person within. The son of a very respectable bank manager, he had been at both Repton and Cambridge with Christopher Isherwood and Edward Upward. Like Isherwood, Vernon Watkins could not face completing his Cambridge course, but his return home to Swansea in 1927 had been accompanied by a nervous breakdown. He travelled back to Repton and burst in on the headmaster, Geoffrey Fisher (a future Archbishop of Canterbury), and accused him of destroying Youth. Committed to an asylum, Vernon then had a series of disturbing visions inspired by the drawings of William Blake, but he was apparently saved from madness by a renewal of his Christian faith. He had been writing poetry since the age of seven.

Vernon was still living with his parents in the village of Pennard on the Gower Peninsula, and that is where Dylan first met him, one Saturday afternoon in 1935. Vernon was struck by Dylan's initial shyness, which soon gave way to an intense and eager manner, restless and very humorous. They went for a walk along the cliffs, and before long Vernon realized that this deceptively cherubic young man took nothing for granted. When they got back to the house, Vernon dragged out a trunk full of his poems and read some to Dylan. There began one of the most central friendships in Dylan's life, which on Vernon's side soon bordered on love. Vernon was not physically attracted to Dylan, but he was captivated by his new friend's precocity and talent, and he grew to value their conversations about poetry more highly than almost anything on earth.

Dylan was soon off again, however. Geoffrey Grigson had a friend living in British Grove in Chiswick called Norman Cameron, a poet who made his living as a copywriter at the J. Walter Thompson advertising agency (as well as translating Rimbaud on slack afternoons). Cameron, who was the same age as Vernon Watkins, assumed the role of concerned elder brother to

Dylan, easing him out of Chelsea pubs when he thought the youth had had too much to drink, and sometimes providing him with a bed for the night. He was fond of Dylan, but also exasperated by him, as comes over very forcefully in the poem he later wrote about him, 'The Dirty Little Accuser'. Norman Cameron decided that the best thing for Dylan in the spring of 1935 was to get away from the temptations of London. So he arranged for him to go and stay with his friend the historian A. J. P. Taylor and his wife Margaret at their cottage at Higher Disley outside Manchester, where Taylor was a lecturer at the university.

As A. J. P. Taylor recalled in his autobiography, *A Personal History*, Dylan arrived in April, supposedly for a week or two, but he stayed a month. Taylor came to loathe Dylan so fiercely for the bewitching hold he won over his wife Margaret that one has to treat some of his recollections of him with caution. None the less, it is clear that Taylor took a pretty dim view of his house-guest almost from the moment he arrived. He found they had no intellectual interests in common and he became infuriated by what he described as Dylan's cruel giggle. This giggle manifested itself when Taylor quizzed Dylan about his method of composition. Dylan would sit by the window, looking out towards Kinder Scout, as he worked on a line of a poem, crossing out words with a pencil. When Taylor looked at the revisions and pointed out that the result was more obscure than the original, Dylan giggled and said that the idea was to make it more difficult for the reader.

The cruel giggle also manifested when Dylan told A. J. P. Taylor a story about his time sharing lodgings in Earls Court with Fred Janes. Janes was reputedly surviving on £3 a week from his parents (three times the amount Dylan was receiving from his mother). The money was sent in a registered letter which arrived every Friday. One Friday, when Fred Janes was out and Dylan was broke and in need of a drink, he signed for the letter when it arrived. He opened it and helped himself to the money. According to A. J. P. Taylor's account of Dylan recounting this story,[11] Dylan giggled when Taylor asked him what Janes did then, before announcing gleefully, 'He starved!'

Taylor disbelieved some of the things Dylan said, such as his claim that he had torn the wings off flies when he was a child. But in Taylor's eyes even more distasteful than Dylan's boasts and deceits was his sponging. He had told Taylor that he was used to drinking fifteen to twenty pints of beer a day and Taylor, who kept a barrel of beer at the house, had no intention of having his stock drunk dry. Accordingly he rationed Dylan to one pint of beer at lunch, and two at dinner. He suspected, though, that Dylan helped himself at other times when no one was around. Otherwise, Dylan would amble down to a nearby pub called the Ploughboy, where a group of trendy Lefties was usually willing to stand him drinks.

Margaret Taylor (née Adams) was a rebellious creature from an affluent family, who had studied piano in Vienna. The very fact that she was not a virtuous blue-stocking had made her attractive to A. J. P. Taylor. In contrast to her husband, however, Margaret Taylor was enchanted with Dylan from the moment he first arrived at the cottage claiming to have seen the Queen of Sheba on the train. Having by now discovered that her husband was not only not as unconventional as she, but positively stuffy by comparison, Margaret latched on to Dylan's calculated bohemianism with glee. She also regarded his poetic creation with awe.

When Dylan finally left Higher Disley, he borrowed a couple of pounds off A. J. P. Taylor (not surprisingly never repaid), on the pretext that he had lost the return half of his railway ticket back to London. When Taylor handed over the money, he hoped he would never see the young man again. But Margaret Taylor was looking forward to deepening their friendship.

A. J. P. Taylor was not the only one to find Dylan's attitude to other people chilling. Geoffrey Grigson dubbed him 'The Changeling', having woven the fantasy that Dylan had been found under a foxglove plant and left in a decent Calvinist Welsh bed. Another of Grigson's nicknames for him was the 'Disembodied Gland'. Norman Cameron christened Dylan 'Ditch', and their mutual friend Bernard Spencer came up with the most lasting epithet of all: 'The Ugly Suckling'. As Grigson commented, this last nickname captured Dylan's wilful and at times nasty babyishness. Like so many other people in 1930s' literary London, however, Grigson was torn by contradictory feelings towards Dylan: 'When he disappeared, it was a relief; when he reappeared, a pleasure.'[12]

However, the novelist Evelyn Waugh decided that Dylan was a pleasure he could do without. Waugh met Dylan at a dinner party given by Cyril Connolly at his flat in the King's Road in Chelsea, probably in late May 1935. Other guests included Desmond Mac-Carthy, Robert Byron and Anthony Powell. Dylan arrived late and rather drunk, and tried to regale the assembled company with smutty schoolboy jokes. Evelyn Waugh fled, telling Cyril Connolly that Dylan was just like himself at Oxford and he couldn't bear to be reminded of it. Dylan cackled devilishly when the conversation turned to the poet Swinburne's taste for flagellation, which provoked a frisson of unease. As Connolly's kind intention had been to use the dinner party to help launch Dylan in literary society, he did not consider the evening a success.

Meanwhile, Pamela Hansford Johnson, who was starting to enjoy real success as a novelist, had finally come to terms with the fact that there was no future in her relationship with Dylan. She had contributed some basic furniture to the London ménage he shared with Fred Janes and Mervyn Levy, but she realized that she was superfluous and out of place in the riotous conversations the young men had together, speculating how many mice it would take to pull a train, or gossiping about other Swansea friends. She felt even more uncomfortable in the Fitzroy Tavern, where she was unable to summon the confidence to join in the repartee. Dylan tried to paper over the cracks in their relationship by repeatedly urging that they get married. On one occasion he even suggested they post a notice of their intention to do so the following day at the Chelsea Registry Office. Pamela spent a sleepless night, torn between her ongoing love for Dylan and the realization that she could never live with him. Somewhat to her relief, when morning came, there was no sign of Dylan, so no trip to the Chelsea Registry Office either.

By the summer of 1935, Dylan had himself grasped the situation. As he wrote to Bert Trick, Pamela had spurned him 'as a small, but gifted, Welshman, of unsocial tendencies and definitely immoral habits'.[13] Pamela found some consolation in the friendly attentions of Dylan's pal Trevor Hughes. But later in the year she met an attractive young francophile Australian, Neil Stewart, whom she married towards the end of the following year. By then, direct contact with Dylan was broken, although Pamela remained on good terms with his parents. She visited them in 1936, getting to know Uncle Dai, Auntie Dosie, Auntie Polly and other members of Florence's family as well. Pamela Hansford Johnson wrote her best novels after the war, and after her divorce from Neil Stewart, she married C. P. Snow.

Dylan's comments about Pamela to Bert Trick came in a letter written when he was in Ireland. Geoffrey Grigson, encouraged by Norman Cameron, had decided it would be good to get Dylan even further away from London than Disley, and so arranged for the two of them to stay at a ruined cottage in the wilds of County Donegal, at the splendidly named Meenacross at Lifford, on the west coast. The property had been acquired by the American artist Rickwell Kent, who had fixed up a makeshift studio in a donkey shed there before losing interest in the place.

Geoffrey Grigson and Dylan travelled to Ireland via Harrow, where they stayed with Daniel Jones. Dylan noted that Dan was cleverer than ever and reading all the time, unlike Dylan himself, who had virtually stopped reading anything except magazines and detective novels, some of which he reviewed for Grigson's *New Verse*. Dylan informed Bert Trick that Dan Jones's mind was in a mess, as he couldn't make up his mind whether to pursue litera-ture or music. In the event, Dan opted for music, attending the Royal Academy in London before taking up a Mendelssohn tra-velling scholarship to Rome and Vienna (1936–7).

Geoffrey Grigson believed that the two weeks he and Dylan spent together in Donegal were the high point of their friendship. They went for enormous walks over the wild countryside, often in the pouring rain, and would then dry themselves out in front of a turf fire. They quaffed poteen – colourless whiskey made in an illicit still – from a quart bottle hidden in a potato patch outside the shed. A deaf local farmer, Dan Ward, and his Gaelic-speaking wife Rose, kept them supplied with food, milk and buttermilk. Drink-ing large quantities of the latter, Dylan remained relatively sober but started to put on weight.

The main idea of being in Ireland was that Dylan should begin serious work on putting together a second book of poems. For much of August, after Geoffrey Grigson had returned home, Dylan would rise at nine, have breakfast and then work until lunch. Then he would walk over the cliffs and down by the sea, watching the gannets and the puffins and the seals. He mused about dead Irish souls in the smooth, white pebbles on the beach. Or he would hike several miles over to the little town of Glendru-makie, to stock up on cigarettes or visit the pub. Back in the 'studio' at Meenacross, he would have tea and then write till dusk.

But it was in the evenings that Dylan's imagination ran wild. As he wrote in a letter to Daniel Jones, harking back to the Gothic fantasies of their 'Warmley' days, when he looked out of the window of the hut at night, he saw a strange Hungarian gentleman, Count Antigarlic, who had come down the hill wearing a cloak lined with spiders. The door was locked and Dylan hurried to bed, frightened. Only in the morning (or so Dylan's fantasy went on), when he found traces of blood on the window-pane, and a dry, dead mouse on the window-sill, did the visitation of the night before come back to him. 'It's hard to pick up the night threads,' he told Dan Jones. 'They lead, quite impossibly, into the socket of a one-eyed woman, the rectums of crucified sparrows, the tunnels of coloured badgers reading morbid literature in the dark . . .'[14]

In September, as the days grew shorter, Dylan became bored with Meenacross, and started feeling nostalgic for the reassuring warmth of his father's study in Swansea, complete with its plaster statues of Greek gods. So one day he simply walked away from the hut and caught a bus, without letting the Wards know or paying them the agreed fees for his upkeep. Geoffrey Grigson was furious when he found out, as he knew Dylan had money with him – some of it borrowed from himself and Fred Janes. Grigson and Norman Cameron (or 'Normal', as Dylan preferred to call him) had to pick up the bill. The affair undoubtedly soured Geoffrey Grigson's attitude to Dylan himself, but he was also becoming less interested in Dylan's work. Although *New Verse* published three of Dylan's poems that December, the association was subsequently terminated.

Dylan was getting work accepted for publication elsewhere, however, including poems in *Comment*, the *Scottish Bookman* and the Majorca *Caravel*. From Ireland he had also written to both John Lehmann (who was co-editing *The Year's Poetry* with Denys Kilham Roberts), and Robert Herring, who had recently taken over the editorship of the magazine *Life and Letters Today*. Both Lehmann and Herring printed some of Dylan's writing. Dylan's letters to the two men were short, businesslike and fairly formal, but as a foretaste of his practice with editors and radio producers from then on, Dylan asked Robert Herring if it would be possible to have some of the fee for his work in advance. Acquiring advances on work – sometimes delivered, sometimes not – became a major source of income for Dylan, to supplement 'loans' extracted from friends like Geoffrey Grigson and Rayner Heppenstall, or even from people he was meeting for the first time.

After a brief stop in London, Dylan arrived in Swansea in the latter half of September and promptly retired to bed. In an odd letter to Geoffrey Grigson, half self-pitying, and half bantering, Dylan implied that this was because he had contracted gonorrhoea. This was a story he leaked to various friends over the next couple of years, and his future wife Caitlin was convinced it was true. The fact that the girl he was meant to have caught it from didn't come on the scene until more than six months *after* Dylan's letter to Grigson is just one of a myriad inconsistencies in Dylan's versions of his life story. Anyway, for an up-and-coming poet about to celebrate his twenty-first birthday, the idea of having a venereal disease was a satisfactory second-best to not dying of TB.

Haydn and Nancy Taylor sent Dylan a cheque for his birthday, which he claimed to have spent on a grey hat and a 'book of ballads'. In the same letter[15] he referred to a new tweed suit covered in coloured spots. Whether it actually existed is a matter of conjecture, but Dylan certainly did take considerable interest in his own appearance, even if some of his choices were alarmingly garish and all pretence at elegance was in any case thwarted by his failure to keep his body and hair well-groomed or even clean.

As far as Florence was concerned, her darling boy was having a minor breakdown – but nothing so serious that five or six weeks in bed being fed boiled sweets and salted bread in milk wouldn't cure. Wrapped in shawls and propped up on pillows, Dylan happily carried on his literary self-promotion from his bed at 5 Cwmdonkin Drive, writing to editors and other people of influence. One such was Richard Church, who was working for the publishers J. M. Dent. Thanks to an intervention by Ralph Abercrombie of the Parton Bookshop, whose father, the poet Lascelles Abercrombie, was friendly with Richard Church, a copy of Dylan's *18 Poems* was sent to Church, and Dylan complemented these with examples of his more recent work. When he finally got to meet Richard Church in London, though, he startled the poor man by asking him if he could lend him half a crown.

Dylan was extremely rude about Richard Church behind his back (as indeed he was about other people who helped him, such as Stephen Spender, whom he renamed 'Chapfork Bender'). He thought Church was a real fuddyduddy, and it was true that

Richard Church was quite shocked by the erotic overtones of some of Dylan's poems. To his credit, this did not prevent him acknowledging Dylan's talent, or ensuring that J. M. Dent became Dylan's publisher. However, Dylan was particularly offended that Church described some of the first poems he sent him as 'surrealist'. Church implored Dylan to produce more simple poems that everyone could understand, which sent Dylan scuttling back to his notebooks to see what could be revised from there. As he was now doing most of his work back at his parents' home, Vernon Watkins was able to help him with the selection for his second book, *25 Poems*. It was mainly on Vernon's insistence that this time 'And Death Shall Have No Dominion' was included.

Meanwhile, Dylan had acquired a new and unexpected fan: Edith Sitwell. Although he had been interested in Edith Sitwell's poetry as a schoolboy, Dylan had turned against her when she wrote a scathing criticism of one of his poems ('Our Eunuch Dreams') in her book *Aspects of Modern Poetry*, published in 1934. This had prompted Dylan to vituperate against her in a letter to Glyn Jones, in December 1934, as a 'poisonous thing of a woman, lying, concealing, flipping, plagiarizing, misquoting' and producing 'virgin dung'.[16] Belatedly, Edith Sitwell had read Dylan's *18 Poems* (which she was to review most flatteringly in the *London Mercury* in February 1936) and had completely changed her mind about this newcomer on the literary scene. She wrote Dylan a charming letter of encouragement and praise in January 1936, to which Dylan replied most properly and respectfully. Miss Sitwell was a formidable friend to have on one's side, and she worked assiduously to promote Dylan, while simultaneously giving him motherly advice about looking after himself well and getting a job.

In fact getting a job was the last thing on Dylan's mind. He was feeling more than satisfied about having pulled off – in this year of his legal majority – the remarkable coup of being accepted as a full-time poet and pub raconteur. Temporarily based in Swansea, he made frequent trips to London, bumping along happily with the continuing support of his family, the generosity of his friends and the kindness of strangers.

It appears that by the spring of 1936, Dylan had won as much renown as a bawdy troubadour of the taverns of Soho–Fitzrovia as he had as a serious poet – a reputation that still prevails today albeit on a far greater scale. He had learned to exploit his Welshness in

London, as he played what the painter Nigel Henderson has astutely defined as his Pied Piper Act. Dylan kept smart young ladies out slumming in Fitzrovia agog with his completely fictitious accounts of how Welsh miners bathed lasciviously after a day down the mines. His steady flow of scabrous stories in bars, and his naughty-boy behaviour, could win devotees in a matter of minutes, as people were charmed as irresistibly as the rats of Hamlin. At this time Henderson was connected with Rupert Doone's Group Theatre, which put on the Auden–Isherwood collaboration plays and other politically motivated works, and was himself trying to become a poet. When he rashly showed Dylan some of his work, Dylan pronounced, after a drawn-out pause, 'Ah! Fucked-out Yeats!'[17]

Dylan was holding forth at the Wheatsheaf in Rathbone Place on the evening of 12 April 1936, when a beautiful young Irish would-be dancer, Caitlin Macnamara, saw him for the first time. She had heard Dylan described by the artist Augustus John – who was both painting and bedding her – as a 'bright young spark'.[18] Standing there in his tweed jacket and corduroy trousers, rolling out the stories, Dylan didn't seem to notice Caitlin at first, as she sat on a stool by the bar. But then suddenly his head was in her lap and he was burbling endearments to her. He didn't just say how attractive she was; he told her he loved her and was going to marry her.

A Pleasant and Eccentric Marriage

(1936–1938)

Dylan Thomas aspired to be a free spirit, able to follow his poetic calling and basic instincts, but Caitlin Macnamara was this to the manner born. The Macnamaras were well-established members of Ireland's Protestant eilite, with a Georgian country mansion at Ennistymon in County Clare, where Caitlin's grandfather had been High Sheriff. Her father, Francis Macnamara, had been marked out for a career in law. He studied at Magdalen College, Oxford and law school in London until he rebelled against the prospect of a comfortable, staid life and determined to be a man of letters instead. Over six feet tall, with golden hair and bright blue eyes, Francis Macnamara carried himself like a conqueror. Brave and adventurous, he had a restive imagination and a ready tongue. He settled in London on an allowance of several hundred pounds a year from his father, becoming a self-styled poet, philosopher and – less convincingly – a financial adviser. He assiduously courted friends among the more virile members of the capital's artistic and literary community and he became a popular figure because of his energy and gift of the gab. A strong drinker in his later life, he published a volume of poetry called *Marionettes*, and wrote free-verse soliloquies put into the mouths of figures from Irish legends, which he circulated among his friends.

In 1907, at the age of twenty-three, Francis Macnamara married an attractive half-French, half-Irish girl, Yvonne Majolier, whose father, Edouard, was a scion of a very well-known family of French Quakers from Congenies, near Nîmes. Edouard Majolier was not a practising Quaker himself, and indeed developed an addiction to actresses and brandy. He settled in England and kept a grand house in Bramham Gardens, Earls Court, where Yvonne grew up. Only after his death did his family discover that he also maintained an establishment in Thurloe Square, South Kensington, complete with a mistress and a second set of children.

Yvonne Majolier eloped with Francis Macnamara, though this seems to have been rather unnecessary as her family quite approved of the young man, apart from the fact that he didn't have much money. The couple married at Paddington Registry Office and moved to Hammersmith, where they produced four children in fairly rapid succession: a son, John, and three daughters, Nicolette, Brigit and Caitlin. By the time Caitlin was born, on 8 December 1913, Francis had become a good friend of Augustus John, who was six years his senior. In fact, in the summer of the previous year, Francis had taken great delight in introducing Augustus John to his home territory of County Clare, Galway and Connemara. Every summer Francis took his children to Ireland, where he had a little house of his own at Doolin, a small fishing village seven miles from Ennistymon.

While Caitlin was still tiny, however, Francis Macnamara put his belief in free love into practice and went off with a married woman called Euphemia, whose previous husbands and lovers had included the painters Ambrose McEvoy and Henry Lamb. The affair with Euphemia did not last long, and Francis kept in contact with his family. But to all intents and purposes, his marriage to Yvonne had broken up. Disoriented and often strapped for cash, Yvonne moved with her children firstly, in 1916, to a house in Cheyne Walk, Chelsea, owned by Gerald and Nora Summers, a wealthy couple who had studied at the Slade School of Art with Augustus John, and then the following year to Augustus John's own home at Alderney Manor in Dorset.

Augustus John was the ultimate bohemian. Tall and bearded (half-Christ, half-gypsy) he had an excess of life-force, which he channelled into painting and procreation. He claimed not to know how many children he had fathered, but was happy for people to speculate that it was scores. He had five sons by his first wife, Ida Nettleship, and by the time Yvonne Macnamara and her brood arrived at Alderney Manor, he had another son and two daughters by Dorelia 'Dodo' McNeil (another son of theirs had died of meningitis in 1912). The Macnamara children became part of one big liberated family, in which the adults and the older children wore long, loose peasant-style clothes, and the smaller ones – in summer, at least – often ran around naked. Augustus himself presided over this ménage as a captivating but also rather ferocious father-figure. As Nicolette Macnamara recalled in her riveting autobiography, *Two Flamboyant Fathers*,[1] there was a regular stream of Bloomsburyite visitors such as Henry Lamb, Lytton Strachey and Lady Ottoline Morrell, who Nicolette thought was a witch. It was a heady but unsettling atmosphere for young children to grow up in.

In 1923, after Nicolette, Brigit and Caitlin had spent a few months at Congenies, Granny Majolier bought Yvonne an old farmhouse and former inn, called New Inn House, in the village of Blashford, Hampshire, a couple of miles from Ringwood. Four years later, Augustus John and his family moved to Fryern Court, about seven miles away, and as Gerald and Nora Summers were now living even nearer than that, the Macnamara children's curious extended artistic family life resumed. John Macnamara had been sent off to prep school and went on to be trained for the Navy, but his sisters were mainly taught at home, by governesses or anyone else who happened to be around. Their particular friends in Augustus John's household were his daughters Poppet and Vivien, and the five of them commuted between New Inn House and Fryern Court, riding, bathing, dancing and sleeping in each other's beds.

Francis Macnamara was a regular visitor to Fryern Court. Nicolette looked on him with a detached curiosity, whereas Caitlin developed a considerable loathing for her father – largely because of the way he treated women. He vied with Augustus John for a reputation as a great Lothario. When Francis teased Dodo one day by complaining that Augustus would take a woman off to a pub to get her drunk, so he could then do what he liked with her, she countered by accusing Francis of taking women off for thirty-mile hikes, after which they were too exhausted to resist his advances.

Caitlin later believed that it was partly in response to such behaviour that her mother Yvonne turned to lesbianism, allegedly
taking Nora Summers as her lover.[2]

As far as the Macnamara girls were concerned, the most intriguing of Augustus John's sons was Caspar, who was born in 1903,
while John was still married to Ida Nettleship. A chubby child who
developed great physical and emotional strength, Caspar was the
first of Augustus's sons to beat his father in the fights that Augustus sometimes provoked. Like Augustus, Caspar was expert at
acting the role of a simpleton, which meant that the Macnamara
girls always considered him rather slow-witted. This did not stop
both Brigit and Caitlin falling in love with him, however. Brigit was
briefly engaged to be married to Caspar, and Caitlin looked on him
as the love of her life. She claimed in her autobiography that had
Caspar turned up on a white charger during her years with Dylan,
she would have happily gone off with him.[3] Caspar realized that
Caitlin was getting sweet on him, and suddenly broke off their
relationship, without ever explaining why. She felt bitter about this
ever after, and even wondered whether the fact that Caspar later
lost both his legs in the war was some form of divine retribution.
All the sisters were astounded when he went on to become an
Admiral of the Fleet and was knighted.

Brigit and Caitlin also shared the honour of being chosen by
Augustus as models, though honour may not be the apposite
word. The girls were relatively safe while they were still young
teenagers, but after Caitlin had gone to London (and later Paris) in
the early 1930s to train to be a dancer, Augustus considered her
fair game for one of his notorious pounces at his studio. At the end
of her first sitting for a new portrait, he leaped on her, ripped off
her clothes and penetrated her like some mindless hairy goat.
Exactly the same thing happened the following day. Though she
didn't complain to anybody at the time, Caitlin later looked back
on these leaps as rape, and declared that the brutality with which
she had lost her virginity to Augustus John explained why she
became basically anti-sex[4] – and by extension, somewhat anti-men
– despite her self-confessed promiscuity towards the end of and
after her marriage to Dylan. Even with the assaults, however, she
continued to sit for Augustus John. Although she disliked the
sexual act that terminated the sessions, she loved being taken out
by him to fine restaurants like the Eiffel Tower in Fitzrovia. While

up in London, she often stayed at John's flat in Fitzroy Square, or with her father Francis at a lovely apartment he had acquired in Regent's Square.

The Dylan Thomas who suddenly plonked his head in Caitlin's lap in the Wheatsheaf pub on 12 April 1936 was a very different man from Augustus John and Francis Macnamara. Far from feeling threatened by this amorous young Welshman, she thought he was rather sweet, and almost instantly wanted to mother him. She spotted that for all the bravura of the troubadour performance she had witnessed earlier in the evening, Dylan was actually rather nervous and very docile. The two of them followed Dylan's drinking companions to another pub or a club, and then went on, at Caitlin's suggestion, to the Eiffel Tower, which was situated just round the corner from the Wheatsheaf, in Percy Street. Above the restaurant were hotel rooms, which the German proprietor, Rudolf Stulik, would make available to his raffishly artistic clientele. Caitlin knew that Vivien John sometimes used to stay there and charge the room to her father Augustus's account. Stulik of course recognized Caitlin as one of Augustus John's lady-friends, and made no objection when she checked in with Dylan on the same basis. Dylan loved the idea that Augustus John would be picking up the bill.

When the couple got up to their room, Dylan was shy about undressing. Caitlin noticed that not only did he have no underpants on but his trousers were so stiff that they remained standing up when he stepped out of them.[5] He came to bed in his long shirt, and immediately snuggled down under the blankets. His lovemaking was gentle and unspectacular; Caitlin claimed that she did not experience an orgasm with him, either on that first night or ever during their years together.

Dylan and Caitlin clung together for the night and stayed on at the Eiffel Tower for nearly a week. Every morning at eleven, when the pubs opened, they would go down to one and Dylan would line up a row of beers which he then downed one after another. Caitlin wasn't very enamoured of Dylan's conveyor-belt drinking and was dismayed to discover that he rarely stopped for food. He did manage to break away from his routine one lunchtime, however, to have a meal with 'the Pope', T. S. Eliot, whom on this occasion Dylan considered quite charming.

Caitlin believed she had found her rightful place among the chattering literary and artistic boozers like Rayner Heppenstall, George Barker, the South African poet Roy Campbell, Norman Cameron and Louis MacNeice, and above all alongside Dylan. She didn't find many of Dylan's pub anecdotes very funny, but she was won over by his endearments and by the way he kept telling Roy Campbell and the others that she was the girl he was going to marry.

By the third week of April, however, Caitlin had returned to Blashford and more sittings for Augustus John, while Dylan's friends had once more decided it was time to get him away somewhere quiet to work. Earlier in the year, Norman Cameron had thought it would be a very good idea if Nigel Henderson's mother Wyn invited Dylan down to stay at her cottage at Polgigga in Cornwall, a couple of miles from Land's End. A forty-year-old publisher and occasional journalist, Wyn Henderson was willing to take on the role of surrogate mother to Dylan. He could joke with her and he especially liked her when drunk, though when she was sober she was a little bookish for his taste. He stayed with her for six or seven weeks, first at Polgigga and then at another house that she took at Mousehole.

Keeping Dylan from spending too much time in the pubs was one of Wyn Henderson's main tasks. On one occasion, she had to enlist the help of some local farm labourers to get him home when he claimed to have drunk forty pints of beer. He raved on about vampires and insisted that all the windows in the house be firmly locked. As sometimes happened when Dylan drank far too much, he shat in his trousers, and Wyn Henderson ended up washing him clean in a tub, just like a baby.

In between the drinking, though, Dylan wrote long letters to chums like Vernon Watkins and Oswell Blakeston (who was a good friend of Wyn Henderson's). Curiously, none of those that have survived makes any mention of Caitlin. Instead, there is a lot of gossip about literary friends in London and some plans to have various pieces of work published. While he was at Polgigga, Dylan heard from Richard Church that J. M. Dent would publish his second book, *25 Poems*. Several of Dylan's letters ended with postscripts begging for money. When he responded on 6 May to T. S. Eliot's accepting his story 'The Orchards' for *Criterion*, he asked Eliot if he could put some money up front too. The story, in which the mythical Welsh village Llareggub appears in print for the first time, was published in the July issue of the magazine.

Despite Dylan's anger at being called surrealist by Richard Church, one of the first things he did when he got back to London in June was to go to see the great Surrealist Exhibition that ran from 11 June to 4 July in the spacious New Burlington Galleries. The show had been organized by the painter and collector Roland Penrose, with assistance from other artists and writers such as Paul Nash, Henry Moore, Herbert Read and David Gascoyne. From the Continent came some of the great names of Surrealism, including André Breton, Salvador Dali and Paul Eluard. On the opening day, Dali arranged for a woman whose face was completely covered with roses to circulate among the visitors. Dylan went to the exhibition several times, as well as giving a poetry reading there on 26 June alongside Paul Eluard and David Gascoyne.

One afternoon, Daniel Jones accompanied Dylan to the exhibition and the two of them stared long and hard at a huge picture of a nude woman that was two-dimensional on the left-hand side, but blossomed out into three dimensions on the right. From the woman's projecting right nipple hung a chain with a little cage on the end. Inside the cage was a white mouse that seemed to spend most of its time cleaning its whiskers, except when its daily moment of stardom came and it was taken for a walk round the gallery on a lead attached to a tiny diamanté collar. According to Dan Jones, this excursion was listed in the catalogue as item 451b, 'La Promenade du Souris' (Not for Sale).[6] Dylan seems to have entered into the spirit of the occasion, as one day he reportedly went round offering visitors portions of boiled string. It wasn't that he thought that all the exhibits were great art; rather, he applauded the concept of cocking a snook at the critical establishment.

In the first half of July Dylan was working hard, polishing some of the poems for his second book. But he did also give some thought to a possible collaboration with Rupert Doone's Group Theatre, largely at Nigel Henderson's suggestion. As he told Henderson in a letter,[7] he envisaged 'a Horrible play' which would be mainly in prose, but with verse choruses. He said he had got most of the plot mapped out, but was putting the project on one side until he had had a chance to talk to Rupert Doone about it. Nothing seems to have come of it in the end.

Meanwhile Dylan learned that Caitlin would be staying with Augustus John at Richard Hughes's house by the castle in Laugharne during the National Eisteddfod, which was taking place that year at Fishguard. He wrote disingenuously to Hughes, asking whether as he and Fred Janes were making a trip to Fishguard in Fred's father's car on 15 July it would be all right if they called by to say hello to Hughes. The two of them duly turned up at Castle House at lunchtime. Augustus John, who had arrived with Caitlin only the night before, was far from pleased. Richard Hughes was a gracious host, however, and invited Dylan and Fred to return that evening to have dinner with him and his wife, Augustus and Caitlin. He himself would spend the day making something special, to be washed down with one of his selection of fine wines.

The four guests left together for Fishguard after lunch, Augustus and Caitlin in one car, and Dylan and Fred Janes in the other. But the journey turned into a pub-crawl, as they pulled in at every hostelry between Laugharne and Fishguard for a pint of beer. They weren't much in the mood to stay long at the Eisteddfod when they got to Fishguard, so they soon left and pub-crawled back. At some stage, Dylan abandoned Fred and climbed into the back of Augustus John's big black Wolseley along with Caitlin. Soon they were kissing and cuddling while Augustus John fumed and drove even faster than his usual hair-raising speed. When he got to the St Clears' turn-off for Laugharne, he drove straight on instead, until he reached Carmarthen. There he pulled into the car park of the Bull's Head, where the three of them went in for yet more drink. As they left the pub, however, a scuffle broke out between the two men, from which Dylan not surprisingly came out the worse. Augustus drove off with Caitlin, leaving him lying on the ground. There was no sign of Fred Janes; not only had he been unable to keep up with Augustus's car, but his own vehicle had broken down. Dylan made his way to his parents' house in Swansea. Back in Laugharne, hours overdue, Augustus and Caitlin discovered Richard Hughes disconsolately surveying the charred remains of his special dinner.[8]

Apart from a quick whizz to London for the August Bank Holiday, Dylan stayed on in Swansea for the rest of the summer, complaining bitterly to anyone whose attention he could hold about his chronic lack of money. On 10 September Dent published *25 Poems*. Despite the fact that Dylan had rudely stood Edith Sitwell up at a meeting they were meant to have had earlier in the year, she reviewed Dylan's new book most warmly in the *Sunday Times*, calling it 'nothing short of magnificent'. She went on: 'I could not name a poet of this, the youngest generation, who shows so great a promise, and even so great an achievement.'[9] Such an accolade from so respected a critic in a mass-circulation newspaper undoubtedly helped sales of the book, which went into a second printing in December.

D. J. Thomas retired from his teaching post at Swansea Grammar at the end of that Michaelmas term, after thirty-six years in the profession. His staff colleagues presented him with a small cheque and the boys gave him some books, but he was morose. He felt he had achieved very little. That Christmas was the last the Thomas family spent at 5 Cwmdonkin Drive, as D. J. and Florence moved out in the spring of 1937, to a smaller house at Bishopston in the Gower Peninsula, still within easy striking distance of Swansea. For Dylan, this move was not just the end of an era but also the loss of a secure home base, to which he had always been able to return. Even though he kept in close contact with his parents, 'home' would now have to be somewhere else. Judging from the intensity of the letters he was sending to Caitlin Macnamara at this time, it is clear that he felt she might be part of this new home scene. Though he was by no means ready to stop sowing his wild oats, he cherished the idea of domestic calm, in which he would provide poetic love in return for Caitlin's looking after him.

Caitlin herself needed some loving support, as she had had to go into hospital to be treated for gonorrhoea. Augustus John seems not to have been alone in suspecting that she caught it from Dylan. But in her autobiography, Caitlin says that she picked it up from someone at a party, though she wasn't sure from whom. After leaving hospital she spent a short spell at Blashford with her mother, before going over to Ireland to stay with her father. Francis Macnamara was now master of Ennistymon House, which he had decided to turn into a hotel. He was not a natural business-man, however, with the result that the Falls Hotel, as it was called, was more like one long house-party than a commercial venture. Francis enjoyed drinking and gossiping with the hotel guests, while Caitlin sat behind the bar as barmaid, dreaming and dabbling with water-colours. In the evenings she would go off dancing with some of the wild local Irish boys, whose zest for life she found exhilarating.

While Caitlin was in Ireland, Dylan fulfilled his need for sexual and emotional satisfaction elsewhere. He was involved with at least two older women at this time. One was an American writer, Emily Coleman, who David Gascoyne believed was in love with Dylan. The other was Veronica Sibthorp, a wealthy friend of Wyn Henderson's whom Dylan had met while staying with Wyn in Cornwall. She was six years older than Dylan and had a handicapped leg. She later claimed that Dylan wanted to marry her. The set-up between Veronica Sibthorp and Wyn Henderson was rather complex, as Veronica's current husband (the second of three), Waldo Sibthorp, a painter, had previously been Wyn Henderson's lover.[10] It was typical of the 'free love' ethos surrounding this group of friends that not only did both Wyn Henderson and Veronica Sibthorp have sexual relations with Dylan, but the Sibthorps also offered him hospitality (with or without Caitlin) in their London flat in Great Ormond Street in the spring of 1937, and at their cottage at Lamorna Cove near Mousehole in Cornwall that summer.

Just before going down to Cornwall for this second visit, Dylan made his radio debut. It nearly ended in farce. The BBC's West and Wales station had contracted him to do a fifteen-minute live reading of poems, to be broadcast on 21 April from its Swansea studios. Unfortunately, however, Dylan had apparently used some money obtained from J. M. Dent as an advance for a book about Wales to go up to London on another spree, and to meet up with Caitlin on her return from Ireland. He failed to catch a train back down to South Wales in time, but an old friend of his, John Pudney, who was now working for the BBC, arranged for him to do the broadcast from Broadcasting House in London instead. The session seems to have gone well, but afterwards the BBC management got into a panic about whether Dylan had obtained permission from the poets concerned to read their work. Knowing him, that would have been most unlikely.

In fact, Dylan was so hopeless about dealing with the tedious paperwork that accompanies being a freelance writer and broadcaster that Edith Sitwell insisted he get a literary agent. Accordingly, he signed up with David Higham, who was one of the most shrewd (though eccentric) figures in the business. David Higham only once bothered to take Dylan out to lunch, in the way literary agents entertain their clients, as on that occasion Dylan had had so much to drink that he couldn't manage to eat anything at all. Higham made it clear from the beginning that it was no use Dylan trying to borrow money off him personally, but he became expert at obtaining advances on Dylan's behalf.

Dylan and Caitlin spent four months in Cornwall in the late spring and summer of 1937, initially at the Sibthorps' cottage. It was from there that Dylan wrote to his parents on 10 June announcing that he was planning to get married to Caitlin the following week. D. J. was horrified on two counts. First, he could not see how Dylan could possibly afford to keep a wife, let alone any family that might ensue. And second, he thought marriage would get in the way of Dylan's work. He therefore contacted Haydn Taylor to see if he could dissuade his brother-in-law. Haydn rather forlornly phoned round various people, trying to track Dylan down. He even phoned Yvonne Macnamara and peremptorily requested that she try to get Caitlin to say no. But Haydn realized he had been given a hopeless mission. All he got for his pains was rebuffs and yet another begging letter from Dylan, asking for money.

Dylan and Caitlin didn't actually get married until 11 July, at Penzance Registry Office. The delay seems to have been caused by a lack of sufficient funds to buy the marriage licence; every time the couple saved up enough, they ended up spending it on drink instead. In the end, Wyn Henderson paid for the licence. She was one of the very few guests present at the wedding. Caitlin wore a simple blue cotton dress, while Dylan had on his usual corduroy trousers, tweed jacket, a checked shirt and no tie. He had however acquired two little Cornish silver rings to be exchanged at the ceremony, which was presided over by a stony-faced Registrar who had doubtless noticed that both bride and groom were pretty well primed with drink.

In a letter to Haydn and Nancy, Dylan described his new domestic arrangement as a 'pleasant and eccentric marriage'. On both sides, though, family and friends divided into two opposing camps. Some thought that Dylan and Caitlin were made for each other, noting how similar they were in many ways. But the other camp avowed that Caitlin was the worst possible thing to happen to Dylan because of her wildness and what her sister Nicolette called her grudge against the world.[11] Dylan himself maintained that

Caitlin was the only wife he ever wanted, and he seemed to need her fiery temperament just as much as her coddling.

After the wedding, Dylan and Caitlin moved in with Wyn Henderson at Mousehole, where Wyn was running a restaurant called the Lobster Pot, with her mother's help. The restaurant provided a focal point for the circle of friends from London who came down to Cornwall that summer. These included Rayner Heppenstall and his recently acquired wife, Oswell Blakeston and Wyn Henderson's son Nigel. Many hours were spent drinking and talking in nearby pubs. One day, Wyn surprised Caitlin by asking if Dylan and she would sleep on top of her if she pretended to be a mattress. Caitlin saw no particular objection to fulfilling this curious fantasy, but Dylan was shocked.[12] Despite his own wild behaviour, a little bit of the Welsh puritan Non-conformist always remained within him.

By the beginning of August, Dylan and Caitlin had moved again, to Newlyn, where they rented Max Chapman's studio. According to a letter from Dylan to Pamela Hansford Johnson, they lived mainly out of tins heated up on a primus stove. He joked that they tended to eat in the morning because after a day's drinking they were too unsteady to open the tins at night.[13] A generous wedding present from Edith Sitwell enabled them to pay off various pressing bills, however, as well as to buy towels and other basic necessities.

Dylan was getting on with some work. Although he only composed one major poem during 1937 ('I Make This in a Warring Absence'), he wrote several short stories. Having totally failed to get to grips with the proposed book on Wales for J. M. Dent, his idea now was to produce a collection of stories which would take its title from the one entitled 'The Burning Baby'. George Reavey of the Europa Press was meant to be publishing it, in both an ordinary popular edition and a collectors' special edition priced at one guinea. Despite endless to-ings and fro-ings well into 1938, the project fell through. None the less, much of the material that would have been included was accepted by J. M. Dent for a volume to be called *The Map of Love*, published in 1939.

In the meantime, Faber and Faber reprinted Dylan's story 'The Orchard' in two of their anthologies in 1937: *Welsh Short Stories* and *The Faber Book of Short Stories*. Various small assignments for magazines included a short piece on W. H. Auden for an Auden double number of *New Verse*, which appeared in November 1937. In a postscript to the covering letter Dylan sent to Geoffrey Grigson, he added cheekily: 'Good luck to Auden on his seventieth birthday . . .'[14]

Dylan spent most of September 1937 at his parents' new house at Bishopston, before Caitlin and he moved into her mother's house at Blashford. The contrast between the two households was striking. Florence Thomas in her spick and span home urged Caitlin to start putting half-crowns aside every month, so that when Dylan or she died there would be enough for a decent funeral, while Yvonne Macnamara thought even to mention money was vulgar. Unfortunately, Caitlin inherited her mother's disdain for paying bills on time, which only aggravated the problems caused by Dylan's own inefficiency in this respect.

The atmosphere at Blashford was cosily untidy. Cast-off clothes littered chairs upstairs and down and nothing ever seemed to get thrown away. Books, magazines, papers and letters lay everywhere, enabling Dylan to get back to some serious reading. Caitlin's mother had very little poetry in the house, but Dylan whiled away the long winter hours reading dozens of thrillers, some Turgenev and the whole of Jane Austen. There was an annexe to the house, known in the family as the 'big room', which had originally been a woodshed, but had been comfortably converted into a large sitting-room at Francis Macnamara's expense. This was where Dylan chose to work, writing for two or three hours every morning.

Caitlin's eldest sister Nicolette (who had married the handsome painter Anthony Devas in 1931) came to stay for several weekends during Dylan's six months at Blashford. She thought he looked very much at home and was amused when he said how nice it was not to have someone fussing behind him with a dustpan and brush. The house was draughty and cold, however, and this went to Dylan's weak chest. He retired to bed and asked for bread and milk. But when this arrived, Mrs Macnamara had torn the bread into rough chunks. He insisted that these be taken out and cut into the regulation squares his own mother made.[15] Dylan also got the women to play parlour-games with him, of which one favourite was called 'Tortures'. The idea was to dream up the worst possible things to be done to oneself. Dylan squirmed and squealed like a child as he imagined himself eating a sandwich of mouse and honey. Even worse was the imagined torture of lying naked in a bath of white mice.

At the end of January, Dylan went up to London to address the poetry club at Goldsmiths' College. This was run by the critic and anthologist Hermann Peschmann, who had persisted with invitations to Dylan to talk about his work until he agreed. A few days after the event, Dylan wrote at great length to Peschmann in response to a request from him to explain the meaning of the poem 'I Make This in a Warring Absence' (which had been published in the January/February issue of *Twentieth Century Verse*). The promptness and care with which Dylan fulfilled this task was indicative of the seriousness with which he addressed genuine interest in his work. But it also reflected a deep streak of goodwill in Dylan's nature, which somehow coexisted with an often cavalier disregard for other people's feelings which at times became sheer malice.

However, Dylan's patience was sorely tried by the poet and writer Henry Treece, who contacted him early in 1938 to inform him that he was writing a book about Dylan's poetry. This book did not in fact appear for another eleven years. Superficially, Henry Treece and Dylan had a lot in common, in that Treece was consciously reacting against the politicization of much 1930s' verse. Three years older than Dylan, he belonged to the neo-Romantic Apocalyptic school along with people like J. F. Hendry. But, over the years, Dylan had to cope with a lot of questions from Henry Treece, who he became convinced didn't really understand him at all.

In March, Dylan's story 'A Visit to Grandpa's' appeared in the *New English Weekly*, of which his friend Desmond Hawkins had become the literary editor. This was to be the first of ten stories forming a provincial autobiography, written during 1938 and 1939, and published in book form in 1940 as *Portrait of the Artist as a Young Dog*. In these stories, Dylan could develop the comic talent that until then he had kept mainly for his pub performances rather than his writing. He always dismissed the stories as nothing like as important as his poetry, yet they marked a major new stage in his development as an artist. They also gave rise to a sort of patriotic nostalgia in Dylan, not only for his lost childhood and innocence, but also for Wales itself. In April he and Caitlin moved back to his parents' at Bishopston, but this was only a stepping-stone. Dylan knew that the place he wanted to settle was that 'strangest town in Wales' that he had tasted so tantalizingly briefly, once with Glyn Jones and once with Caitlin: Laugharne.

6

POVERTY WITH DISTINCTION

(1938–1940)

In April 1938, Dylan wrote most politely to Richard Hughes at the Castle House in Laugharne, asking him whether he could find a cottage for himself and Caitlin to rent in the town. As Caitlin remembers it,[1] they stayed briefly with Richard Hughes and his wife Frances at Castle House before taking possession of the property the novelist obtained for them. Richard Hughes probably never realized just how rude Dylan could be about him behind his back, while Caitlin considered their host both stingy and a snob. She thought that the success of his book *A High Wind in Jamaica*, published in 1929, had gone to his head. Hughes did a lot of his writing in a tiny one-room gazebo up on the battlements of the ruined castle itself, and he let Dylan use this as well. It was there that some of the stories in *Portrait of the Artist as a Young Dog* were written, both during and after the period when Dylan and Caitlin were the Hugheses' house-guests.

One day, when Caitlin was up in the gazebo with Dylan, enjoying the view over the estuary, they spotted Richard Hughes going down into the bowels of the castle and returning with a bottle some time later. Obviously he had laid down a wine-cellar there. As both Caitlin and Dylan resented the fact that Richard Hughes allegedly never offered them wine at dinner, while serving it to more important visitors passing through Laugharne and drinking it himself, they decided it was only fair that they should go down into his secret wine-cellar and help themselves. They found that he had some very good vintages there. At first they only took the odd bottle, but when they realized that Richard Hughes hadn't noticed, they left with armfuls. Soon, of course, the thefts became evident. Dylan and Caitlin sympathized effusively with Hughes when he railed about the fact that many of his very best bottles had disappeared, and they persuaded him it must have been the work of men from the Territorial Army who were encamped nearby.

By then, Dylan and Caitlin had probably moved into their first proper home in Laugharne, called 'Eros'. Some previous occupant must have had a warped sense of humour as 'Eros' was in fact a poky little two-bedroomed fisherman's cottage in Gosport Street, with no bathroom and an outside loo. There was, however, a long garden which ran down almost to the estuary, where Caitlin would take herself off to swim. Swimming, like dancing, was a part of her private being which Dylan could never share, and both were a useful outlet for the sudden bursts of energy to which Caitlin was prone in between much longer periods of lethargy. She became pregnant about the time that the two of them moved into 'Eros'. This would bring to an end a habit Caitlin sometimes had of picking Dylan up and holding him under one arm as she forded a stream out on a country walk. Besides, Dylan was putting on a lot of weight. Still, that didn't prevent him from assuming his little boy's act and cadging piggy-backs from fishermen in Laugharne and friends like the painter Rupert Shephard (who was to become Nicolette Macnamara's second husband) when he was in danger of getting his feet wet.

Dylan had been in 'Eros' for only a few days when he received a most welcome cheque from America. This was from James Laughlin, a wealthy young man who had started his own avant-garde publishing house called New Directions. Laughlin had arranged to buy sheets for an American edition of the collection of Dylan's short stories, *The Burning Baby*, from George Reavey's Europa Press, which had hoped to publish the book in June 1938. But Reavey had not reckoned on the puritanism and power of British printers, who stubbornly refused to set the title-story that had grown out of Glyn Jones's conversation with Dylan in Aberystwyth back in 1934. In the end, Laughlin produced instead a selection of

Dylan's prose and poetry entitled *The World I Breathe*, which came out in December 1939.

James Laughlin, like J. M. Dent, came in for a lot of criticism from Dylan as the years went by, though Dylan was none the less at pains to keep both of them sweet by writing them carefully crafted letters that played up to his image as a brilliant but rather defenceless young poet who needed a lot of support (preferably in cash). Laughlin was meant to go to Wales to meet Dylan in June 1938, after seeing another of the poets on his list, Ezra Pound, in Italy, but the visit fell through.

The first visitor to stay at 'Eros' was Vernon Watkins, some time in May. He had kept up a regular correspondence with Dylan and they had seen each other whenever Dylan was in Swansea, discussing each other's poetry for hours on end. It was largely at Dylan's urging that Watkins started getting some of his own work aired in publications such as the new magazine *Wales*, edited by Keidrych Rhys. Dylan acted as an editorial adviser to Rhys, and Vernon was hurt when he discovered that Dylan had changed a line in one of Vernon's poems, printed in *Wales*, without his approval. Typically, Vernon went round all the Swansea bookshops surreptitiously altering all the copies he could get hold of back to his original version.

Vernon was still living with his parents at Pennard and Dylan had taken Caitlin there to meet them. On that occasion they had all ended up playing Lexicon, a popular playing-card precursor of Scrabble. Vernon was amused and admiring when Caitlin had tried to put down the word 'fucking', only to be prevented by Dylan who insisted that she really couldn't, despite her protests that she would get so many points for 'K' and 'ING'.

Vernon thought Caitlin extremely beautiful, but she was convinced that he was in love with her husband. Caitlin and Dylan enjoyed speculating about their friends' sexual orientation and appear to have devised a test for Vernon on his first visit to see them at Laugharne. They informed him, incorrectly, that there was only one bed in the house – the double bed in which they slept themselves. That meant he would have to muck in with them. As Vernon had been cycling round Wales on holiday he was tired and went to bed first. By the time Dylan and Caitlin came up to join him, he had rolled down into the dip in the middle of the bed and was fast asleep. Dylan had to wake him and push him to one side while he himself climbed into the middle, with Caitlin on his other side. Nothing untoward happened during the night, but Vernon did wake up several times to find Dylan cursing and Caitlin giggling merrily.[2]

Vernon was almost certainly still a virgin at the time, though he had been in love with the soprano Elizabeth Schumann from a distance. He was also notoriously gullible. In his semi-fictional youthful autobiography *Lions and Shadows*, Christopher Isherwood recorded how at Cambridge he and Edward Upward ('Chalmers') ragged Vernon ('Percival') unmercifully because he would believe anything they told him. Vernon's own future wife Gwen once got him to eat sardines with chocolate sauce, having told him that that dish was currently all the rage. In his innocence, Vernon seems to have taken the double-bed incident with Dylan and Caitlin at face value and not to have noticed that there was another bedroom in the cottage with two single beds in it. Certainly he wrote to a mutual friend saying that it was no use hoping to stay with the Thomases if he came as part of a couple, as they could only accommodate one guest.

Vernon met Richard Hughes for the first time on that first visit to Laugharne, when Hughes called round one morning to see how Dylan and Caitlin were getting on. Hughes seemed to Vernon to be like a 'very rich, bearded telegraph post',[3] tall, thin and enigmatic. Hughes mystified all three of them by looking up at the newly painted white rafters in the cottage and complementing them on their lilac-coloured beams.

Vernon was back again in June, after visiting Ireland to see W. B. Yeats. This time he was accompanied by a handsome young French teacher, Francis Dufau-Labeyrie, who had a great admiration for Dylan's work and indeed translated some of it into French. Dylan had known Dufau-Labeyrie in Swansea, where the young man had been the French *assistant* at Swansea Grammar School. They had become drinking companions and Francis had witnessed one of Dylan's few acts of unpleasantness to his own mother. Francis had been invited to dinner at 5 Cwmdonkin Drive for the first time, and Florence went to a lot of trouble to make something special. Dylan took Francis down to a pub for a pre-dinner drink – and kept him there drinking until closing time. Florence was still waiting up with the meal keeping warm in the oven, but D. J. had retired to bed in disgust.[4]

Vernon was struck by the contrast between W. B. Yeats and Dylan, both of whom he considered to be geniuses. He was disappointed that Dylan responded coldly to his enthusiasm for Yeats's pronouncements during the visit he and Francis Dufau-Labeyrie had just made to Ireland, despite the fact that Dylan had admiration for Yeats's work. When Vernon reported wistfully that Yeats had said that young poets toil too much, Dylan deflated the atmosphere by commenting, 'He should come *here*!'

However, it was not Yeats but Auden and Spender who were the flavour of the year in 1938, and Dylan became visibly irritated at being repeatedly asked what he thought of them and their work. In a letter to James Laughlin, Dylan said that he thought Auden sometimes wrote with great power, but that he was considerably overpraised. Dylan saw Auden as exactly what the English literary public thought a poet ought to be: perfectly and expensively educated, yet eccentric and a rebel. He admitted he had never met Auden, and he didn't want to either, as he saw him as a 'heavy, jocular prefect, the boy bushranger, the school wag, the 6th form debater, the homosexual clique-joker'.[5] Dylan had already used the analogy of a school prefect to describe Auden six weeks before, in a letter to Henry Treece. In this, he lambasted the contemporary concept of the Brotherhood of Man – 'love thy neighbour and, if possible, covet his arse'.[6] He also said he found Spender's communism unreal, and damned him as the Rupert Brooke of the Depression who 'condemns his slight, lyrical, nostalgic talent to a clumsy rhetorical death'. As early as 1934, in a review for the magazine *New Verse* of Spender's slim-book-length poem *Vienna*, Dylan had written uncompromisingly that 'as a poem, *Vienna* leaves much to be desired; in the first place, it leaves poetry to be desired'.

Such opinions did not prevent Dylan from writing to Stephen Spender, soliciting his support in obtaining a grant from the Royal Literary Fund, whose aim was to assist destitute writers of quality. The cheque that James Laughlin had sent Dylan had not gone far. Dylan did make some small economies, such as not putting stamps on the letters he sent to family and friends. But when he had money, it quickly evaporated. Dylan was a generous companion to other drinkers in pubs when he had cash on him, and expected others to behave the same way when he was skint. His generosity did not always extend to his wife, however. Just as Fred Janes used sometimes to have to hold Dylan upside-down at their lodgings in Chelsea, in the hope that some money might fall out of his trousers that could be put towards the rent, so Caitlin took to rifling Dylan's pockets at night to try to find something to help with the housekeeping.

By the time Dylan sent off his formal application to the Royal Literary Fund, in August 1938, he and Caitlin had moved into a much grander house in Laugharne, called 'Sea View'. None the less, the tone of his letter was calculatingly pathetic. He maintained that he had been content living in poverty for the past five years, surviving off the tiny income his work generated in literary magazines, but now, with his wife pregnant, his situation had changed. In support of his application, he cited T. S. Eliot, Cyril Connolly, Richard Hughes, Richard Church (of J. M. Dent), Charles Fisher (of the Oxford University Press) – and W. H. Auden. He admitted that he hadn't actually asked all these gentlemen if he could use their names (though in fact in Eliot's case, he had). He also did a great deal of lobbying among others: Edith Sitwell, in particular, backed his case enthusiastically. But as Dylan told the critic and occasional writer John Davenport in a letter about six weeks after the application to the Royal Literary Fund went in, they turned him down on the grounds that his literary claims were not considered sufficient for the purposes of that august society.[7]

Dylan and Caitlin rented 'Sea View' at seven shillings and sixpence a week from Tudor Williams, brother of Ebie Williams, the landlord of Brown's Hotel in Laugharne's main street, King Street. 'Sea View' is a striking but odd building, resembling an early Victorian dolls' house; broad, tall and symmetrical but only one room deep. At first Dylan and Caitlin lived mainly in the kitchen and a room immediately above, as they had hardly any belongings other than a few things they had picked up from Dylan's parents. Then they bought a fine bed on hire purchase, for which the weekly payments were only sixpence less than the rent. At first, they put the money regularly aside in a tea-caddy, but soon they started raiding that to buy drink. The payments on the bed stopped and men came to take it away, after which they slept on a mattress on the floor. Then one of Caitlin's aunts died and Yvonne Macnamara sent down the aunt's cane furniture to Laugharne, supplemented with some things of her own.[8]

In a letter to Henry Treece, Dylan described his early life with Caitlin as 'poverty with distinction', and certainly they were determined not to allow their penury to cramp their style. Visitors were encouraged to stay; in their first few weeks at 'Sea View' they played host in quick succession to Henry Treece, Augustus John, Mervyn Levy (who was hitch-hiking en route to Ireland) and Yvonne Macnamara. Dylan enjoyed taking visitors off to savour the delights of the local pubs, of which the Brown's Hotel bar had already become his favourite. The landlord's wife, Ivy, became one of Dylan's closest friends and confidantes, although Caitlin could never quite understand what he saw in her. Ivy was in fact a younger, more quick-witted and broad-minded version of his own mother, and a never-ending source of local gossip. Dylan carefully stored away some of the stories she told, as well as the phrases she employed, sometimes openly writing them on the backs of envelopes or the insides of cigarette packets, for future use. In return, Dylan kept Ivy amused with his wicked imagination and he shared with her some of the juicier products of contemporary Anglo-American literature, such as Henry Miller's *Tropic of Capricorn*, which was published in Paris that year. Ivy kept that book hidden in the oven so her husband Ebie wouldn't find it.

Even though Dylan found Henry Treece something of a nuisance, he put a great deal of effort into their correspondence, which is as important as those he had with Pamela Hansford Johnson and Vernon Watkins in its insights into Dylan's literary tastes and methods of working. For this, Treece rewarded Dylan with regular small presents. It was to Henry Treece that Dylan confided that he saw his poems as individual watertight sections of a stream that is flowing all ways, in which all warring images would be reconciled for a small stop of time.[9] The conflict of images was inevitable, he believed, because of the contradictory, destructive, creative and recreative nature of the 'womb' from which the poems emerged: himself. Dylan also confessed to Treece his complete detachment from the terrible events that were happening on the Continent. Adolph Hitler's forces marched into both Austria and Czechoslovakia in 1938, but Dylan informed Henry Treece that Treece was right when he suggested that Dylan considered a squirrel stumbling at least of equal importance as Hitler's invasions, murders in Spain and other contemporary outrages.[10] Now distant from Bert Trick's influence, Dylan had let his superficial political principles fly out of the window.

While Britain and France were ignominiously acquiescing to the German occupation of Czechoslovakia in September 1938, Dylan, Vernon Watkins, Vernon's sister Dot and his old friend from Repton, Erik Falk (nicknamed 'Fig') were racing across Pendine Sands in a borrowed car. Though 'racing' is perhaps not the right word to describe Dylan's progress when he got his turn behind the wheel, grinding through a patch of soft sand at ten miles an hour on full throttle before coming to a halt, after which everyone had to help dig the vehicle out.

By mid-October, the Thomases' financial situation was getting desperate. A number of the local traders had extended them credit, but there was a limit to patience, even in Laugharne. Dylan calculated he needed £30 urgently. He would sit worrying over the figures he had totted up on the sheets of paper on which he was in principle meant to be writing poems. Having failed to get a grant from the Royal Literary Fund, he set about trying to find a patron. Among those he approached for suggestions of people to whom he could send a 'special sponger's song' was John Davenport. Dylan confessed that if no appropriate sponsor turned up, then he and Caitlin would have to do a bunk from Laugharne, where he couldn't get in touch with anybody 'with more money than a betty with no cunt or more generosity than a fucked weasel'.[11] Davenport couldn't immediately think of any patrons in search of a good cause, but he sent £5 himself.

One ray of light on Dylan's otherwise cloudy horizon came from the BBC, which invited him up to Manchester on 18 October to take part in a late evening broadcast of poetry-reading alongside W. H. Auden, Stephen Spender, Louis MacNeice, Kathleen Raine and Charles Madge, whom Dylan described later to John Davenport as a 'mincing lot', all born in the same house, of the same mother.[12] The programme was presented by Michael Roberts (or 'Minnie', as Dylan preferred to call him). Dylan read one of his works from 25 Poems, 'The Hand That Signed the Paper', for which he was of course paid a fee. He also insisted that he be paid his train fare up to Manchester and his subsistence allowance in advance, as otherwise he wouldn't be able to get there.

Dylan took advantage of his meeting with Wystan Auden to see if Auden could use his influence with John Lehmann at Leonard and Virginia Woolf's Hogarth Press to get another book of his verse published. Dylan had been putting together a new collection of poems, which he had provisionally entitled *In the Direction of the Beginning*. As Dylan wrote to his agent David Higham the following week,[13] Auden thought that the Hogarth Press might indeed be interested, and that if so, he could expect an advance in the region of £50. In fact, nothing came of this, and Higham wished that Dylan would stop going behind his back, trying to fix up new deals, in case it soured the arrangement with J. M. Dent.

Listening to the Laugharne postman scrunching up the cockle-shell path to the front-door of 'Sea View' was becoming a nightmare of anticipation for Dylan, not of cheques but of yet more bills. And as Caitlin was by now six months pregnant, he decided it was time for them to seek sanctuary elsewhere. Accordingly, by the third week of November, they had decamped back to Hampshire, to stay with Caitlin's mother, having paid off at least some of the most outstanding debts in Laugharne.

Dylan complained to David Higham that his second lengthy stay at Blashford was marred by his being half-starved, worrying and escaping from things. However, apart from the fact that he became increasingly cold as winter set in and there were no opportunities for romantic walks in bluebell woods with Caitlin as there had been in the spring, he had little to complain about legitimately. There was no danger of eviction from his mother-in-law's house, and as usual he was waited on by the women as he sat bundled up in two or three sweaters and a coat. Besides, London was considerably more accessible from Hampshire than it had been from Laugharne, and official penury was not going to keep him away from his favourite playground.

Dylan also had something to celebrate. At the beginning of December he heard that he had won the Blumenthal Prize for Poetry in America, which carried not only prestige but also a cash award of $100 (then worth approximately £20). This considerably brightened Christmas, which he spent not in Wales, for once, but at a house party not far from Mrs Macnamara's, playing charades and children's games out of a compendium that Vernon Watkins had sent as a present.

None the less, when Laurence Durrell wrote asking whether Dylan could meet him in London towards the end of the month, as he wanted to introduce him to Henry Miller, Dylan begged the train fare off him. The cost of the ticket was 18 shillings, and Durrell sent him a pound. This Dylan was able to add to his general funds, as he managed to get a lift up to London in someone's car.

Durrell had been living in Paris, working for the Obelisk Press, and his own *The Black Book* had been published there earlier in the year. He liked Dylan's work and was fascinated that Dylan's small, neat handwriting uncannily resembled that of Emily Brontë. Durrell knew that in turn Dylan greatly respected the novels of Henry Miller. But the first meeting he arranged between the two men almost turned into a disaster, as Dylan had one of his periodic fits of shyness. As Durrell recalled in an article in the magazine *Poetry London–New York* in 1956, Dylan did not turn up at the appointed hour for dinner at the flat in London where Durrell was currently staying. They had virtually given him up when the phone rang and a sheepish Dylan said he couldn't find the address. When Durrell offered to get in a taxi and fetch him, Dylan admitted that in fact he was drinking in a pub immediately opposite, but couldn't pluck up the courage to come up. So Durrell went over to the pub and had a drink with him there, to try to calm him down. He was shocked by the change in Dylan's appearance since they had last met, probably two or three years previously. He looked as though he had been sleeping in a haystack. He was not just dishevelled but jumpy, and his face was almost hidden behind a giant muffler. After Durrell had described how poor Henry Miller was pacing round the dining-table in the flat in increasing agitation at Dylan's non-appearance, Dylan agreed to go up. Once inside, he suddenly relaxed, and he and Miller got on famously. Dylan found Miller to be a dear, mad, bald man of fifty and he invited him to go down to stay with him and Caitlin in Laugharne the following spring.

Dylan was now in two minds about London itself. Its social life and literary contacts were an irresistible magnet. Yet as he wrote to Laurence Durrell after this visit, London gave him the willies. Similarly, he had told Vernon Watkins on his return from a previous visit to the capital before Christmas that he saw it as an insane city, a city of the restless dead, which filled him with terror.[14]

At least part of Dylan's instability at this stage was attributable to the imminent birth of his first child. His nervousness increased as the baby was several days overdue. When Caitlin finally went into labour and was admitted to Poole General Hospital on 29 January, Dylan stayed behind at Blashford, and then disappeared. Later, Caitlin was convinced that he had spent the night of his son's entrance into the world on 30 January in the arms of a tall girl dancer they had nicknamed 'Joey the Ravisher'.[15] The birth was lengthy and difficult and the nurses kept telling Caitlin to tone down the noise when she screamed. When they urged her to push harder she thought she would shit the bed. The baby was only a little over 6 pounds in weight and Caitlin chose the name Llewelyn (for being such a nice-sounding Welsh name) and Edouard (after her French grandfather). Somewhat to her own surprise, she was enchanted with the baby, and she found herself consumed by maternal instincts. Llewelyn became the centre of Caitlin's world for the next few months, though her mother wisely got in a nanny to help for the first fortnight.

Dylan was rather startled by the baby's virtually hairless, bright red head and squalling voice, and he dubbed him the 'Mongolian monkey'. But he wrote proudly to a few close friends announcing his son's birth. Vernon Watkins, who was made one of Llewelyn's godfathers, along with Augustus John and Richard Hughes, was unable to enthuse as sincerely as he would have liked, as he was in deep mourning for W. B. Yeats, who had died just two days before Llewelyn was born. Caitlin realized that Dylan was in fact jealous of the new arrival. He didn't pick the baby up, as most fathers would have done, and he resented the way that all Caitlin's attention was now being focused on the infant. As Dylan had also now decided that he hated his mother-in-law, and would sit locked in the lavatory muttering to himself about her, he was soon anxious to get back to Wales.

In the meantime, David Higham had finalized arrangements with J. M. Dent for a contract for the mixed book of poetry and prose, *The Map of Love*. The title was chosen by Richard Church at Dent's. Higham obtained an advance of £50 for Dylan (the same that he could have hoped for from the Hogarth Press), but £20 of this had to be handed straight over to George Reavey at the Europa Press, as repayment of his advance on the aborted book *The Burning Baby*, in which some of the same material would have appeared. Dylan had received the first advance cheque from David Higham by the beginning of March, which temporarily eased his finances. And he obtained permission from Augustus John to reproduce a fine portrait of himself that John had done in 1937. This appeared as a frontispiece in the book, though considerably diminished by being reproduced only in black and white.

Dylan whiled away some of the time at Blashford by writing book reviews, which was a useful way of picking up a guinea or two. The books sent to him by various periodicals extended beyond his preferred fields of detective stories and poetry. It is striking how many of his book reviews were essentially negative; only a very few lucky authors, such as Djuna Barnes (whose *Nightwood* had appeared in 1936), met Dylan's high standards. He had not lost the iconoclasm first displayed in the columns of the *South Wales Evening Post*.

After a quick visit to Bishopston, to display the wizened baby to D. J. and Florence, Dylan and Caitlin were back at 'Sea View' in Laugharne by early April. They had got one of the local Mrs Williamses to clean the place up before their arrival, and they employed a girl to help round the house and with the baby. Poor they may have been, but there were some things they were not prepared to do without. Besides, as Dylan reportedly never spent a single evening of his married life at home, preferring to repair to the pub, Caitlin needed someone in the house from time to time, otherwise she would have been trapped alone with Llewellyn.

At times she felt she had two babies on her hands, as Dylan could be as demanding as any child. Yet he could be equally easily soothed. Florence had briefed Caitlin well on Dylan's likes and dislikes, and the rest she had quickly learned. An essential part of keeping her husband happy was to give him the freedom not only to be off to the pub when he wanted – which, from his background, was what he expected – but also to stay out at night or even disappear for a few days. But one of the best ways of keeping him at home was to make sure he was supplied with his little treats: dolly mixtures, boiled sweets, pickled onions and other favourite delicacies, laid out around the house in little bowls. When he took his bath, the soap rack would be filled with a buffet of sweets and savouries, while a big bottle of pop stood beside the tub.

Vernon Watkins added to Dylan's home comforts by giving him a radio. Once one of the Williams men had worked out how to instal it, this radio came into its own during the cricket season.

Dylan would sit glued to the set, especially when there was a test match, and woe betide anyone who disturbed him.

Vernon himself visited Laugharne in the third week of May, and noted that Dylan had swollen to an alleged 12 stones, 8 pounds. Vernon looked on Caitlin suckling Llewellyn by the side of the evening fire with the romantic vision that only a bachelor in his thirties could have: they were madonna and child. He wrote a sonnet about this, 'The Mother and Child', and later produced a whole series of poems dedicated to his godson.

Vernon visited Dylan and Caitlin several times during that troubled summer of 1939, walking on the sands with Dylan and listening to him reading some of the stories that were to form part of *Portrait of the Artist as a Young Dog*. In turn, Vernon would read his own poems out loud, or those of Yeats and Rilke. They spent one whole sunny afternoon in the ruins of Laugharne Castle, reading the 'Duino Elegies'.[16] Less seriously, Vernon would declaim extracts from an absurd Italian grammar he had found years before in a second-hand bookshop in London's Charing Cross Road: Carlo Barone's *Manual of Conversation English–Italian*. This became a cult book for Vernon and Dylan, as they acted out the little situations in the book, with their defiantly incorrect English. Dylan particularly savoured the role of Barone's dentist, who has to cope with an outraged patient, played by a giggling Vernon. 'But sir, I was anxious to keep that tooth!' Vernon would recite. 'That was impossible. It is black and decayed,' Dylan would respond. 'Besides, you have none but old stumps in your mouth.'[17] The two friends also composed obscene verses together, which Dylan suggested they send to the children's comic *Puck*, saying they could always claim later that they had misread the publication's title.

For all the mutual pleasure of such tomfoolery, however, there was an imbalance of affection within the friendship between Vernon and Dylan. This was starkly demonstrated in July, when the Swansea Little Theatre put on two performances of Vernon's masque *The Influences*. Vernon was naturally keen that Dylan attend, but Dylan said he was so impoverished that he could only come if Richard and Frances Hughes gave him a lift over from Laugharne. In the event, the Hugheses did go to see the masque, but there was no sign of Dylan. It was a cruel absence, as he knew Vernon would value his opinion of the work more highly than anyone else's. Later he gave the excuse that he and Caitlin had colds. But the plain truth was that he would not put himself out for anyone, not even his closest friends, unless it suited his mood. Indeed, on numerous occasions in his life Dylan's actions seem to have been calculated to wound those who loved him most.

If anything, having a child as well as a wife to provide for made Dylan even more self-centred than before and helped him develop a sense of grievance against the world. Although he did endeavour to get more of his material sold and published – for example, in the magazine *Poetry London*, launched by his seductive contemporary from Ceylon, Tambimuttu, in 1939 – he felt that he was owed a living simply for *being* a fine poet. That summer he worked on a scheme which he mock-dismissively referred to as his 'Five-bob Fund', but whose intention was far from frivolous. The idea, as expounded to John Davenport,[18] was that ten people of assured means should be found who would be prepared to contribute 5 shillings a week to Dylan's upkeep. The resultant £260 a year would, he believed, make all the difference. Then, he argued, he would have the peace of mind to get on with serious work, without the constipating distraction of finding ways to clear off debts.

Dylan's list of possible donors to be solicited to subscribe to the Five-bob Fund included Richard Hughes, Augustus John, Edith Sitwell, the wealthy American patron of the arts Peggy Guggenheim (with whom Dylan had only the slightest acquaintance), Norman Cameron and John Davenport himself. One has to admire his cheek. Davenport, ever the generous friend, responded promptly with a cheque; Norman Cameron also indicated his willingness to chip in. But others were less forthcoming, and some wondered, not unreasonably, why Dylan didn't devote more time to writing things which he could probably sell to magazines without much difficulty, rather than spending so much time composing begging letters.

A fortnight at his parents' in Bishopston in July brought home to Dylan the stark contrast between their attitude to money and his own. He was half-touched and half-despairing at their penny-cautious concern for security, and at their desire for his success. Yet even with two books in the pipeline, the fruits of his current literary success would be insufficient to support his little household. His only hope seemed to be to try to get both James Laughlin and J. M. Dent to advance money on books not yet even conceived, let alone written. Almost hysterical, he wrote to David Higham saying that unless the publishers could be persuaded to part with some more money, then he and his family would have to surrender their few possessions to creditors, abandon 'Sea View' and become homeless. Thirty pounds was once again the magic figure he cited that would keep the wolves from the door.[19] Higham managed to extract exactly that from Dent's, to be followed by monthly payments of £8.

The Map of Love came out at the end of August. It contained seven short stories (some distinctly surrealist) and sixteen poems, including 'I Make This in a Warring Absence' and 'After the Funeral'. Dylan's friend Desmond Hawkins was given the book to review for the *Spectator*, and was so baffled by some of its contents that he wrote to Dylan asking for a few clarifications. Dylan responded at considerable length, demonstrating yet again how painstaking he could be in explaining his work when it really mattered. Cyril Connolly, in the *New Statesman*, wrote discouragingly that while Dylan's technique remained, the inspiration that had marked his earlier work had gone. Many of the images in the poems in *The Map of Love* were nonsense, Connolly complained, and the writing was 'inflated and faked'.

Other critics were kinder, but the book failed to take off. J. M. Dent had printed an edition of 1,000 copies, as well as running off 2,000 extra sets of sheets. But by the end of the year, after four months in the bookshops, fewer than 300 copies of *The Map of Love* had been sold.

The reason for the book's failure was undoubtedly the outbreak of war, which made some of the stories, in particular, seem singularly irrelevant to the times. Dylan, Canute-like, had tried to keep the growing European crisis at bay, but its ripples had reached even Laugharne. A discussion between Dylan and Keidrych Rhys on modern Welsh poets that the BBC had planned to record in the first week of September was cancelled, and the Corporation asked for the train fare it had advanced Dylan to be returned. On 1 September, two days before war was declared, Dylan wrote plaintively to David Higham asking whether war would interfere with the financial arrangements he had come to with Dent's.

Dylan had already decided he was a pacifist who could not kill, and who felt no enmity towards the Germans. So an immediate preoccupation was how to avoid being conscripted into the armed forces. He wrote jocularly to Desmond Hawkins that he might declare himself to be a neutral state,[20] but behind the levity was a deep-seated wish that the war would go away and leave him alone. He realized that many of the small magazines which had printed his work would be likely to go out of business in wartime, thus reducing even further his chances of earning money. On the face of it, there seemed no alternative to getting a job, preferably in a reserved occupation which would keep him safe from the call-up. Accordingly, on 14 September, he wrote to the highly cultivated civil servant Sir Edward Marsh, who was a noted patron of the arts, asking him if he could get him a position at the Ministry of Information. Dylan acknowledged in a letter to John Davenport the same day that 'all the shysters in London . . . all the half-poets, the boiled newspapermen, submen from the island of crabs' would be trying to find a safe niche in the Ministry of Information as well. Sir Edward confirmed that this was indeed the case. Dylan also asked Davenport if he could use his own influence to see if there was any opening in the film world which would save him from active service, as 'my one-&-only body I will not give'.[21]

Anxiety prevented Dylan from doing much work on poems or prose, as he spent countless hours writing to everyone he could think of who had any position of influence in London. But he recognized that his qualifications for most alternatives to military service were practically non-existent. As he confessed to Desmond Hawkins, he knew no foreign languages, and was incapable of deciphering other people's poems, let alone the cryptic messages used in intelligence work. He was not prepared to contemplate the Army Medical Corps; quite apart from the fact that he had no relevant training, he didn't want to patch up poor soldiers so they could be sent back to face more bullets. But the prospect of going before a tribunal to obtain exempt status held terrors in itself. How would he react, he mused to Desmond Hawkins, if he were asked (à la Lytton Strachey in the First World War) what he would do if he saw a soldier raping John Lehmann?[22]

At Hawkins's suggestion, Dylan contacted the Welsh Secretary of the Peace Pledge Union, who confirmed that membership of that organization could help one's case to be accepted as a conscientious objector. He made the sensible point, however, that tribunals were unlikely to be impressed with the pacifist credentials

1. Dylan's schoolmaster father, D. J. Thomas, before he went bald.

2. Dylan with Nancy (*left*), Florence (*seated*) and an unidentified family friend, c. 1917.

3. The family home, 5 Cwmdonkin Drive, Swansea (right-hand semi).

4. The first girlfriend: Pamela Hansford-Johnson and Dylan at Caswell Bay, The Mumbles, 1934.

5. Pamela Hansford-Johnson, Auntie Polly, Florence Thomas, Uncle Dai, Auntie Dosie and Uncle Bob at Blaen Cwm, 1936.

6. Caitlin dancing by the River Avon, 1936.

7. The Bohemians: Dylan writing, Caitlin painting, Blashford 1937.

8. Dylan at Sea View, Laugharne, 1938.

10. (*right*) Caitlin and Dylan at the Manresa Road studio, Chelsea, 1944.

9. Dylan avoids getting his feet wet, Laugharne 1940.

11. Dylan recording for BBC Radio, London 1947.

12. The Swansea gang: Vernon Watkins, John Prichard, Alfred Janes, John Griffiths (*standing*), Daniel Jones and Dylan at the BBC studios, 1949.

14. Playing nap with Ivy Williams, Brown's Hotel, Laugharne.

13. The Boat House, Laugharne.

15. Revisiting Fernhill with Florence, 1953.

16. Family group: Dylan and Llewellyn (*standing*); Florence, Colm and Caitlin (*sitting*), with a glimpse of the dog Mably in the foreground.

17. John Malcolm Brinnin and Dylan, Milbrook NY, 1952.

18. Dylan and the climbing vine, Milbrook NY, 1952.

19. Dylan at the bar of the White Horse Tavern, New York, 1952.

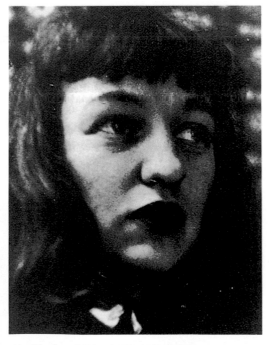

20. The last girlfriend: Elizabeth Reitell.

21. Dylan at the first public performance
of *Under Milk Wood*, New York 1953.

22. Florence Thomas at the Boat House
in Laugharne, 1955.

of someone who had joined the PPU *after* war had broken out. Moreover, Dylan knew he would be unable to argue conscientious objection on the grounds of being a Christian, though he thought he was one.[23] Sitting in the public gallery of the tribunal in Carmarthen once, as a string of Chapel-goers proclaimed their "ligious' objection to killing, convinced him he couldn't carry it off.

Instead, Dylan sought a kind of spurious safety in numbers by writing round to a number of friends asking them to send him pieces about why they, as artists, objected to war, as he assumed – not always correctly – that they did. Dylan hoped to get these published alongside an essay of his own in the periodical *Life and Letters Today*. Desmond Hawkins, Glyn Jones and Keidrych Rhys were among those who obliged. Dylan said he wasn't seeking political statements, from either Left or Right, but rather individual testimonies to the value of each creative person's continued output. Undoubtedly there was an element of cowardice in his own wish not to go to war, but more important was his passionately held belief that a poet's calling was to write poetry, not to bear arms.

The Cambridge University English Society contacted Dylan in November, asking him to give a reading early the following month, but they got cold feet when he demanded expenses, and put it off. But at least Dylan went into the winter with the consolation of James Laughlin's publication on 20 November of his first volume in America: *The World I Breathe*. This comprised forty poems culled from *18 Poems*, *25 Poems* and *The Map of Love*, and eleven short stories. Then on 9 December, Dylan was able to send the manuscript of *Portrait of the Artist as a Young Dog* to Laurence Pollinger at David Higham's agency, for forwarding to J. M. Dent. Higham himself had enlisted for active service as soon as war was declared.

Dylan's sister Nancy, who had walked out on Haydn Taylor in 1938, picked Dylan, Caitlin and Llewellyn up in her car in the third week of December and drove them to Bishopston for a family Christmas with D. J. and Florence. From there they decamped to Yvonne Macnamara's at Blashford, where they stayed about two months. But by the first week of March 1940, they were back at 'Sea View' in Laugharne, where Dylan started pulling strings again to try to get gainful employment in London. Augustus John had told him that Sir Kenneth Clark at the National Gallery had some links with the film world and liked helping out young men who painted or wrote. Augustus John was going to lobby Sir Kenneth on Dylan's behalf, but for good measure Dylan also wrote to Stephen Spender (with whom he was now on first-name terms) to see if he or any of his friends could put some pressure on Clark too.

Meanwhile, Vernon Watkins kept sending little gifts of money to help Dylan out, and to buy nappies and other necessities for Llewellyn. On occasions Dylan asked Vernon to type out neat copies of poems for him, and Vernon continued to play the role of tame literary critic. In mid-March Dylan sent him for comment a 100-line satirical poem, 'The Countryman's Return', which was published in the Summer 1940 issue of a publication called *Cambridge Front*.

Portrait of the Artist as a Young Dog was published in England on 4 April, in an edition of 1,500 copies. The reviews were mixed. *Time and Tide* hailed it as a 'superb evocation of boyhood and adolescence', but the *Times Literary Supplement* judged more disdainfully that the book had little to offer other than a convincing atmosphere of 'schoolboy smut and practical jokes'. With half the British people braced to repel a German invasion at any moment, the book's timing could have been more propitious. Yet again sales were slow.

Moreover, any pleasure Dylan may have gained by the book's appearance was overcast by a summons to register for military service that same week. There seemed no escape into civilian employment, as Kenneth Clark wrote to say there were no safe jobs towards which he could steer Dylan. But Sir Kenneth's wife Elizabeth suggested that Dylan try to join the curious anti-aircraft battery run by her friend Captain Victor Cazalet, MP, which became a haven of civilized wartime service for a number of London's literati. She wrote to Victor Cazalet pleading Dylan's case. First, though, Dylan would have to go through a medical check-up, to receive his classification for service.

There are conflicting stories about exactly what happened at the medical, and indeed whether there was only one – in Wales – or another in London as well. Dylan himself recounted several versions. In his letters, he referred to himself being classified 'C3' (the lowest grade of fitness) because of scars on his lungs, though no such scars showed up at his post-mortem thirteen years later. More plausible is the story he put about the pubs he frequented in London and Wales that he made himself ill the day before the check-up by downing a frightening cocktail of sherry, whisky and gin. This meant that he turned up at the medical looking as if he could put the whole war effort in jeopardy if enlisted: pale and spotty, shaking and coughing, and in a half-faint. According to Caitlin, when he got back to Laugharne, he was as happy as a child, saying, 'I've done it! I've done it! I've got away with it!'[24] He then went out to celebrate, seemingly not realizing how deeply offensive his boasting about this 'victory' was to pub-goers in Laugharne whose sons had gone into the forces to do their bit for King and Country, whether they really wanted to or not.

Dylan had in any case acquired a reputation as a 'conchie' in Laugharne, which was causing a certain amount of friction. On one occasion, he was taken out of Brown's Hotel and duffed up for decrying the war. However, what was really beginning to make life in Laugharne increasingly uncomfortable was the daily pressure from local tradesmen who were getting restless about Dylan and Caitlin's failure to settle their bills. Things got to such a state that at the beginning of May the Thomases moved over to Florence and D. J.'s at Bishopston for a couple of weeks, to avoid the knocking of irate creditors at their door.

Dylan turned for help to Stephen Spender, who set about raising a rescue fund. With the help of Herbert Read, Henry Moore and Peter Watson (a wealthy patron of the arts who helped Stephen Spender and Cyril Connolly get the literary magazine *Horizon* launched), Spender drafted a written appeal which was sent to a carefully selected list of literary figures, including Richard Hughes, Cecil Day-Lewis, Richard Llewellyn, J. B. Priestley, Hugh Walpole and H. G. Wells. The aim was to raise £70, which would pay off everything that Dylan and Caitlin had had on tick. Knowing the Thomases' inability to manage their own finances, Spender arranged for them to send him all the bills, which he would pay directly out of the proceeds from the appeal. This proved to be even more successful than Dylan had hoped, as there was nearly £20 left over after all the bills had been paid, which Stephen Spender sent to him. So within a matter of weeks, Dylan had had a double reprieve: from military service and from having his goods seized by bailiffs.

Yet Dylan could see his position was untenable. The monthly cheque from Dent's had stopped, and they had turned down his suggestion of issuing a new book of poems, which would have included all those already published in his *18 Poems*. The firm had lost quite a lot of money on Dylan and saw little reason why that situation should change unless he produced something remarkable and completely new. Some royalties were coming in from New Directions in America, but the sums were paltry. So when John Davenport suggested that Dylan and Caitlin join a prolonged summer house-party for musicians and writers at his splendid manor-house at Marshfield in Gloucestershire, they abandoned Laugharne and moved in with him.

7

POETRY, GUILE AND BEER

(1940–1942)

John Davenport, who was six years Dylan's senior, was a larger-than-life character figuratively as well as physically. Short and almost square, he weighed nearly 19 stones. A former amateur heavyweight boxer, he had been a promising poet while he was an undergraduate at Corpus Christi College, Cambridge, where he edited *Cambridge Poetry*. But then his Muse had deserted him. In 1931, he went to seek advice from T. S. Eliot, who recommended that he stop trying to force something that would not come naturally, and take a break from poetry for ten years. By that time the Muse was past summoning, and this sometimes rankled with him. Late one night, the Irish writer Constantine FitzGibbon, who became one of Dylan's earliest biographers, had to stop Davenport throttling Dylan out of jealousy that he *had* established himself as a recognized poet.

In the mid-Thirties, Davenport went to Hollywood to seek his fortune writing for the movies. He worked for Robert Donat, among others, notably on some of the awful European historical costume dramas that were so popular at the time. He married Clement, the daughter of a wealthy Boston family, and in 1937 both of them separately inherited substantial sums of money. This was just as well as, back in England as story editor for MGM, John

Davenport had his contract cancelled as soon as war broke out.

Davenport used up most of his windfall buying a large Georgian house, The Maltings, at Marshfield, and filling it with first-class modern paintings (including works by Picasso, Rouault and Tanguy). There were two grand pianos and a fine wine cellar. The Maltings became a sanctuary for musicians and writers who had no wish to get sucked up into the war. When Dylan and Caitlin arrived there with baby Llewellyn in July 1940, fellow guests included the composers Lennox Berkeley and Arnold Cooke, William Glock (later to be the BBC's Controller of Music) and the novelist Antonia White.

Soon after the Thomases moved in, Antonia White was alarmed to hear screaming coming from one of the rooms upstairs. When she went up to investigate, she found it was only Dylan protesting shrilly while Caitlin was giving him a bath. Even more disturbing for Miss White, however, was Dylan's dog routine. When he scampered round her on all-fours, yapping and pretending to nip her ankles, some of the other residents of The Maltings were convinced he was trying to drive the already unstable novelist completely mad.

Night-time would often bring terrors for Dylan himself, as enemy aeroplanes droned overhead on their way to drop their loads on English and Welsh towns. While the planes passed, he would hide under the blankets, at the bottom of the bed, trembling and whimpering like a puppy, while Caitlin lay there reading or just thinking, quite certain that nothing could possibly happen to them. As Dylan confessed in a letter to Vernon Watkins, he had terrible nightmares invoked by the Battle of Britain that August, including one particularly unsettling image of airmen being fried alive in a huge frying pan. The knowledge that Swansea and even the Gower Peninsula were being bombed appalled him.

None the less, Dylan and Caitlin spent many enjoyable afternoons cycling round the Gloucestershire and Wiltshire countryside, as if life were perfectly normal. At other times, Caitlin would dance alone, in a large, empty private chapel at The Maltings, to music on records lent to her by John Davenport. Dylan, meanwhile, would be cloistered with Davenport in a room in the big house that had been converted into a bar, working on what Dylan described as a 'fantastic thriller': *The Death of the King's Canary*. As Constantine FitzGibbon explained in the introduction to the book, when it was finally published in 1976, the idea for *The Murder of the King's Canary*, as the novel was originally titled, first came to Dylan in 1938, when he wrote to his old friend from *South Wales Evening Post* days, Charles Fisher, asking him to collaborate on a detective story to end all detective stories. This would use stereotyped characters and situations that no contemporary author would dare employ any more, dragging 'hundreds of red herrings, false clues, withheld evidences' into the story, falsifying every issue and making 'many chapters deliberate parodies, full of clichés, of other detective writers'.[1]

Charles Fisher produced a first chapter of the proposed book, which was also briefly mooted as a radio play. That chapter set the scene of a committee assembling to choose the next Poet Laureate (hence the expression 'the King's Canary'). Then the project fizzled out. With nothing else to do in the wonderful long, hot but war-worrying summer of 1940, Dylan resuscitated it, with John Davenport standing in for Charles Fisher. They half-hoped that the book would become a useful little earner for them, but Davenport, at least, must surely have realized that it was little more than an elaborate private joke. Moreover, it would be unpublishable for many years because so many of the literary figures lampooned in it were instantly recognizable, and their originals would undoubtedly sue.

Almost the whole galaxy of British contemporary poets, including Dylan himself, appears in the book, along with parodies of their work. Later, Dylan used to disclaim having written much of *The Death of the King's Canary*, other than a parody of his friend William Empson, which appeared as a separate piece in the magazine *Horizon* (presumably with the target's approval) in 1942. Yet Dylan undoubtedly wrote a great deal of the book, or at least threw in his share of ideas and phrases, just as he had done in earlier, more self-consciously frivolous collaborations with Daniel Jones and Vernon Watkins. Right from its opening Firbankian line, 'His nerves had not been soothed by the bishop's unctuous platitudes', the book is a playful romp, but it is unlikely that it would ever have been published without Dylan's famous name attached to it.

Largely thanks to the BBC radio producer John Royston Morley, with whom he had had contact before the war, in Royston Morley's incarnation as editor of the magazine *Janus*, which had published his story 'The Horse's Ha', Dylan got some script-writing work for the BBC Overseas Services while he was installed at The Maltings. His first script was for the Portuguese-language section of the Latin American Service, on the nineteenth-century Brazilian military hero and conservative statesman the Duque de Caxias. This was broadcast on 26 August and earned him a fee of 12 guineas. A second script was then commissioned for a programme on Christopher Columbus – also for the BBC Latin American Service – which was to last nearly an hour. The script for this took Dylan much longer to write, and it was not considered entirely suitable when it was submitted. So he received only two-thirds of the 15-guinea fee contracted for. The programme was broadcast on 13 October. Even more problematic was a third commissioned script, on the Czech Legion set up in Russia in the final stages of the First World War, about which Dylan knew absolutely nothing. Even the public library in Bristol could not provide him with much relevant information, so he wrote to the Czech Legation in London asking if they could send him some. Bland Czech officers' reminiscences of taking 'Omsk and Tomsk and Bomsk'[2] drove Dylan, with his thirst for human detail, to the verges of despair. When the script on the Czech Legion was finally delivered to Royston Morely, after much delay, he found it unusable.

This rather unsatisfactory experience put paid to the hopes that Dylan had at this time of actually getting a job at the BBC. But it did give him the opportunity of going up to London for numerous brief visits in 1940 and 1941. He would usually scrounge a bed off friends, though on occasions he was lent vacant flats. That practice became rarer as his frightening reputation as a lodger grew. The painter Rupert Shephard and his first wife Lorna Wilmott got well and truly stung. In April 1940, Dylan had stayed at Lorna's flat, and according to Rupert Shephard,[3] they got back unexpectedly, to find Dylan polishing some of Lorna's silver. Their initial surprise and pleasure at this uncharacteristic act of domesticity turned to outrage when they discovered that Dylan had already pawned the rest of the silver in the flat (along with Lorna's gramophone, typewriter and fur coat). He had been preparing to do the same with the pieces he was cleaning. Lorna threatened to bring in the police, but decided to drop the matter when most of the items were recovered. However, appropriate warnings went out to other friends. This did not stop Dylan repeating the offence in households that had not taken the necessary precautions.

Caitlin became convinced that Dylan took advantage of his visits to London for casual encounters with other women, and she decided to wreak her revenge. There was a fairly libidinous atmosphere at The Maltings, as its transient population of musicians, artists and writers paired off in different combinations, and Caitlin fell heavily for the musician William Glock, who was already having an affair with Clement Davenport. Although Caitlin was usually attracted to dark men, Glock was very fair, though undeniably handsome. Later Caitlin thought it was probably his piano-playing and his gentle romanticism that appealed to her.[4] She would sit listening while Glock played Schubert and Mozart, and then they would hold hands chastely in the garden.

After a while, Caitlin decided she wanted to consummate the relationship with William Glock and devised a scheme whereby they could spend a night together in Cardiff. She told Dylan that she thought it would be a good idea to go over to Laugharne, to make sure that everything was all right there. This would also give Caitlin the opportunity of stopping off to see Florence and D. J. at Bishopston. As the scheme matured in her mind, Caitlin realized she wanted to mark this special event of her calculated infidelity by wearing memorable clothes. As she did not possess any smart dresses or suits, and had virtually no money, she arranged to sell what few possessions she and Dylan still had in Laugharne. Ivy Williams at Brown's Hotel helped Caitlin dispose of the Welsh blankets and lovely crockery she had acquired in Carmarthen market over the past two years, and with the proceeds Caitlin bought the most elegant outfit she could find in the dress-shops of Cardiff.

William Glock was waiting for Caitlin at a hotel, as arranged, and after a few drinks and dinner, they went up to the bedroom. She sprayed herself with perfume, put on her Isadora Duncan dancing tunic (which she felt was fitting for such an occasion) and lay down on the bed, waiting for Glock to take her. But nothing happened. According to her memoirs, they just lay there next to each other, staring at the ceiling, neither of them making any move, until they fell asleep. The following morning, they parted with hardly a word.

Unfortunately, Dylan realized his wife's deception when Florence Thomas told him that Caitlin had stayed only two nights at Bishopston, rather than the three that she had claimed. He swore fiercely at Caitlin, in the way that he used to swear at his sister Nancy. And just as he had once threatened to strangle Nancy, so he threw a knife at Caitlin – which missed by miles. For a while after that, when Caitlin and Dylan were in bed together, he would just turn his back to her, and refuse to have sex. Clearly there was one rule for the goose and another for the gander.

This situation considerably soured the atmosphere of Christmas 1940, which was spent once again at Bishopston with D. J. and Florence Thomas. Florence's opinion of her son's 'little madam' had plummeted, and she was exasperated that Dylan himself had contrived to lose his ration-book, which complicated the process of buying enough food for them all to eat. Moreover Dylan was preoccupied with yet more attempts to solicit financial support from potential benefactors. The Davenports had had to bring their generous hospitality to an end, as they too were beginning to run out of money, not to mention wine. Their house-guests scattered. Though staying with his parents was a helpful stop-gap, Dylan recognized that it was no long- or even medium-term solution, partly because D. J. could not afford to keep them, and partly because he felt stifled in the Bishopston house with its little rooms.

The ever-loyal Vernon Watkins – who had applied to join the Royal Air Force police – sent a pound or two whenever he could, but Dylan needed much more than that. On Christmas Eve, no less, he wrote to Lord Howard de Walden, who was a well-known patron of music and drama in Wales, and had helped out once before, asking him if he could send some money. This time the request was ostensibly so that Dylan and Caitlin could rent a cottage somewhere in Wales, probably in Pembrokeshire or Carmarthenshire,[5] where Dylan could get on with more writing in peace. The vagueness about the place suggests that Dylan realized it would probably be as well to avoid Laugharne for a while.

As so often in his begging letters to rich friends and acquaintances, Dylan held out the prospect of work to come. In other words, they could consider themselves to be sponsoring something of lasting literary value which might otherwise never appear. In Lord Howard de Walden's case, Dylan did indeed have a book in the pipeline: a novel called *Adventures in the Skin Trade*. This was to be a fictionalized follow-up to the autobiographical stories in *Portrait of the Artist as a Young Dog*. The hero of the book (Samuel Bennet) is, like the young Dylan, a South Walian boy with an older, hockey-legged sister (Peggy). In a symbolic break with his upbringing, Bennet rips his sister's photograph to pieces, and smashes some of his mother's best china, before taking off to sample the fleshpots in London. There he meets up with various decadent or delapidated characters; he flirts with the girls and finds himself dancing with an unattractive older gay man. The book was meant to be amusing, in a rather heavy-handed way, but the humorous innocence of *Portrait of the Artist as a Young Dog* had gone.

During the first half of 1941, three chapters of *Adventures in the Skin Trade* were written, parallel to continuing work on polishing *The Death of the King's Canary*. Dylan typed much of these texts on Vernon Watkins's typewriter. This Vernon had loaned to Dylan in an extraordinary act of sacrifice, given that he himself was preparing his first book of poetry, published as *The Ballad of Mari Lwyd* in October 1941. Vernon only got his typewriter back when his initial training with the RAF was over, and he received his first posting.

In February 1941, Swansea was hit by a series of shocking air-raids, which devastated the town centre. Bert Trick ran into Dylan and Caitlin the morning after the third and worst raid. This was the last time Bert Trick saw Dylan. He was standing with Caitlin on the corner of a shattered shopping street, looking dazed. As Trick recalled, firemen's hoses snaked among the blackened entrails of what had been Swansea market. Dylan, with tears in his eyes, declared, 'Our Swansea is dead!' [6]

Better news came that month when the Royal Literary Fund responded to a second application from Dylan, this time awarding him £50. In his letters to H. J. C. Marshall, the Secretary of the Fund, soliciting a grant in January, Dylan had been economical with the truth in several respects. He claimed that he had volunteered for service in the armed forces, but had been turned down because of the poor state of his lungs. Then he said that the BBC had not replied to his application for a job, allegedly with the Monitoring Service, though it is hard to imagine what Dylan might have done there, as he knew no foreign languages. Finally, he also maintained that he was about to become homeless, as he really could not impose on his parents for more than another week, and he and his family had nowhere else to go. In fact, Caitlin and the infant Llewellyn stayed on at Bishopston for more than another three months, until the last week of April, while Dylan himself divided his time between there and London.

As before, Dylan had lined up an impressive range of literary celebrities to back his application to the Royal Literary Fund. This time they included Hugh Walpole, J. B. Priestley and Edwin Muir. Alec Waugh, Evelyn's novelist brother, took a dim view of Dylan's seemingly boundless energy for writing round to friends and strangers alike, begging for money. Yet he too wrote a strong letter to Mr Marshall in support of Dylan's application, saying that although he personally didn't like Dylan's work, or indeed anything he had heard about him as a person, he none the less felt that Dylan deserved a grant because 'he is producing work that is respected by people competent to judge'.[7] But the thing that probably clinched the Royal Literary Fund's decision in Dylan's favour this time round was the fact that he had published three more books since the previous application: *The Map of Love*, *Portrait of the Artist as a Young Dog* and the American miscellany *The World I Breathe*. However poor the sales of these books may have been, he had proved his literary worth.

Dylan revealed his true feelings about earning a living and helping the war effort to Clement Davenport at the beginning of April. He told her that he feared that unless he was very careful or lucky, he would end up making munitions in a factory, condemned to the mind-numbing routine of clocking in, turning a screw and winding a wheel, whereas 'deary me I'd rather be a poet anyday and live on guile and beer'.[8] Guile was especially important, as he could deploy it to ensure that he had the liberty to write, and the money to pay for the beer.

Obtaining the grant from the Royal Literary Fund was not the only money-raising exercise Dylan embarked on. He had realized that there was probably money to be made in selling off his juvenile poetry notebooks, which had been the source of so many of his poems right up until 1940. The notebooks were still at the Davenports' house in Marshfield, but he got Clement to send them on. Through the London bookseller Bertram Rota, who specialized in modern first editions and literary manuscripts, Dylan was then able to raise over £20 by the sale of five notebooks and other manuscripts to the Lockwood Library at the State University of

New York in Buffalo. Subsequently, he asked Bertram Rota how much various first editions of works by authors such as Evelyn Waugh, Richard Hughes, H. G. Wells and William Faulkner were worth, as he wanted to sell off any books from his own small library that might fetch some money. Once he had done that successfully, he showed that he was not averse to selling off books from other people's libraries as well, as some of his hosts in London discovered to their cost.

One therefore needs to take Dylan's claim of being penniless at this period with a large pinch of salt. As ever, the real problem was that he did not know how to manage money when he had it. Similarly, it was not true that Dylan was writing nothing as a result of the strains of penury, although this was the impression he liked to give. Apart from the two prose works in progress – neither of which would be published in his life-time – Dylan had written several poems in recent months. These included his first war poem, 'Deaths and Entrances' (with its ominously repeated line 'On almost the incendiary eve'), and what was for him the exceptionally long 'Ballad of the Long-legged Bait'.

The latter was finished in April 1941, and it appeared in *Horizon* two months later. Dylan was furious with Cyril Connolly at the way the 216-line ballad was set; like all wartime publications, *Horizon* had to economize with paper, and Connolly had the poem laid out in parallel columns. But such appearances in magazines gave Dylan considerably more public exposure than he had had through any of his books. He could have had more, had he produced more poems. John Lehmann, who had launched the hugely successful magazine *New Writing*, badgered Dylan for contributions, but eventually had to settle for reprinting extracts from *Portrait of the Artist as a Young Dog*, with the permission of J. M. Dent.

Dent's had agreed to pay Dylan for sight of the early chapters of his novel in progress, *Adventures in the Skin Trade*, but when he submitted the first 15,000 words or so, their reaction was deeply hostile. As the editor John Hadfield wrote to Laurence Pollinger at David Higham's, not a single publisher's reader to whom the typescript was sent for an opinion gave it a favourable report. Hadfield felt that it was at best 'a fragment of frolicksome dirt'. The material was not deemed good enough for publication, and Dylan needed to be told so plainly. In Dent's opinion, Dylan had reached a crucial point in his literary career. He had made a flying start, but had not maintained the position he had achieved through his early poetry. Hadfield advised Pollinger that he should persuade Dylan to abandon *Adventures in the Skin Trade* – which Dylan had himself described as a mixture of Dickens's *Little Dorrit*, Kafka and 'Beachcomber', the humorous columnist in the *Daily Express* – and instead buckle down to a more carefully thought-out piece of work. In the words of one of the readers' reports: 'unless he pulls himself together, he is going to fizzle out as an author most ignominiously'.[9]

Vernon Watkins was with Dylan when he received the publisher's verdict in June. A few weeks previously, Dylan, Caitlin and Llewellyn had moved back to Laugharne, where they were being put up in Castle House by Frances Hughes (Richard Hughes being away working for the Admiralty). As Vernon wrote in his preface to the posthumously published fragment of *Adventures in the Skin Trade*, Dylan opened the letter eagerly, but when he read its contents he was indignant as well as amused. As they walked together later in the garden of Laugharne Castle, Dylan asked Vernon why publishers always wanted writers to impress readers rather than entertain them. For Dylan, there was no serious intent to the picaresque adventures of Samuel Bennet. They were merely meant to amuse. Vernon, for one, thought some of the passages in the early chapters were extremely funny, and John Lehmann accepted the first one for publication in his *Folios V* that autumn. Having received such a strong slap on the wrist from his publisher, however, Dylan shelved the project.

The day after Vernon left, the literary editor of *The Listener*, J. R. Ackerley, turned up in Laugharne, on the recommendation of a friend who had been there the year before. Dylan had recently turned down a commission to do an article for *The Listener* on the relationship between poets and institutions like the BBC, but he found Joe Ackerley to be charming, with a nice smile and a lazy, affected, very pleasant voice.[10] Ackerley spent only about three or four days in Laugharne, going off each day on long walks. He would meet up with Dylan in the evenings at Brown's Hotel, and then go round with him to Frances Hughes's for more drinks. Ackerley, who was nearly twenty years older than Dylan, used his position at *The Listener* to help promote a fair number of young writers. Not for the first time in his life, however, Dylan failed to capitalize on the opportunity offered by the distinguished editor's presence.

In contrast, he did take advantage of the contact he had made through John Davenport with the trainee American film director Ivan Moffat, to seek out film work. Although Dylan almost never referred to the cinema in his letters, he was an enthusiastic cinemagoer. This was not only because a matinée performance was a useful way of filling in the afternoon hours in London when the pubs were closed, though that undoubtedly contributed. Film was a medium in which enormous stylistic and visual liberties could be taken. It could embrace surrealism or gothic horror almost as easily as it could portray more straightforward stories. Above all, through careful casting and the use of close-ups, the cinema could put the most extraordinary people under the microscope in a way that appealed to the voyeuristic side to Dylan's character.

Documentary film-making – so different from the fictional floss and fluff that was blowing out of Hollywood – had come into its own in Britain in the 1930s. This was thanks largely to the remarkable talent of the producer John Grierson and the director with whom he collaborated, Basil Wright. Grierson set out his ground-breaking principles of documentary-making as an instrument of educational and sociological change in 1932, and he produced a series of powerful documentaries, first for the Empire Marketing Board and then for the GPO (Post Office) Film Unit, which was based in London's Soho Square. He believed in using proven writers who did not necessarily have any established connection with film. One of the most successful of these was Wystan Auden, who worked on *Coal Face* and *Night Mail*, which became classics of the genre.

Probably Grierson's most promising disciple was Donald Taylor, who eventually left to set up on his own, founding the more commercially-minded Strand Films. This company had its offices first in Upper St Martin's Lane and then in Golden Square. Like Grierson, Donald Taylor brought in first-class writers to work on his films: one of the earliest was Graham Greene; another was the then popular novelist Philip Lindsay. So when Donald Taylor's young American apprentice Ivan Moffat (who was the son of the actress Iris Tree and the painter Curtis Moffat) introduced Dylan Thomas as a penniless, sickly but brilliant poet in need of a job,

Taylor was favourably inclined. According to Constantine FitzGibbon's wife Theodora (commonly known as 'Tony'), the first meeting between Dylan and Donald Taylor occurred in a pub in St Martin's Lane – probably The Salisbury – on a lovely evening early in September 1940. Taylor was familiar with some of Dylan's earlier poems, and the two men got on well.

Yet it was nearly a year later before Dylan decided that he should install himself in London and try to establish a career in film-writing with Donald Taylor's help. Caitlin and he left young Llewellyn at Blashford with Mrs Macnamara and Caitlin's sister Brigit, and arrived in the capital in August 1941, staying where they could. During these war years, they became expert at just turning up on people's doorsteps, often late at night, with their few possessions in a bag or a laundry basket, knowing that friends and relations could hardly refuse them entry. On occasions the taxi that had deposited them would still be waiting, while Dylan and Caitlin extracted money from their 'hosts' to pay the fare. Caitlin's sister Nicolette had to put them up sometimes, at her home in Markham Square in Chelsea. On one occasion, Dylan repaid her hospitality by peeing all over her lounge wall. At another friend's house, he shat on the floor. More fortunate victims merely had their larders raided or clean shirts pinched. Dylan had a very communal attitude to property.

Yet Dylan's outrageous behaviour in friends' homes and in pubs was counter-balanced by a tremendous professional seriousness and even correctness when he did succeed in getting a job with Strand Films. Donald Taylor took him on at the not ungenerous salary of £8 a week (later raised to £10), which meant that he had a good regular income for once. Taylor had a fairly relaxed attitude towards how and where his writers did their work, but Dylan would conscientiously come into the office, perfectly sober, no matter how wild the evening before. He even managed to look smart, often sporting a bow-tie.

Because so much film-writing is team-work, it is difficult to know exactly what Dylan produced in his years with Strand Films. But during 1942 he certainly worked on a series of short documentaries commissioned by the Ministry of Information, including a portrait of the Council for the Encouragement of Music and Art (CEMA). One of the more commercial ventures he was involved in was a five-minute documentary for the chemical giant ICI, entitled 'This is Colour'.

One evening in March 1942, Dylan, Caitlin and Llewellyn – who had been temporarily retrieved from Blashford – descended on Lady Herbert, the wife of the writer and politician A. P. (Alan) Herbert, who was away on war business. The Herberts lived in Hammersmith Terrace, only a step from where Caitlin had been born, and the Thomases had heard from the Herberts' son-in-law, the poet John Pudney, that Sir Alan's studio next door was empty. Lady Herbert let them stay there for a few weeks. They all recognized it was not a very satisfactory arrangement, however, particularly given the dangers of German bombing. So in May the Thomases decided it would be as well if they lived separately for a while. Dylan would remain in London, Llewellyn would go back to his grandmother's, and Caitlin would go to stay at Talsarn in Cardiganshire with Vera Killick, who had known Dylan in Swansea in his dame-school days and had become close to Caitlin as well.

Dylan hoped he would be able to move into a house-share in St Peter's Square, Hammersmith, though in fact that arrangement came to nothing. While it was still a possibility, he wrote to a new admirer of his, Ruth Wynn Owen, asking if she knew of anyone in London with any furniture that needed a home. All he had, he claimed, was a deckchair with a hole in the canvas, half a dozen books, a few children's toys and an old iron. There were times, he wrote half-jokingly, half-self-pityingly, when it would be nice to be able to sprawl in one's own bourgeois chair and to have someone to bring one's slippers.[11]

Ruth Wynn Owen was a young actress from Anglesey, who had met Dylan that spring in Bradford, while she was touring in a play and he was working on a documentary about wartime theatre. According to the account she gave to Paul Ferris, she had spotted 'this little man' in the wings of the theatre where she was playing, and was intrigued when he said to her: 'Now that I've found you, don't go and die!'[12] Like Dylan, Ruth Wynn Owen was married, but this did not stop her falling in love with him. This obviously flattered Dylan's vanity, though she refused to sleep with him. They corresponded for about eighteen months, and occasionally met in London. Dylan's letters to her contain a number of endearments, but he was not going to let this become a grand affair that would threaten his relationship with Caitlin. Rather, he seems to have valued Ruth Wynn Owen's friendship. His gossipy accounts of life at Strand Films, with its 'queers in striped suits' talking about cinema and its repressed women secretaries 'punishing typewriters', are more missives to a chum than to a lover. There was all the difference in the world between them and the lengthy protestations of undying love that Dylan was sending to his one-and-only Cat and darling wife in Wales.

None the less, Caitlin was deeply dissatisifed. It was not just her fear that Dylan would find girlfriends to tide him over while they were apart. Equally important was the resentment she felt towards the film world – and Donald Taylor in particular – about the way they were allegedly 'corrupting' Dylan and preventing him from getting on with writing poems. She knew Dylan's working pattern well enough to realize that he would never be able to get much serious writing done after a day at the office. Evenings were for socializing and for drink. Up to a point, of course, Caitlin was right. Yet it may well have been that film work was exactly what Dylan needed at this unsettling time of war, especially as he himself seemed to be going through a period of transition. His disposal of his early poetry notebooks was symbolic of a desire to cease reworking the outpourings of his youth and to try to find a new direction.

During August, Dylan was able to spend some time with Caitlin and Vera Killick at Talsarn. It was good not just to get away from the air-raids of London, but also to be in a place where there was plenty of milk and cheese and eggs. Caitlin was two months pregnant and not in the mood to face the coming difficult months without her husband, however. So sometime in the autumn, Dylan found them a home-base in Chelsea where they could be together: a dilapidated one-room apartment at 8 Wentworth Studios in Manresa Road. This had a kitchen area separated off by a curtain, and an antiquated bathroom. When Caitlin was in town, the flat stank of the broth that seemed to be perpetually bubbling away on the stove. When she was away, there was utter squalor.

Wentworth Studios were single-storey buildings with giant artists' windows in the roof that somehow survived the war, though they have long since been demolished. Constantine FitzGibbon recalled that when it rained, water dripped down from the roof and even came in under the door. A few prints were pinned up on the walls, as well as some of Dylan's own drawings and cartoons, which he referred to mockingly as his 'literary pictures'. There was a large double bed in the room and a fine old circular table; the latter is prominent in a well-known photograph of Dylan and Caitlin taken at Wentworth Studios by Bill Brandt in 1944. Behind them in a bookcase can be seen some of the rows of Daniel Jones's precious library, which he had left with Dylan for safekeeping. This proved to be a foolish act of trust. A few of the books were probably stolen, or lent and never returned. But the vast majority were converted by Dylan into cash. When Dan Jones eventually came to retrieve his treasures, there were only about fifty of the more obscure and least valuable left.

Dan Jones saw quite a lot of Dylan in the middle years of the war. Together they would frequent the Chelsea pubs, like The Crossed Keys or The King's Head and Eight Bells by the river, where Dylan would beat Dan at shove-ha'penny. Dylan had a liking for such entertainments, as well as simple card games, but he became irritable and uncooperative when Dan Jones tried to teach him anything much more sophisticated.

Similarly, Dylan's attitude to music was like that of an unformed child. When Dan met up with him in a Chelsea pub one day, Dylan told him excitedly that someone had lent him an old gramophone and a recording of Verdi's opera *Il Trovatore*. 'It's great!' Dylan kept repeating between gulps of beer. When they got back to Wentworth Studios, Dylan produced the machine, whose turntable regulator had stuck so that by some extraordinary quirk it played the 78 rpm record at twice its proper speed. The music thus came out an octave above its usual pitch and the 'Anvil Chorus' sounded like the frenzied hammerings of dwarfs. Seemingly unaware of the distortion, Dylan was particularly delighted by the *presto* passions of the opera's male lead. As he enthused to Dan Jones, 'Those Italian tenors wear their testicles in their throats!'[13]

Dan Jones was less enchanted on the rare occasions when he went into Soho pubs with Dylan and felt marginalized by Dylan's growing band of camp-followers. These London friends of Dylan's could spend hours listening to his risqué stories and his merciless imitations. The composer Elisabeth Lutyens, for example, thought he was the funniest man in the world. Moreover, it was not just a case of Dylan the actor performing for a passive audience. As Ivan Moffat told Paul Ferris, he had the knack of taking over people's concerns and worries, blowing them up into fantastic and often ludicrous proportions, so that they turned into his own grotesque nightmare about which one could only laugh. As with many clowns, however, there was a profound core of personal disquiet, even misery, inside Dylan, which in years to come would show itself in open bitterness and verbal cruelty.

8

NEW DIRECTIONS

(1943–1945)

Constantine FitzGibbon saw a lot of Dylan during 1943, when FitzGibbon was working as an Intelligence officer at the United States Embassy in Grosvenor Square. He had rented a small furnished house with his wife-to-be Theodora in Godfrey Street, Chelsea, just a couple of minutes' walk from Dylan and Caitlin's studio in Manresa Road. The house had a small spare room with a desk in it, which FitzGibbon put at Dylan's disposal so that he would have somewhere quiet to write on those afternoons when he didn't have to go in to Strand Films. This meant that Dylan had a key to the FitzGibbons' house. One afternoon, Theodora was astonished to bump into him in the King's Road with her sewing-machine in his arms, on his way to the pawn-shop. Caitlin felt he had really gone too far this time, but Dylan just thought it was funny to be caught out red-handed.

In February, the publisher James Laughlin of New Directions in America brought out a slim volume of Dylan's verse written since the miscellany *The World I Breathe*. The book was entitled simply *New Poems*, and appeared in a series called 'Poets of the Year'. For some reason, Dylan thought the series was called 'Poet of the Month', and he found this deeply insulting. He turned down his literary agent's suggestion of trying to get J. M. Dent to publish the volume in England as well, as he thought only seventeen poems were not enough for a commercial publication and that it would be better to wait until he could add others to produce a book that would have a greater impact.

On 15 February the BBC Welsh Service broadcast a fifteen-minute autobiographical sketch called 'Reminiscences of Childhood' which Dylan had written at the end of the previous year. This was the first of what proved to be a hugely popular irregular series of Dylan's childhood recollections, put out on BBC radio. The combination of his booming voice, his sensitivity to the sound and rhythm of words, and his acute eye for nostalgic detail made Dylan a natural radio broadcaster. He came across as a man of great warmth and self-deprecating humour, far different from the carousing performer his London friends and fellow-drinkers knew in the Soho and Chelsea pubs.

When the first version of 'Reminiscences of Childhood' was actually broadcast, however, Dylan and Caitlin were far more preoccupied with the imminent arrival of their second child than with Dylan's past. Caitlin went into St Mary Abbots Hospital, Kensington, for the birth itself, which took place on 3 March 1943: as had happened in the case of Llewellyn, Dylan completely disappeared. The new baby was a girl, called Aeronwy (or Aeron for short), after the River Aeron in Cardiganshire. Vera Killick's cottage at Talsarn was in the valley of the River Aeron, and Caitlin had calculated that that was where Aeronwy had been conceived.

A tremendous air-raid was going on at the moment of Aeronwy's delivery, which mercifully was easier than Llewellyn's had been. As Caitlin wrote in her memoirs, it was comforting to know that there was something even worse than childbirth going on outside. It was a week before Dylan summoned up the courage to go to see his wife and new daughter in the hospital, and he arrived looking 'completely shagged out'. He was wearing an old dressing-gown that was not his own, and bedroom slippers. His hair was in a mess and he hadn't shaved; he had clearly been on a bender for days. Caitlin was hurt that he did not seem particularly concerned about her or the baby's condition.

When the day for Caitlin's discharge from hospital came, there was no sign of Dylan, so she bundled up Aeronwy, ordered a taxi and went home to Manresa Road. The scene that awaited her was harrowing. Never tidy at the best of times, the studio was now a filthy, chaotic mess. Dylan had obviously done no washing-up the whole time Caitlin had been in the hospital. Dirty dishes and empty beer-bottles lay everywhere, while the carpet was strewn with old newspapers and cigarette butts. Caitlin just stood there holding the baby in her pristine white baby-clothes, unable to find any suitable place to put her down. Then she saw the rumpled bed and knew instantly that Dylan had had another woman sleeping there.

Dylan arrived back in the evening the worse for wear from drink, accompanied by Constantine and Theodora FitzGibbon. In later years Caitlin had no inhibitions about attacking her husband physically as well as verbally in front of friends, but for the time being she felt she could not create a scene. On the verge of tears, she choked back her anger, and buckled down to clearing up the studio.

Later Caitlin felt that the need and desire to look after Aeronwy prevented her from walking out on Dylan at his period. She looked on the little baby with wonder, thinking that she resembled a tiny, prettier version of Dylan. They got a bassinet for her, over which an umbrella was placed when it rained, to stop her being splashed by leaks from the roof. Yet of an evening, Caitlin would still keep her routine of going out to the pub with Dylan from seven till ten, leaving the baby alone. One day she came back to find a Dutch woman neighbour who kept several smelly Siamese cats holding Aeronwy in her arms. Far from being grateful for the neighbour's helping out, Caitlin was disgusted at the idea that hands that had stroked the cats were now touching her child.[1]

Often the Thomases had to search round different pubs to find one that actually had alcoholic drink to serve; Caitlin's favourite spirits were particularly difficult to get in wartime. But The Eight Bells in Cheyne Walk was the main Chelsea haunt of the crowd with which Dylan, Caitlin, Constantine and Theodora mixed. This included other writers and poets such as John Davenport, Norman Douglas, Philip Lindsay and Brian Howard, as well as the painter Francis Rose. The ambience was heavily orientated towards the arts, and with so many gay and lesbian or bisexual men and women in the area, there was considerable sexual ambiguity and camp ragging, into which Dylan entered with gusto. Just as before his marriage to Caitlin he had once gone flouncing around Leicester Square with Nigel Henderson, as they pretended to be a pair of mincing queens, so now Dylan would sometimes put a gaudy flower in his button-hole and play the role of an outrageous arty queer, especially if there were men in uniform around.

Teasing soldiers and sailors during the war seems to have been one of Dylan's regular pastimes. Perhaps this was partly a way of sublimating subconscious guilt over avoiding active service himself. Constantine FitzGibbon recalled how Dylan bristled once when Daniel Jones came into a pub wearing army uniform. Dylan's aggressive attitude to men in uniform got him into some nasty scrapes. Far from avoiding these, he would provoke them. Just as a Yorkshire terrier will sometimes go for an Alsatian, yapping at its flanks, so pint-sized Dylan (albeit with his quart of flesh squeezed into his tweeds) would goad the burliest servicemen in pubs until they were riled. In that respect he was no coward.

Caitlin took Aeronwy to Wales on a number of occasions during 1943, staying with Frances Hughes at Laugharne Castle, or Vera Killick at Talsarn, or with Dylan's parents. D. J. and Florence had moved from Bishopston to get away from the Swansea bombing, and had settled at one of Florence's family's cottages, Blaen Cwm, at Llangain. The Rev. David Rees and Auntie Dosie had lived there after the minister's retirement, but both were now dead. In the cottage next door lived Florence's chatterbox sister Auntie Polly, and their taciturn unmarried brother Uncle Bob. D. J. would mutter under his breath about being surrounded by 'cows and clots',[2] and would often go off on long walks to escape.

During his separations from Caitlin in the summer and autumn of 1943, Dylan would write to her insisting how much he loved and missed her and Aeronwy and Llewellyn, and how much he hated film work. He said he found this particularly burdensome when he had to be based at the film studios at Elstree, when he lodged at The King's Arms at Barnet in Hertfordshire. The hours were long, which meant there was no opportunity to get to London to see his friends and wind down. He also claimed that the subject matter of the documentaries he was working on bored him, although in fact he enjoyed sending up some of the more pompous wartime themes.

Dylan's irreverent attitude even permeated one of the films he helped make, *Is Your Ernie Really Necessary?* The title was a pun on the ubiquitous wartime slogan 'Is your journey really necessary?', which was aimed at discouraging people from travelling unless they really had to, thereby conserving fuel. Dylan worked with the comedy director Oswald Mitchell in producing a script that took a light-hearted look at transport. One actor, Haypetrie, played all the parts. In one scene, he appeared in drag as a girl in a revue, and was then turned into a whole chorus line by the use of mirrors. But the thing which really seems to have upset the Ministry of Information, which forbade the release of the completed film, was a scene in a railway signalbox, in which the signalman played 'The Bells of St Mary's' by pulling the signal levers. Such flippancy was considered unhealthily subversive by the Ministry.

There were also problems with a film about Wales, called *Green Mountain, Black Mountain*, for which Dylan wrote an Audenesque script, with long verse passages stressing both the beauty of the landscape and the misery of the coalpits and unemployment. The British Council, which had originally commissioned the film for distribution overseas, thought the overall impression of life in wartime Wales was too negative, so it was offered to the Ministry of Information instead. The MOI's Welsh Office then came up with the objection that Dylan wasn't Welsh enough, with his cut-glass voice and London lifestyle; they wanted him replaced by a *real* Welshman. But more senior civil servants in London put their foot down, and in the end the film was issued as made.

The most vivid portrait of Dylan at Strand Films has been left by the writer Julian Maclaren-Ross, who was himself a notable figure on the Soho–Fitzrovia scene in the second half of the war. Only recently out of army uniform in the summer of 1943, Maclaren-Ross habitually wore a teddy-bear coat and dark glasses, and carried a silver-topped cane, which made him stand out in a crowd. Donald Taylor took him on to the payroll at Strand Films on the recommendation of the writer Arthur Calder-Marshall. Maclaren-Ross started work there the day after the August Bank Holiday, and found himself travelling up in the lift with Dylan to their offices in Golden Square. They didn't speak as they didn't know each other. Instead, as Maclaren-Ross recalled in his *Memoirs of the Forties*, they examined one another with mutual distaste. Dylan's eyes travelled from the silver-topped cane to Maclaren-Ross's white corduroy jacket, cream silk shirt and peach-coloured tie, and then turned away so abruptly that Maclaren-Ross looked down to check whether his flies were undone. Dylan himself had on a green pork-pie hat pulled down almost level with his eyes, and a grubby mackintosh hung from his shoulders like a cape. Underneath he wore a dark blue suit, a white shirt and a bow-tie, which made him look like a salesman up from the provinces. One arm was in a filthy sling; he had hurt his wrist falling down a flight of stairs. A damp cigarette-end hung from his lower lip, and his bulbous nose shone. Later Dylan informed Maclaren-Ross that he polished his nose by rubbing it with his fist every morning in front of the mirror.

Dylan shot out of the lift when it arrived at the right floor, so he didn't see Julian Maclaren-Ross follow him into the same suite of offices, where he was greeted by Donald Taylor and ushered into the room he would share with Dylan. When told that the two of them would be working together, Dylan visibly recoiled. None the less, Maclaren-Ross discovered that it was largely on Dylan's recommendation that he had been offered employment at Strand Films, as Dylan had been impressed by some of his stories that he had seen in magazines.

Dylan thawed when his new colleague asked him why his arm was in a sling. Apparently he had hurt his wrist trying to stop the other full-time scriptwriter, Philip Lindsay, falling down stairs. He explained that Lindsay – an even greater drinker than himself – was always falling over, so that he tended to wander round bruised and bloodied. Allegedly the hospital which had tended Dylan's wrist had asked him to return twice a week for treatment, but he had refused. 'I said to myself: "No bloody fear!" Start going to hospitals and you never know what they'll find wrong. Might begin taking my liver out and scraping it again.'[3] He claimed that this was a regular occurrence, and that he was probably suffering from cirrhosis.

His attitude to Maclaren-Ross changed even more when Julian suggested that they go out to the back-bar of the Café Royal to discuss the project they would be working on together: a film about the Home Guard. That first lunch-time, Dylan stuck to beer, and was careful not to get sozzled. But in the evening, first at the Café Royal and then in The Wheatsheaf in Rathbone Place, Dylan quickly got drunker, mixing beer with gin. At one stage he asked Maclaren-Rose why he didn't take off the white corduroy jacket that had caused him such offence in the lift. 'Fucking dandy,' Maclaren-Ross later reported him as saying, 'why don't you try to look more sordid? *Sordidness*, boy, that's the thing!'[4] Yet in the weeks that followed, as their friendship deepened, Dylan became attached to Maclaren-Ross's jacket and cane, and grew extremely belligerent when a stranger in a pub was critical of his colleague's get-up. He could be very protective about his friends, and on several occasions turned on people who he imagined were sending them up.

However, when Maclaren-Ross suggested that he and Dylan could go halves on a bottle of Irish whiskey and keep it in the office for the occasional restorative nip, Dylan was appalled. Drink and work didn't mix. Even if sometimes he was counting the minutes until pub opening time, he wouldn't have a bottle on the premises. This corroborates the impression his friends had that he was never an alcoholic. In fact, Maclaren-Ross, who could happily down whiskies one after another, was surprised by how relatively little Dylan drank, considering the hangovers he sometimes got. In their lunch-times, a double Irish whiskey and a pint of beer with his ham sandwich was enough to satisfy Dylan. The fact that he was drinking whiskey at all, however, suggests that he was influenced by his new friend's tastes. Left to his own devices, he almost always just drank beer.

The Wheatsheaf was at the height of its popularity during the second half of the war, attracting a wide variety of literary and local personalities with whom both Dylan and Julian Maclaren-Ross felt at ease. The pub had good blackout boards fitted over the windows, and even on winter evenings it was bright and warm inside. There was scarlet lino on the floor and the walls were a fine example of British mock-Tudor kitsch, with squares of different Scottish tartans set between wooden panels. A large china swan had pride of place in the big bow window at the bottom of the bar. The licensee was a short, plump spinster called Mona, who had the final say about who could or could not come into the pub, though as far as the customers were concerned the landlord was her equally portly brother Redvers (universally known as 'Red'). He usually served in his shirt-sleeves and braces, except on Sundays when he wore a suit. Red's tall, slim wife Frances, looking severe in pince-nez and tweeds, completed the trio behind the bar.

At first Red and Frances did not think much of Dylan, with his show-off ways, although they changed their minds when he became famous from his radio broadcasts. However, fortunately for Dylan Mona did not disapprove, so he was spared the indignity of being barred. Not all the Wheatsheaf's customers were enthusiastic about him, either. In particular, his detractors included a permanent evening fixture called Mrs Stewart, a tiny, neatly dressed elderly lady who lived in a tenement block nearby, and who arrived at the pub on the dot of six. The subject of a notable portrait by Nina Hamnett – with whom she had coincided in Paris before the war – Mrs Stewart would sit in the same spot on a bench along the wall at The Wheatsheaf, night after night, sipping Guinness, with a couple of evening papers and an alarm clock spread out in front of her, timing herself as she did the crosswords. Mrs Stewart loathed anyone offering to help her with the puzzle clues, and it is possible that that is how Dylan got into her bad books, as he had become used to helping D. J. do the *Times* crossword over the years.

Another of the Wheatsheaf's regulars was a very elderly member of the Home Guard, whose tunic was bedecked with lines of medals, some of which looked as if they dated from the Crimean War. Julian Maclaren-Ross used him as a model for the old sweat who was to appear in the film on the Home Guard that he was writing with Dylan. Then there was Sister Ann, a most respectable-looking prostitute in tweeds, who wore subdued makeup and hung around the lobby between the pub's public and saloon bars. Sister Ann was often to be seen during the evening rush-hour standing beneath the Guinness Clock in the Tottenham Court Road, catching prospective clients as they made their way to the Tube.

At half-past ten in the evening, when the pubs on the north side of Oxford Street closed, there would be a mass migration of hardened drinkers into Soho proper, where pubs like The Highlander in Dean Street were open for another half-hour. It was in The Highlander in 1943 that Julian Maclaren-Ross first met the painters Robert Colquhoun and Robert MacBryde, who were among the most colourful of Soho's figures in the 1940s and 1950s. Aged about thirty when Maclaren-Ross encountered them, they had been lovers since they had studied at Glasgow School of Art. Belligerently Scots, with their broad accents and kilts, they took a dim view of fellow-Celts who they felt had succumbed to pernicious English ways. Robert Colquhoun once upbraided Dylan in a taxi for being a 'phoney Welshman' because of the way he talked. Colquhoun also considered it an insufficient excuse on Maclaren-Ross's part that he himself had no Scots accent, despite his name, just because he had been brought up in England and France.

Colquhoun was both the taller and the stronger of the two Roberts. He was a handsome man with striking curly hair, a fiery temperament and a laugh that resembled a snarl. He would bang on the bar counter when he wanted a whisky and swear at people he didn't like the look of. Yet to Dylan's amusement, numerous women would swoon at the sight of Robert Colquhoun's mouth, which one of them described as 'so masterful and clamped so determinedly tight'.[5] Any designs the women had on Colquhoun were in vain, however, as he was fiercely loyal to MacBryde, though sometimes the two of them would fight like dogs, struggling along the length of the bar before falling out into the street. MacBryde kept house for the two of them and did as much as he could to promote his lover's artistic career. None the less, a number of women took it upon themselves to act as the two Roberts' surrogate mothers, just as they did with Dylan.

Apart from the pubs, there were a number of afternoon drinking clubs in Soho, to which Dylan would sometimes retire with Julian Maclaren-Ross or Philip Lindsay for 'script conferences'. A particular favourite of Dylan's was the Horseshoe Club in Wardour Street, which was reached by a flight of exceptionally sordid stairs – the stairs that Dylan had tried to prevent Philip Lindsay from falling down. There was a spy-hole in the door at the top; when anyone arrived, a panel would slide aside and an eye would appear at the aperture before the door was opened. Dylan loved the conspiratorial nature of this, thinking that it made the Horseshoe resemble an American speakeasy during Prohibition, or an opium den.

To Maclaren-Ross, at least, the inside of the Horseshoe Club was much less exciting. The clientele was predominantly middle-aged, with a liberal sprinkling of lesbians and arty types. Dylan was particularly fond of the fifty-year-old art critic T. W. (Tommy) Earp, who hung out there. He had hair like fur and big round staring eyes, and Maclaren-Ross considered him not only creepy but a thumping bore. Yet Dylan enthused about what he saw as Earp's deadpan wit and his talent for punning word-games. Like many of Dylan's friends, Maclaren-Ross was intrigued by his devotion to older men like Earp, who became a favoured correspondent. Dylan's attitude incorporated the almost Oriental concept of equating age with wisdom. When he was with Julian

Maclaren-Ross, for example, he would often reminisce about his old mentor at the *Swansea Evening Post*, Fred Farr.

Maclaren-Ross quickly got bored with the Horseshoe Club, and came to an arrangement with Dylan whereby each of them would take alternative afternoons off from the Strand Films office, while the other held the fort. That way, Dylan could hang out with his cronies on his free afternoons and Maclaren-Ross could go chasing women on his. He was puzzled by the fact that although Dylan loved to talk about sex, he never seemed to go to much effort to chat up girls. Stories (most of them no doubt self-originated) did the rounds of the Soho pubs of how Dylan had spent the night with various women. Yet when Maclaren-Ross asked Dylan whether one such story was true, namely that Dylan had smuggled a girl in his sleeping-bag up on to the roof of the Strand Film offices in Golden Square, when it was his turn to spend a night on fire-watching duty there, Dylan just giggled and said: 'Then she must have been a very *little* girl!'[6] As he explained to Maclaren-Ross, having had the good fortune to marry a girl he considered to be the prettiest he had ever met, he had few illusions about the grass being greener on the other side of the fence.

Besides, a lot of Dylan's sexual banter was aimed at amusing or shocking people, rather than boasting about actual conquests. Ivan Moffat was delighted by one occasion, when the two of them were working on a film entitled *Balloon Site 568*. This gung-ho documentary was designed to encourage women to volunteer for the anti-aircraft balloon service, and much of the filming was done at a Women's Auxiliary Air Force base at Cardington. One day, as Ivan and Dylan were sitting on an outside dais at the base, reviewing a march-past of a couple of hundred WAAFs, Dylan turned to the matronly commanding officer and said: 'You have the most superb body, ma'am . . . ', pausing long enough for an expression of outrage to suffuse her face before continuing, ' . . . of women.'[7]

When Ivan Moffat and Dylan went drinking, as they often did, they tended to favour the York Minster pub in Dean Street, more popularly known as 'The French' for its now legendary landlord, Victor Berlemont, who had moved over from France with his wife in 1900. He was said to be the only foreigner to hold an English pub licence, and his establishment was a natural home for the exiled Free French during the war, including Charles de Gaulle when he was in London. Victor Berlemont, whose huge, curving moustaches reminded Constantine FitzGibbon of Napoleon's Old Guard, had devised an extraordinary contraption that could pour water into four glasses of Pernod simultaneously. In good French café tradition, 'The French' also served decent wine by the glass.

It was through Ivan Moffat that Dylan also became a regular at another of the great social institutions of the period, the Gargoyle Club, which occupied the three top floors of a building on the corner of Dean Street and narrow Meard Street. It had been founded in 1925 by the rich, attractive and eminently well-connected Cambridge graduate David Tennant, who was a younger son of the first Lord Glenconner. Tennant's original idea was that the Gargoyle should be a chic nightclub where wealthy people could dance, but which would also attract the avant-garde. It was stylishly decorated, with a number of important works of modern art, including a huge Matisse that was taken down for safety during the war and subsequently sold.

From the mid-Twenties to the end of the 1940s, when it started to go out of fashion, the Gargoyle brought together the cream of London society and Bohemia, counting among its loyal patrons such heteredox figures as Edwina Mountbatten, Randolph Churchill, T. S. Eliot, Noël Coward, Virginia Woolf, Gladys Cooper, Guy Burgess and Tallulah Bankhead. Though it did function as a luncheon club as well, the Gargoyle was considered especially interesting and racy in the late evening, after the pubs had closed. While not exactly encouraging people to behave outrageously, the management was extremely tolerant so long as violence did not break out and people paid their bills. Thus the painter John Minton, with his inevitable flotilla of uniformed sailors in tow, was able to hold court or dance frenetically on his own there, and assignations of every possible kind were made by the club's table-hopping clientele.

In letters to his 'Dear Cat', Dylan affected to dislike the Gargoyle, referring to it once as 'horrid, low-ceilinged [and] devil-enveloping'.[8] On at least one occasion the Thomases seem to have been barred from the club, on account of bad behaviour. But Ivan Moffat was proud to take Dylan along to the Gargoyle as one of the Young Turks he had promised David Tennant he would bring to rejuvenate the place during the war. The strategy succeeded, as the club was at its zenith at that time, benefiting when that earlier favourite gathering place of fashionable bohemians, the Café

Royal, went into decline. Few of the Young Turks had much money, but their presence encouraged the bigger spenders to stop by frequently.

Dylan's reluctance to splash out at the Gargoyle himself – even with other people's money – was illustrated amusingly one evening when Ivan Moffat confided to him over a drink at 'The French' that he had £100 in his pocket, a considerable amount of money at the time. Dylan bubbled with delight at this news and they agreed to go and spend some of it at the Gargoyle. As they travelled up to the club in the tiny lift, Ivan asked Dylan what his favourite drink would be, in the best of all possible worlds. 'Champagne,' replied Dylan unhesitatingly. When they got to the bar, the *maître d'*, Charles, who was standing in as barman that evening, was astonished when the normally impecunious Dylan resonantly ordered two champagne cocktails. 'That will be three pounds ten each, Mr Thomas,' Charles declared solemnly, to which Dylan responded in a voice that had suddenly fallen by an octave: 'Two milds-and-bitters, Charles, if you please.'[9]

In between the drinking and socializing, Dylan had grand plans for breaking away from documentary film-making into the field of full-length feature films, aided and abetted by Julian Maclaren-Ross and Donald Taylor. The film on the Home Guard for which Dylan and Julian Maclaren-Ross were writing the script was suddenly cancelled by the powers-that-be, despite the fact that the two writers had put so much work into it. They had devised a charming comic thriller, set in an unnamed village deep in rural England, complete with local eccentrics, a group of fifth columnists and a German parachutist who was a master of disguise, having worked as a music-hall artiste in civilian life. Dylan wrote out most of the script in pencil in longhand, as Maclaren-Ross dictated their mutually-agreed text.

Donald Taylor himself was convinced that they would soon all be working on feature films anyway. Strand Films was to be wound down by the spring of 1944, and Taylor was to set up another, more broadly-based, company called Gryphon Films. Philip Lindsay had in fact already been working for some time on a feature film project for Donald Taylor, based on the true-life murder committed by the US-born Dr Hawley Harvey Crippen, who killed his second wife Belle, an unsuccessful opera singer, and then dissected her body. Dr Crippen burned Belle's bones in a fire and stored what remained in his cellar. His capture, trial and execution gripped the nation. This was just the sort of gruesome story that Dylan would dearly have liked to get his teeth into himself, and for a while he would greet Philip Lindsay sardonically: 'How's Crippen, crappin'?'[10]

In fact, Dylan and Julian Maclaren-Ross kept a feature idea of their own in a drawer, which they worked on in idle moments, under the alternative titles *The Whispering Gallery* or *The Distorting Mirror*. The story-line grew out of an original concept by Dylan that involved a party of visitors being shown round an historic house by a guide. When they get to the house's whispering gallery, a mysterious voice suddenly says: 'I'll have this place.' No one in the gallery knows who spoke. In fact, it is the voice of someone who will inherit the property if he or she manages to dispose of everyone who stands before him or her in the line of succession. The sexual ambiguity of the mass-murderer is deliberate; as Dylan saw it, the lead character would have a sex-change operation halfway through the film. While Julian Maclaren-Ross happily played along with this game, he knew that there was no way in 1940s Britain that any such film would ever get past the censors.

Donald Taylor actually encouraged such extra-curricular activities. Moreover, he hoped that a film could one day be made of Dylan's own partly completed novel *Adventures in the Skin Trade*, whose typescript had been passed around the Strand Films office. But even more, Donald Taylor wanted Dylan to write a script based on the case of the nineteenth-century Irish body-snatchers William Burke and William Hare, who turned to murder to keep up their supply of bodies for dissection to the Edinburgh anatomist Robert Knox. Donald Taylor was intrigued by the implications of the case regarding the old philosophical dilemma of whether the ends justify the means. Moreover, it was a wonderfully ghoulish story, which Dylan did indeed turn into the script *The Doctor and the Devils*, after the war. This was published in book form in 1953. It was made into a film more than thirty years later, starring Timothy Dalton (as the anatomist), Jonathan Pryce and Twiggy. The film was directed by Freddie Francis, and Mel Brooks was the executive producer. The script of the movie as made was reworked by the South African-born playwright Ronald Harwood – who, incidentally, as a young man was so dismayed by the sight of

Dylan being particularly drunk and disgusting in a pub that he turned down the offer of being introduced.[11]

Donald Taylor also encouraged Dylan to act out some of his own different personae while out in public. Perhaps that is one reason why Caitlin considered Taylor to be such an unhealthy influence. He recognized that Dylan was basically a chameleon, who could adapt himself to any company and play any role. According to a short memoir Donald Taylor left of Dylan,[12] when the two of them knew they would be going out drinking together later in the day, they would decide in the morning what roles they would play. One of Dylan's favourite parts was that of the Welsh country gentleman: a sort of tweedy Evelyn Waugh caricature from the Brecon Beacons: he even acquired a knobbly walking stick as a prop for this gent. At other times he would pretend to be a plummy-voiced BBC reader. But Taylor maintained that the most effective role Dylan ever played was that of a drunken Welsh poet, who tended to dress in a dirty raincoat and a polo sweater, and who could talk endlessly with a fag hanging out of the corner of his mouth. Dylan could assume that personality for several days on end, before tiring of it like the rest.

Constantine FitzGibbon also witnessed Dylan as the actor performing on the natural stage offered by a pub. One day, Dylan had to go to Fleet Street, to call in at a newspaper office, and he arranged to meet Constantine in The Cheshire Cheese, just a few steps away from Dr Johnson's London house. Constantine, dressed in his American army uniform, arrived first, and was immediately cornered by a local pub bore, who started to recount stories about Dr Johnson, in the hope of being bought a drink. Dylan then arrived, and immediately sized up the situation. Without any warning to Constantine, he adopted the identity of an eminent (non-existent) Welsh professor of English literature, whose speciality just happened to be Dr Johnson. He proceeded to amaze the Cheshire Cheese bore with a series of far-fetched alleged Johnsonian anecdotes, which, of course, the man had never heard. The victim of this prank was so impressed that within no time at all it was he who was paying for rounds of drinks.[13]

At the very beginning of 1944, London started receiving new German aerial bombardments, after a lull of several months. Donald Taylor wisely suggested that it would be a good idea if Dylan moved out of Chelsea, with Caitlin and Aeronwy (who had been yo-yoing back and forth from Wales), and went to live within a reasonable commuting distance of London. Accordingly, the Thomases took a little house, 'Far End', at Bosham in Sussex. However, Dylan kept on the Manresa Road studio for a while, and went up to London once or twice a week, notably on a Friday, which was pay-day.

Dylan disliked Bosham, despite the good view and their acquisition of a pet dog, of which he soon got bored. It always seemed to be raining, planes buzzed low overhead and the whole area was crawling with British and North American troops. None the less, while at Bosham, Dylan was able to work on a film called *Building the Future*, which was about the planned post-war resurrection of the much-bombed city of Coventry. This required several visits to Coventry, as well as script conferences in London.

However, the most substantial film project Dylan was involved with in 1944 was a fifty-minute documentary called *Our Country*, which, unlike several of the other projects, was both made and released, receiving widespread favourable comment in the press. Directed by John Eldridge, with music by William Alwyn, *Our Country* took a leisurely, lyrical look at wartime Britain through the eyes of a merchant seaman home on leave. To a most un-seamanly but often moving poetic commentary by Dylan, this focal figure travels from Liverpool docks to the airfields of Kent, a South Wales mining village and even the bizarre lumber camps in Scotland where black West Indians worked.

After about three months in Sussex, the Thomases went to stay for several weeks with Donald Taylor at his cottage at Hedgerley Dean, not far from Beaconsfield, in what these days tends to be called the 'gin-and-Jag' belt. This was far more to Dylan's liking, despite the fact that the dry, thin, affluent people in the area 'grieved over their petrol-less motorcars and played bridge like ferrets'.[14] Despite his affectation of revelling in squalor, Dylan actually relished bourgeois comforts.

By the end of July, though, Dylan, Caitlin and Aeronwy were all ensconced in D. J. and Florence's tiny cottage at Blaen Cwm by Llangain, well away from the dangers of flying bombs, rockets and other real or imagined horrors that Hitler might have up his sleeve. Dylan found that his father was now one raw, bald nerve, and he was keen to get away to a rented house or even a few rooms, preferably at Laugharne. That was easier said than done, given the amount of billeting and requisitioning that had gone on during the war.

None the less, despite the cramped conditions at Blaen Cwm, Dylan was writing poems again. He had completed another war poem, 'Ceremony after a Fire Raid', and was working on two others, 'Vision and Prayer' and 'Poem in October'. Both of these were new departures. Over 200 lines long in its final form, 'Vision and Prayer' is set out as a series of six diamonds and six hour-glasses, moving symmetrically from shorter to longer lines in the former case, and longer to shorter in the latter, like the ebb and flow of the tide. But even more striking than its format and rhythm is the poem's clarity of language: the complex, clever, sometimes impenetrable early Dylanese has been replaced by ringing lines of absolute transparence, while still employing favourite tools such as alliteration and internal rhymes. Similarly, the birthday poem 'Poem in October' comes over as a straightforward personal statement, albeit redolent of profound and troubled feelings. According to Vernon Watkins, Dylan had in fact been working on the poem since 1941, and the birthday it was meant to commemorate was Dylan's twenty-seventh. But the delay until August 1944 meant he could look forward to the much more significant milestone two months hence of his thirtieth birthday, which resulted in the eminently more resonant first line 'It was my thirtieth year to heaven'.

The new simplicity undoubtedly reflected some of the lessons that Dylan had learned writing scripts for film and radio. In such scripts, the directness, economy and immediacy of language are paramount. As someone who always believed his verse should be read out loud, Dylan must have realized how much more effectively he would be able to communicate through his poetry if he adopted some of those same rules. Besides, the end-products had wider public appeal. Dylan had little trouble getting his new poems published in magazines on both sides of the Atlantic, enlisting the assistance of the poet and anthologist Oscar Williams as an unofficial literary agent in America. In Britain, *Horizon* took the most. Dylan was also aware that the new material would enable him at last to put together a new book of poems for publication in Britain. This was contracted with J. M. Dent in the autumn of 1944, although the resultant volume, *Deaths and Entrances*, did not see the light of day until 1946, largely because Dylan found it hard to relinquish the proofs.

At the beginning of September, Dylan, Caitlin and Aeronwy at last had a home of their own to move into once again: a simple bungalow made of wood and asbestos, with 'bumpaper thin walls',[15] just outside the small, attractive Cardiganshire seaside town of New Quay. The bungalow was called 'Majoda', after the three children of its owner (Marjorie, John and David), and Dylan joked that he would change it to 'Catllewdylaer', after his own family. The bungalow was about a mile out of town, with windows looking out over the sea, where Caitlin liked to bathe in the rough waters. 'Majoda' was lit by Calor gas and heated by a paraffin stove; there was only an outside loo. The rent was a pound a week and their nearest neighbour was Vera Killick, who had moved with her own baby into a house her family owned.

Hardly had Dylan moved his little family (minus Llewellyn, who was still with his grandmother at Blashford) into 'Majoda' than he was back in London. This visit was not only to reassure Gryphon Films that it was still worth paying his salary, which they were threatening to cut, but also to arrange an advance from the small publisher Peter Lunn. David Gottlieb at Peter Lunn's had been impressed by some photo captions Dylan had done for one issue of the little magazine *Lilliput*, and he wanted to commission an illustrated book about the streets of London, for which Dylan would write a text. Without consulting his agent – who was understandably put out – Dylan went ahead and signed an agreement whereby he would get £50 as the first part of an advance on the book, which he was contracted to deliver in the first week of January 1945.

Dylan seems to have collected £10 in cash out of that first instalment of the book advance from David Gottlieb's office late on the morning of 2 October, having first spent some hours at Gryphon Films. The date and Dylan's movements are significant because at 2 p.m. on that day he was due to be best man at Vernon Watkins's wedding. Vernon was to marry his longstanding girl-friend, Gwen, at St Bartholomew the Great in the City, after lunch in a small private room at the Charing Cross Hotel. Vernon and Gwen had only managed to get forty-eight hours of overlapping leave from their respective war duties and had therefore planned the wedding to be a quick and intimate affair.

Vernon started getting nervous when Dylan wasn't at the hotel for lunch, but he asked for a plate of food and some beer to be set aside for his friend after a secretary from Gryphon Films rang to say that Dylan was on his way in a taxi. By the end of the meal, however, he still had not turned up. Nor was he at the church. Only the Lady Chapel at St Bartholomew's still had a roof as a result of bombing, and the forlorn couple hung around there until the vicar said he really couldn't wait any longer for the best man to arrive. Fortuitously, Vernon had run into another male friend on the way to the church and had invited him along on the spur of the moment. So that fellow found himself being dragooned into standing in. Vernon still looked hopefully around for Dylan outside the church, and back at the hotel, and it was only when Gwen and he were on a train leaving St Pancras Station that he accepted that his best man and best friend had stood him up. 'That's the end of Dylan as far as I'm concerned,' Vernon told Gwen bitterly. 'The only possible excuse is that he's paralysed from the neck down, or dead.'[16]

It was four weeks before Vernon received an apology of sorts. The letter, dated 28 October, enclosed a dirty, creased and semi-incoherent pencil-written missive, full of crossings-out, which Dylan claimed to have composed two days after Vernon and Gwen's wedding, but which he said he had just found in his overcoat pocket, having forgotten to post it. The missive, entitled 'On Not Turning up to Be Best Man at the Wedding of One's Best Friend', recounted a convoluted cock-and-bull story about having been delayed on a train from Coventry, having left the details of the wedding back at New Quay, and having gone to the wrong church. It was clearly a pack of lies. Gwen Watkins was convinced Dylan had only just written the supposedly earlier letter and then soiled it to make it look as though he had been carrying it about unawares for nearly a month. Vernon, forever the gullible, loving friend, chose to believe Dylan's story. Gwen, who did not know Dylan and therefore viewed the incident more objectively, was unforgiving.

If one accepts that Dylan's explanation for not being at Vernon's wedding was fictitious, then one has to consider the alternatives. The least damning, perhaps, is that he went into a pub with the money he had got from David Gottlieb, with the intention of having a celebratory drink en route to the Charing Cross Hotel, and ended up drinking round Soho for hours instead, oblivious to the time. We know that he had no particular objections to the role of being best man at a wedding, as he had performed that service earlier in the war for William Killick, a young army captain who had married Dylan's childhood friend Vera (née Philipps). It is true that Dylan did have a fear of meeting strangers in situations in which he was not in control, yet that seems an insufficient excuse for funking this occasion, particularly as he knew that hardly anyone else had been invited. The last and most unpalatable plausible explanation is that he deliberately stayed away, knowing how much it would wound his friend. For all his 'dog' antics in pubs, Dylan had little of the faithfulness typical of that animal. In contrast, he could be as selfish, independent, cruel and fickle as any cat.

Back in New Quay, Dylan was having difficulties concentrating on his writing because of baby Aeronwy's wailing, so he hired a room nearby to work in. Various Gryphon Films projects were still up in the air, including a film based on the life of Charles Dickens, which Dylan was in theory to co-write with Philip Lindsay, the Burke and Hare story *The Doctor and the Devils*, and the one which was most preoccupying him at 'Majoda': *Twenty Years A-growing*. The last-mentioned was based on a book by Maurice O'Sullivan about the Blasket Islands, off the south-west tip of Ireland. Dylan was having such trouble with it that he wrote tongue-in-cheek to Donald Taylor suggesting it be retitled *Forty Years A-growing*.

Shortly before Christmas, Dylan and Caitlin dropped Aeronwy off to stay for a week or so with her grandmother and Llewellyn at Blashford, while they went to London to satisfy their hunger for plays, films and spicy meals. Just before he went back to Wales, Dylan spoke to David Gottlieb on the phone and there was quite an acrimonious exchange when it became clear that Dylan had not actually written anything at all of the commissioned book on London streets, despite the fact that the deadline was little more than a fortnight away. This deadline was put back for another month, but in fact Peter Lunn's never received anything more than Dylan's original three-page synopsis for the book. This outline indicated that Dylan was intending to concentrate not on the great thoroughfares of the capital, but rather on the smaller world of back streets, tree-lined suburban roads, and alleyways down by the docks. As Paul Ferris astutely pointed out, Dylan's synopsis made it all sound more like Swansea than London.[17] If it had been a book on Swansea, perhaps he would have written it. But Dylan never was to learn not to take on projects in which he had no interest – and which therefore there was no possibility of completing – because acceptance was an easy way of inveigling money from publishers.

Donald Taylor was also getting a little concerned about Dylan's slow progress on various projects, so he sent a motherly Russian Jewish typist down from Gryphon Films to help him in March 1945. The director James Eldridge and a production assistant went along too. One evening, this group was sitting drinking in Dylan's favourite New Quay pub, The Black Lion, with Vera Killick and her soldier husband, who had recently returned from a hair-raising and heroic commando operation in Greece. Captain Killick had been given the unflattering nickname of 'Drunken Waistcoat' by Dylan and Caitlin, because he always looked so natty and had a strong taste for drink. For some reason the Captain had got it into his head that during his absence Vera had become involved in a ménage à trois with the Thomases. There is no reason to believe there was any foundation to this fear, for although Vera was very pretty and vivacious, Dylan looked on her as a friend. But there is no doubt that Vera Killick was a great fan of Dylan's, and the riotous intimacy between them in clowning sessions provoked her husband's jealousy. The already tense atmosphere within the group at The Black Lion on the evening in question was made worse when the Russian Jewess, who was a communist, made various political remarks which angered the Captain. Already fairly well-oiled, he countered with some anti-semitic comments. At this, the woman leaped at him, clawing at his face, and he hit back. Dylan and the other men then threw him out of the pub.

Later, back at 'Majoda', Dylan and Caitlin were drinking bottles of beer in front of the fire with a group of friends, including Mary Keene, the wife of the film director Ralph 'Bunny' Keene, who was staying with her baby at the Thomases', and a neighbour, the former diplomat and recluse Alastair Graham. Suddenly Captain Killick loomed out of the dark outside, with a sten-gun in his hands. He started firing at the bungalow, whose flimsy walls offered no protection. And although he said later that he was only trying to give the bunch of 'egoists' inside a fright, the bullets were far too close for comfort. Caitlin and Mary Keene raced into another room to make sure their babies were all right, and were reassured to find them both asleep. Captain Killick then burst into the house, looking wild in dark glasses and with the scratchmarks from the Russian Jewess still standing out on his cheek. He fired off more shots into the ceiling, before agreeing to hand over his weapon. Then he pulled out a hand-grenade, allegedly to test the reactions of the people in the room. Most of them were petrified, but Dylan reportedly stayed calm. The Captain threatened to blow everyone up unless they gave him his gun back, which they did, and eventually he went away.

Just as the party at 'Majoda' were resettling their nerves, the police arrived, having been called by a neighbour who had heard the shots. Captain Killick was charged with attempted murder. Dylan and his friends were required to give evidence at a number of hearings, which they did only half-heartedly, as they wanted to try to forget the whole affair. When the case came up before Lampeter Crown Court in June it got wide coverage in the press. The defence's case was that Captain Killick had had no intention of harming anyone, and had been intolerably provoked. In view of the defendant's distinguished war record and the strain his experiences in Greece had put him under, the judge directed the jury to find that there was no case to answer.

Even so, it had been a narrow escape, and embellished accounts of this brush with death became one of Dylan's favourite pub routines. His coolness at the time, though, suggests not just considerable presence of mind but also a lack of great concern about his own survival. Recently he had informed Caitlin, as he had often told his adolescent friends in Swansea years before, that he would not live to see forty. Like a cat with nine lives, Dylan had been given a reprieve this time, but those lives were gradually being used up.

9

CHELSEA, OXFORD, ITALY

(1945–1948)

Well before the European war formally ended on 8 May 1945, Dylan was planning to leave Britain if he could. America beckoned like some mythical land of milk and honey. There, he believed, all his financial worries would evaporate and he would know great public acclaim. As early as February 1945 he had asked his American publisher James Laughlin if he could fix him up with some job lecturing or giving poetry readings, which would allow him to spend at least a few months in the United States. In the meantime, Laughlin decided to bring out another representative volume of Dylan's work, to be called simply *Selected Writings*. This was actually published in November the following year. Then the Chicago-based magazine *Poetry*, with which Oscar Williams had placed several of Dylan's poems, awarded Dylan the Levinson Poetry Prize in the second half of 1945, which brought a cheque for $100 and, more important, further recognition. In Dylan's mind, America was clearly the place to be.

For Dylan to be given a visa that would allow him to go to America, however, he had to persuade the US Embassy in London that he would not be a liability for the US taxpayer. As he had no savings, only debts, this meant that he had to give written proof that some institution or individual over there would be financially responsible for him and his family. Dylan intended taking Caitlin and the two children with him, for as he explained in a long letter to Oscar Williams at the end of July, he did not want to return to Britain for a long time.[1] The fact that the Labour Party had just won an unexpectedly huge majority in the general election made the prospect of remaining in the country even more unappealing. Despite Dylan's supposed former allegiance to socialist principles, he shared the widespread middle-class anxiety that a Labour government would inevitably bring in higher taxes.

Oscar Williams had suggested that either *Time* magazine or the English faculty at Harvard University might have work to offer Dylan, so Dylan asked Augustus John to intercede with his friend the poet Theodore Spencer, who was a member of Harvard's teaching staff, to see if something could be arranged. But nothing came of it. As late as December 1945, Dylan was still trying to procure an American job, or even just a patron who would get him the precious piece of paper he needed for his visa, but none was forthcoming.

Meanwhile, Dylan and Caitlin had temporarily retrieved Llewellyn from his grandmother's and had moved away from New Quay, using Dylan's parents at Llangain as a base once again. Dylan made out to friends that the narrowness of the environment at Blaen Cwm drove him crazy, but in fact, as so often in the past, the fussy stability of domestic life in Wales was an aid to his creative process. It was at Blaen Cwm that he wrote the majestic poem 'Fern Hill', which evokes rhapsodically his happy and easy childhood holidays at Aunt Ann Jones' farm. Dylan managed to squeeze 'Fern Hill' into *Deaths and Entrances* thanks to being so late in returning the corrected proofs of that book to J. M. Dent. Moreover, Blaen Cwm and the proximity of D. J. and Florence were helpful to his work as a reminiscer on radio. Once Gryphon Films folded at the beginning of October, and his weekly salary from them stopped, the BBC became Dylan's main source of income for a while.

Dylan's real breakthrough in radio came with the broadcast on 31 August 1945 of his piece 'Quite Early One Morning', a highly embellished description of life in New Quay. This opens with the locals still asleep as the town is observed, and ends with a series of voices of local characters (including Mrs Ogmore-Pritchard, who is hoping for a snooze) in a manner that presages *Under Milk Wood*. Dylan had actually recorded 'Quite Early One Morning' at BBC

Wales in Carmarthen nine months previously. The producer, Aneirin Talfan Davies, had immediately tried to get his colleagues in London interested in broadcasting the piece nationwide, but initially there was resistance. The Director of Talks in London, G. R. (George) Barnes, objected to Dylan's 'breathless poetic voice' and made the singularly English observation that the wit would have been more effective if it had been put over more drily. But Aneirin Talfan Davies was right in his estimation that both the subject matter and the reader of 'Quite Early One Morning' would have far more than just regional appeal. After the broadcast, both received lavish praise in a review in *The Listener*.

Encouraged by the response, Dylan worked hard through September on a commission from Lorraine Jamieson at the BBC's Cardiff office to do a nostalgic piece entitled 'Memories of Christmas' for the popular Children's Hour programme. The finished product was deliberately in the style of a somewhat toned-down version of his earlier 'Reminiscences of Childhood', an update of which had been broadcast in March. Normally the Children's Hour programme was broadcast live, but Dylan had already acquired enough of a reputation as a 'tricky' collaborator at Broadcasting House in London for the programme's director, 'Uncle Mac' (Derek McCulloch), to insist that in this case the piece should be recorded in advance.[2] This was done in London on 6 December, and it went out ten days later.

While still not abandoning hope that he would be able to get away to America in 1946, Dylan spent much of his spare time in the latter half of 1945 trying to find suitable temporary accommodation for himself and his family in London. He enlisted the help of friends like Donald Taylor, David Tennant and Tommy Earp in the search. Dylan was going up to London regularly on his own, of course, and rather enjoyed his refound bachelor existence in the capital as a house-guest of friends such as the FitzGibbons, the writer and artist Mervyn Peake, and a young poet and engineer called Bill McAlpine and his wife Helen. However, Dylan knew that Caitlin deeply resented being left in Wales with the children and his parents. Loving letters from London were not enough. For the sake of their marriage, they all needed to be together on a more permanent basis.

At first, Theodora FitzGibbon put Dylan and Caitlin and Aeronwy up with her at a small flat in Chelsea that the FitzGibbons were then renting; Constantine himself was away in America. But soon the noise and the confusion that tended to accompany the Thomases wore Theo down and she moved out of her own home to stay with her mother. Then the lady who owned the house, and who lived upstairs, declared that unless the Thomases with their rowing and late-night carousing were told to go, she would cancel the FitzGibbons' lease.[3]

In November, with considerable reluctance, Caitlin's sister Nicolette and her husband Anthony Devas let the Thomases stay in the basement flat in their house in Markham Square, Chelsea. During the war, Anthony Devas had dreaded the repeated nocturnal arrivals of the in-laws he vividly described as 'the Visigoths from Wales'. Both he and Nicolette realized that the less they saw of their basement lodgers now, the better for all concerned. Nicolette and Caitlin had fought like cats when they were younger, rolling around on the floor and pulling each other's hair, and their relationship was still spiced with a high degree of mutual disapproval. Yet Nicolette loyally provided the Thomases with help when she could. When Anthony Devas was not feeling too angry about the latest example of his in-laws' outrageous behaviour, he openly acknowledged Caitlin's beauty and Dylan's talent. Fortunately, despite having common links like Augustus John, the Devases and the Thomases tended to move in separate circles in Chelsea.

Christmas 1945 was spent in Oxford, courtesy of Alan and Margaret Taylor, with whom Dylan had re-established contact. A. J. P. Taylor had become a Fellow of Magdalen College and he and his wife were now living in a College house, Holywell Ford, just outside the College walls. Alan Taylor was far from pleased to see Dylan re-enter his life, but was prepared to put up with him for a while in order to keep his beloved Margaret happy. She was more convinced than ever that Dylan was a genius and she thought it an honour to be able to offer him help. Dylan in turn was prepared to sing for his supper, in that he spent a considerable amount of time and energy writing detailed, kindly criticisms of her own undistinguished verse. What he said behind her back, however, was quite a different matter.

Back in London, Margaret Taylor's faith in Dylan's talent was vindicated with the publication of *Deaths and Entrances* on 7 February 1946. J. M. Dent, who had patiently stood by their difficult and poor-selling author for nearly ten years, sensed that maybe his moment had now come. They therefore printed 3,000 copies of this slim little book of poems, which was small enough to slip into a jacket pocket or a handbag. Their hunch was right. The first edition sold briskly, so the following month they ordered a reprint of a further 3,000.

The critics (with a few exceptions like Geoffrey Grigson) were rapturous. Walter Allen, writing in *Time and Tide*, said the book represented a new maturity in Dylan Thomas, adding that half a dozen of the poems in the volume were 'entrancing'. G. W. Stonier, in the *New Statesman*, went further; he thought that three of them ('A Winter's Tale', 'Poem in October' and 'The Ballad of the Long-legged Bait') were among the most outstanding poems of the age. Vita Sackville-West, in the *Observer*, hailed Dylan's 'rare combination of vigour and virtuosity'. And John Betjeman, in the *Daily Herald*, declared that Dylan was not only the best living Welsh poet, but a *great* poet, *tout court*.

Like a pop star who has just issued his first hit record, Dylan became famous virtually overnight. His reputation was no longer restricted to his countrymen in West Wales, his drinking companions in Chelsea and Soho—Fitzrovia and a few BBC producers. Suddenly, he was acknowledged as a poetic force to be reckoned with, as well as a character whom complete strangers gossiped about and wanted to meet. But in a pattern that was to become all too fatally familiar over the remaining seven years of his life, Dylan was unable to handle the acclaim. In principle he loved it; it was something he had always wanted. Yet he did not have the necessary inner strength to cope. He smilingly accepted the drinks people bought him in pubs and he performed on cue when they urged him to entertain them with smutty stories and rhymes, until his head sank down in a drunken stupour on to the table, or into the lap of someone sitting nearby. Within weeks of *Deaths and Entrances* coming out, he had collapsed.

Dylan was taken to St Stephen's Hospital in the Fulham Road, where he regaled the doctors with accounts of his boozy bohemian existence. Contrary to rumours circulating at the time, however, he did not have cirrhosis of the liver, although heavy drinking had undoubtedly contributed to his run-down state. The doctors' verdict was that, despite traces of alcoholic gastritis, Dylan was basically suffering from nervous exhaustion. He apparently had an unsatisfactory interview with a psychiatrist, who he felt was poking fun at him, and he failed to keep a further appointment. But the doctors' prognosis was clear: he must moderate his lifestyle if he wanted to enjoy a healthy middle age.

This crisis enabled Margaret Taylor to switch into noble guardian angel mode, to her immense satisfaction. She was never happier than when organizing other people's lives, and brilliant, sickly Dylan with his chaotic little family seemed an eminently worthy cause. When she suggested to her husband that the Thomases should come to live in the funny little summerhouse on the Holywell Ford property, down by the River Cherwell, he decided to humour her. After all, it would make a good story at High Table in College to be able to say that he had a poet living at the bottom of his garden. Had Alan Taylor realized that the Thomases would treat the summerhouse as their main base for the next year, however, he might well have raised some objections.

The summerhouse had electricity and gas, but no water, which Caitlin had to fetch from the main house. Aeronwy slept in the main house with the Taylors' own two daughters, and attended a day nursery. For the time being, it seemed impractical to bring Llewellyn over from Blashford. The Thomases had all their meals at Holywell Ford, cooked by Margaret Taylor (very indifferently, according to Caitlin), while Alan Taylor sat severely at the head of the table, rationing Dylan to half a pint of beer with each meal. Taylor himself liked to have good red wine with his cheeses, but like Richard Hughes back in Laugharne, he kept it all for himself or important guests. In the evenings, Margaret Taylor would often go out pubbing with Dylan and Caitlin, which her husband couldn't abide. But bright and early the next morning, she would march briskly into the summerhouse, full of plans for what they could do with their day, even if Caitlin and Dylan were still snuggled up in bed.

Margaret Taylor arranged for Dylan to meet endless people in Oxford who she felt might prove useful to him. However tempted the Thomases were at times to tell her to go and jump in the river, they stayed mute, as she was slipping them regular sums of money. Alan Taylor flatly refused to 'loan' any money to Dylan himself, but he could not prevent Margaret from sharing money of her own that she had inherited. Besides, he consoled himself for a while with the delusion that Margaret's superficially literary obsession with the married Dylan – whom Caitlin would clearly never let her steal – would help her get over what Alan Taylor considered to be a far more dangerous earlier unrequited passion for one of his more talented students at Magdalen, Robert Kee, who subsequently became a successful author and broadcaster himself.

Dylan travelled up to London frequently during the spring and summer of 1946, for engagements at the BBC. Ralph Maud, in his meticulous study of Dylan's broadcasts, records nineteen separate engagements for the BBC between April and July that year. These were for a variety of different BBC outlets, including the Africa section of the Overseas Service, the Light Programme and Home Service domestic stations (the precursors of Radio 2 and Radio 4). Sometimes travel to other cities like Birmingham and Cardiff was necessary. Dylan's broadcasts ranged from straight readings of other people's verse or speaking parts in a documentary, for a standard fee of 7 guineas, to full scripted broadcasts, such as a study of the First World War poet Wilfred Owen, for which he received 20 guineas.[4] Whenever possible, Dylan would get at least part of his fee and expenses in cash (or at any rate in the form of a cheque that he could cash), and then proceed to spend much of it drinking with colleagues and friends. If he missed the train back to Oxford from Paddington, as sometimes happened, he would either find a bed for the night in London, or else hire a car to drive him all the way home to Oxford. On those occasions when he did not have enough money left to pay for this extravagance, he would expect Margaret Taylor to give the driver the difference.

A. J. P. Taylor got a short respite from the Thomases when they went off to Ireland for a holiday with Bill and Helen McAlpine in August 1946. In theory, Dylan was combining the holiday with work, as he had been commissioned by *Picture Post* to do a feature article on the annual Puck Fair in Kerry, to which the little party travelled after four hectic days in Dublin. The lack of seriousness with which Dylan undertook this project is reflected by the vow that he and Bill McAlpine made when they got to Kerry, namely that they would stand drinking Guinness at a bar day and night for the entire four days of the fair, during which the pubs never closed. Meanwhile Caitlin and Helen McAlpine went dancing and flirting with the handsome local lads, and would return every few hours to see how their husbands were getting on. As Caitlin remembers it, Dylan and Bill McAlpine lasted two days and two nights, by which time they were both speechless and collapsing on to the floor. They had to be thrown into the back of a lorry and driven home to their lodgings, where they stayed in bed for a week, feeling ghastly. Caitlin and Helen McAlpine left them to it, as they were determined that they at least would have a proper holiday. Needless to say, the piece for *Picture Post* was never written.[5]

Dylan and Caitlin stopped off at Blaen Cwm for ten days or so on the way back from Ireland, and from there Dylan was able to finalize by post arrangements to collaborate on a series of radio broadcasts to be called 'The Poet and His Critic', which was to feature on the Third Programme, a new, highbrow BBC radio channel due to start at the end of September. This was to become one of Dylan's major outlets, parallel to a series of broadcasts that he did for the Eastern Service of the Overseas Services.

Through new colleagues at the BBC, Dylan became familiar with the pubs around Broadcasting House in Langham Place, where a lot of BBC staff and outside contributors spent their time, both inside and outside working hours. These favoured watering-holes included The Stag and The Dover Castle and, pre-eminently, The George, which the conductor Sir Thomas Beecham nick-named 'The Gluepot', as his musicians were so frequently stuck in there. The nickname stuck too.

One of Dylan's favourite new drinking companions at The George was the burly South African radio producer Roy Camp-bell, who was a most distinguished poet in his own right. Campbell was a controversial figure, not just because of his belligerent he-man personality and tendency to take a swing at people he didn't like. During the Spanish Civil War, for example, he had outraged the left-wing poetic establishment by siding with General Franco, and he had little time for what he considered to be the trendy political posturings of the Spenders of this world. Roy Campbell was, however, a dedicated professional in his work at the BBC. He estimated Dylan to be the finest all-round reader of poetry he ever worked with.

On one famous occasion when he turned up drunk for a live broadcast on the Third Programme, Dylan was fortunate that it was Roy Campbell who was producing. Only twenty seconds or so before the programme was due to go on air, Campbell found Dylan fast asleep and snoring in front of the microphone. He gave him a poke and Dylan lurched into action, declaiming the title of the first poem he was due to read as 'Ode on St Sheshilia's Day'. He then got a grip on himself and was doing fine until he spotted the term 'Religio Laïci' coming up. He waved his arms around frantically in the forlorn hope that someone would be able to communicate to him how to pronounce it. He had three desperate shots at saying it, and then decided to carry on as if nothing unusual had happened. Roy Campbell was subsequently summoned by the new Controller of the Third Programme, who was none other than the G. R. Barnes who had had such a low opinion of Dylan's Welsh reading skills, and who now hauled Campbell over the coals.[6]

Dylan promised that in future he would always turn up sober for broadcasts, and he seems to have abided by his pledge. Numerous producers who worked with him over the next few years commented on the fact that contrary to his wildboy notoriety, Dylan would be both punctual and punctilious. He even acquired a certain reputation for thinking quickly, which always makes a broadcaster popular with the studio staff. On one occasion, for example, when there was deep consternation in a studio about what a key word that was going to be read actually meant, Dylan said reassuringly: 'Never mind, I'll say it with *conviction*.'[7]

John Arlott was one radio producer who particularly enjoyed working with Dylan. Arlott produced Dylan frequently on the Eastern Service, and recalled in his memoirs that to hear Dylan peal out William Blake's 'The Tyger' was a profound poetic experience.[8] Arlott noted, however, that whereas Dylan was a wonderful performer when he was working with poetry that he respected, he could spit out verses he considered inferior with withering scorn. The two men got on particularly well because of their shared interest in cricket. One of Arlott's first live outside broadcasts (for the Eastern Service) on a cricket match was at Oxford, where he sat watching the match with Dylan, Louis MacNeice and Cecil Day-Lewis, and stayed overnight at the Taylors' summerhouse. Arlott went on to become one of Britain's top cricket commentators, and Dylan was one of his most ardent fans.

They would also go out drinking together, and Arlott noted oddly in his memoirs that no matter how drunk Dylan became, his funny stories were never crude. He even had a distaste – or so Arlott claimed – for dirty jokes. Considering how other people would sometimes come away reeling from a session with Dylan, in which he had paraded his obsession with contraceptives ('French letters'), bestiality and the sexual habits of deformed and handi-capped people, one can only draw the conclusion that Dylan the chameleon had decided that Arlott was a man he respected too much to want to shock.

James Laughlin of New Directions visited London in November 1946, at the very time his firm was publishing the new collection of Dylan's work, *Selected Writings*, in New York. Dylan and he met at least once on this visit, but in their discussions they made little progress over Dylan's plans to go to America, before Laughlin had to travel on to Paris. Dylan therefore wrote Laughlin a letter soon afterwards setting out very clearly and rather dictatorially what he hoped for and expected from the United States. He pledged that he would write a lot in America, and that everything he wrote there would go to New Directions. But in return he wanted James Laughlin to start searching immediately, first for an apartment in New York City for Dylan and his family, and then for a house in the country, within easy reach of the metropolis. As if that were not enough, he expected all their fares over to the United States to be paid.[9]

In the same letter, Dylan mentioned that he believed Edith Sitwell would help him find some lecturing and journalistic work in the United States through her many contacts there. Dylan had reforged links with her after a gap of almost ten years, following a highly favourable review by her of his book *Deaths and Entrances* in the April issue of the magazine *Our Time*. As Edith Sitwell told the Oxford don Maurice Bowra, she believed that Dylan was one of the greatest poets Britain had had for the last hundred years. She was also extremely fond of Dylan as a person, feeling a kind of maternal pride in his progress and finding him to be sweet and lovable. She was moved by his explanation that one of the main reasons he wanted to go to America was because of his son Llewellyn's delicate health. But she felt it would be a terrible mistake if Dylan were to go to America with his family to live; it would be far better, she told Bowra, if he just took Caitlin along on a short lecture tour.[10]

As Caitlin witnessed for herself when Dylan took her to meet Edith Sitwell, he was on his best behaviour in the presence of this important patron. Miss Sitwell invited him several times to the celebrity-filled luncheons and teas she gave at the Sesame Club in

Grosvenor Street. Caitlin thought Edith Sitwell quite extraordinary and rather terrifying: a grand English eccentric, in her turbans and bangles and long oriental gowns.

Yet the nice, sweet Dylan whom Edith Sitwell liked so much was the same man who could abruptly brush aside young aspirant poets, as Dannie Abse discovered around this time. Abse was a South Walian Jewish medical student whose real wish was to become a successful poet (an ambition he realized subsequently). He was sitting in a pub in Swiss Cottage one day when Dylan walked in with a friend. Although Abse had never met Dylan, he recognized him instantly, and he felt a thrill of nervous excitement when the poet came and sat at his table while the other man went to the bar to buy their drinks. Dannie Abse plucked up the courage to talk to Dylan, mentioning that he believed that Dylan in his youth had regularly seen a cousin of his called Solomon in Swansea. Dylan denied even recognizing the name of the cousin, and Abse quickly left the pub in some confusion. Years later, he learned from a mutual friend that Dylan had indeed been quite close to the young man in question.[11] Dylan's denial was presumably a ruse to get rid of someone he considered an unwelcome intruder.

Much more hurtful was an incident witnessed by the young Welsh actor Richard Burton, who worked with Dylan at the BBC at this period. One day, Burton was one of a group of hangers-on in a pub, listening to Dylan recounting a long shaggy-dog story about a visit to a barber. One of the group was called away to the telephone and this man interrupted Dylan when he came back to inform his companions that his wife had lamentably just had a stillborn child – the third that they had lost. Dylan looked at him coldly and said, 'Well, lamentably, you're a stillborn little couple, aren't you?' before launching back into his barber-shop anecdote.[12]

With the callousness of youth, Richard Burton thought this a daring put-down. He was even more impressed by Dylan's performance in the radio studio, however, when the two of them were recording David Jones's allegory *In Parenthesis*, in November 1946. Dylan played the part of Captain Dai Evans. The director asked him to imagine himself dying in No Man's Land, where suddenly he hears the Royal Welch sing, and then to scream the words 'Mam! Mam!' As Burton recalled for Paul Ferris: 'Dylan, short, bandy, prime, obese and famous among the bars, screamed as I have never heard, but sometimes imagined, a scream, and we were all appalled, our pencils silent above the crossword puzzles, and invisible centuries-gone atavistic hair rose on our backs.'[13]

Over Christmas, Margaret Taylor nagged the novelist Graham Greene on Dylan's behalf, as Greene was then working for the publishers Eyre and Spottiswoode, and Dylan hoped Greene might be able to help him get the filmscript for *The Doctor and the Devils* published. He needed the money, he said, to pay doctor's bills for Caitlin and Llewellyn. Given Greene's own deep interest in films, Dylan also hoped that he could be of use in rustling up some film work for him. He was embarrassed, though, about the persistence of Margaret Taylor's badgering of this potential benefactor, who found her deeply irritating.

Meanwhile it was beginning to dawn on Alan Taylor that his wife's interest in Dylan might not be so platonic after all. It seemed almost inconceivable to Taylor that a woman as attractive as Margaret could fall for a fat, grubby slob like Dylan, but clearly this was happening. Caitlin sensed it too, which made her hate Margaret Taylor and offered another pretext for blazing rows with her errant husband. Caitlin's suspicions were confirmed when she found a letter from Margaret Taylor in one of Dylan's pockets, in which Margaret said that 'to sleep with you would be like sleeping with a god'. Caitlin inferred from this, with a certain satisfaction, that Margaret had not actually managed to get Dylan into bed. But when she gave Caitlin a lovely purple taffeta petticoat as a present, Caitlin took immense pleasure in cutting it up into tiny pieces which she then sent back to Margaret in an otherwise empty envelope.[14]

Dylan and Caitlin saw the New Year 1947 in with 5,000 other revellers at the Chelsea Arts Ball at the Albert Hall in London. It was a fancy-dress affair, and Dylan went dressed as a Chinaman, while Caitlin was a grand Spanish lady. Dylan then tried to apply his mind to a new potential commission: to write the libretto of a full-length opera by William Walton, who was another of Edith Sitwell's protégés. Dylan boasted that this would be the biggest English opera event of the century. The idea was to set it in the Thames docklands, and early in January Dylan went to the bombed-out communities of Tilbury and Gravesend with the designer Michael Ayrton, to get the feel of the place. But like so many of Dylan's ambitious plans, this came to nothing, as he failed to produce the libretto.

Dylan had now decided that his little family could divide their time between the Taylors' summerhouse and Bill and Helen McAlpine's comfortable home at Richmond in Surrey. But a number of his friends had become worried by his increasingly dissolute lifestyle in London, to which he himself sometimes used to refer as his 'capital punishment'. Accordingly, Edith Sitwell arranged for him to get a travelling scholarship to Italy for a few months, where he would be able to work away from the temptations of London and recover physically from the rigours of what had been one of the worst English winters on record. She chaired the travel grants committee of the Society of Authors, whose other members included John Lehmann. The committee decided to give the whole of the 1947 travel allocation – £150 – to Dylan for Italy. The recipient did not actually have any wanderlust, especially where hot Mediterranean countries were concerned. Indeed, when Lawrence Durrell had tried to persuade him earlier to go out to Greece, he had thought the idea most unappealing. But the possibility of an extended foreign holiday greatly attracted Caitlin, who was tired of the drudgery of her life in Oxford. She savoured not only the prospect of having Dylan to herself for once, but also the opportunity the trip would give the two of them to get to know their son Llewellyn better after the long years of separation.

Caitlin's sister Brigit decided to accompany the Thomases with her young son Tobias, and the extended family group left at the beginning of April by train for the Italian Riviera. They succeeded in losing their luggage on the way, but fortunately retrieved it in Milan. After three exhausting days travelling, they installed themselves in a small, pretty hotel at San Michele di Pagana, a mile outside Rapallo, where they stayed for about a month. The balconies of their bedrooms looked out over the sea, and Dylan marvelled at the meals served in the hotel. A typical dinner was spaghetti in a rich sauce, followed by white meat with artichokes, spinach and potatoes, then bread and his favourite cheese, gorgonzola, all washed down with plenty of the local red wine.[15] Unlike a genuine alcoholic, Dylan took a considerable interest in his food when his stomach wasn't bloated by too many pints of beer.

Dylan and Caitlin went to Rome on a short trip from Rapallo, leaving the children with Brigit. They visited the major tourist sights, like the Sistine Chapel in the Vatican, and were hosted by the British Council in the tapestried rooms of its opulent premises in the Palazzo di Drago. The Director of the British Council in Rome at the time was the poet Ronald Bottrell, who had known Dylan in London. He arranged a sumptuous party for Dylan and Caitlin, where they met a wide selection of people from Rome's literary high society who spoke English.

A few days later in Florence, Dylan and Caitlin ran into Stephen Spender in the street. He was in Italy on a lecture tour. Dylan was unimpressed by Spender's contention that as all poets speak the same language it was important that European intellectuals get organized together. The Thomases had a couple of meals with Spender and his second wife, Natasha, in between visits to the Pitti Palace and the Uffizi gallery. Dylan, who normally preferred to read detective stories, became absorbed in George Eliot's *Romola*, and enjoyed recognizing parts of Florence from that. The main purpose of visiting Florence, however, was to find a house to rent, which they succeeded in doing: the Villa del Beccaro at Scandicci, up in the hills about 5 miles out of town. It was a long, low house, with a beautiful garden full of orange trees and nightingales. It had its own swimming-pool and a sun terrace, from which the great cathedral dome of Florence could be seen. The Thomases took it for two and a half months, at a total rent of about £25.

Dylan's enthusiasm for the Villa del Beccaro quickly waned once he and his entourage had moved in, especially when the weather started to get unbearably hot. The children got on his nerves; Brigit's little boy Tobias screamed like a bull-frog, and Llewellyn moped about complaining that he had no one of his age to play with. Dylan was delighted that his son had turned into a keen reader, though he was a little taken aback when Llewellyn said he hated poetry. Moreover, Dylan couldn't understand why his delicate and currently chubby son showed not the slightest interest in sport.

Dylan tried in vain to persuade English friends like John Davenport to come out to Italy to stay with him. Instead he had to make do with the company of local writers and editors. This was often difficult, as he spoke no Italian and hardly any of them knew any English. However, this did not stop some of them coming up to the villa on unannounced visits, when everyone would sit around the pool feeling rather stupid and uneasy and drinking too much red wine. Unable to communicate verbally with his guests, Dylan would act the clown, standing on his head and on several occasions throwing himself fully clothed into the swimming-pool in the hope of raising a laugh. He came to dread these visits from the locals so much that on one occasion, after he had spotted a group coming up the hill to the villa, he hid in a cupboard so they would think he was out.

To get away from the noise of the children and the distraction of visitors, so that he could write, Dylan arranged to use a small farm cottage not far from the villa. There he wrote one poem, 'In Country Sleep', which several critics have identified as marking a new stage in Dylan's attitude to religion, because of its central theme of Faith. Vernon Watkins was quite convinced that Dylan was becoming a Christian poet and several other friends wondered if he would one day convert to Roman Catholicism. After Dylan's death, the radio producer and critic Aneirin Talfan Davies wrote a whole book assessing his role as a religious poet.[16]

This is not as improbable as it might at first appear from Dylan's attitude to truth and morality. Dylan himself, in his Note to his 1952 *Collected Poems*, said that they were written 'for the love of Man and in praise of God'. Many of his poems are indeed full of the imagery and language of the Bible and the Chapel, reflecting Dylan's West Wales background. Even more important, as the Welsh poet Saunders Lewis pointed out in an obituary piece on Dylan for the BBC Welsh Home Service, Dylan 'sang of the glory of the universe when it was the fashion for every prominent poet in Europe to sing despairingly and with passion and anguish of the end of civilization'.[17] In his reverence for the wonders of the universe, Dylan was as much pantheistic as specifically Christian, and he told several people he did not believe in God, yet there is no doubt that one aspect of his multifaceted personality was 'religious', in the broadest sense of the term.

The production of the one poem 'In Country Sleep' seems to have taxed Dylan's creative capacity in Italy to the limit. Soon Caitlin noticed that he was no longer poring over worksheets in the little farmhouse, but was instead listening to test match cricket commentaries on the radio, having discovered how to pick them up. He was also going down into Florence increasingly frequently, despite the fact that this involved a complicated and tiring little journey, first by horse-trap and then by train. Once he had arrived in the centre of the city he would install himself in a café, looking morose and pining for British beer. All earlier interest in sight-seeing had evaporated.

Dylan started wandering around with bottles of beer in his pockets, as beer was not always easy to get in Italy so soon after the war, and Italians whose homes he visited rarely had any. This habit hardly endeared him to the local literati, who tended to be elegant and rather formal. In her memoirs, Caitlin recalled one particularly embarrassing dinner at the home of the poet Eugenio Montale. Dylan was half-drunk when he arrived at the Montales' house with Caitlin. He proceeded to empty his pockets of his beer bottles, which he then lined up in front of him on the table and drank one after another, as the scandalized hosts and their servants tried to behave as though nothing odd was going on.[18] Of all the Italian writers Dylan met, however, Montale was his favourite, despite Montale's horsey wife, aloof tolerance and 'dry wit, like old Ryvita'. In a letter to Ronald Bottrell Dylan dismissed the other literary luminaries of Florence as living with their mothers, on private incomes, translating Apollinaire.[19]

Things looked up when the Thomases moved away from Florence in the third week of July and went to the island of Elba. This was only made possible because an Italian radio journalist in Florence, who was going to London to work for the Italian Service of the BBC, lent the Thomases sufficient lire. Predictably, Dylan had spent all the money he had brought out with him to Italy and he had been writing round to people desperately asking them to get some money to him (quite illegally, given the strict currency regulations operating at the time).

The hotel the Thomases found at Rio di Marina on Elba was so tiny that Dylan's little party occupied all its bedrooms. The sea-bathing on the island was superb, which pleased Caitlin and the children. Caitlin was also very taken with the handsome, macho and attentive young miners of the district, who would pinch her bottom, Italian-style. As she enjoyed herself in and around the sea, Dylan would sit in a rockpool with water up to his waist, wearing a hat and reading copies of the *New Statesman*,[20] like a caricature of an Englishman abroad. However, he was intrigued by the natural and indigenous brand of communism prevalent in Rio di Marina, the notices in the town's bars saying 'Fighting Prohibited', and the sun-black water-boys diving from cranes. Cognac was threepence a glass.

Brown as berries, the Thomases returned to England in mid-August. They went to stay briefly with the McAlpines, and as their hosts were out when they turned up at the house, Dylan tried to climb in through a window. He fell and broke his arm for the umpteenth time; once again, he was able to wander around happily wearing a sling.

During the Thomases' absence in Italy, Margaret Taylor had acquired for them a little farmhouse, rather grandly called the Manor House, in the village of South Leigh, near Witney in Oxfordshire. It has usually been assumed that she paid for the house herself, though in his autobiography A. J. P. Taylor maintained that the money to buy the Manor House actually came from an inheritance he had had from his mother. He said he agreed to do Margaret this favour on the strict understanding that she would give the Thomases nothing more. He should have known that that was a condition she would be incapable of respecting.[21] What Margaret certainly did pay for, though, was a gypsy caravan, which she parked near the Manor House, so Dylan would have somewhere quiet to work. She rather defeated the object of the caravan, however, by constantly going to pester Dylan in it when she was over on one of her frequent visits from Oxford. The caravan had eventually to be moved much further away from the house, not because of Margaret Taylor but because of Caitlin, who in one of her increasingly frequent rages against her husband tipped it over one day, with Dylan still inside.

The Manor House itself was fairly primitive, with no electricity or gas and only an outside bucket-toilet which had to be emptied regularly. Yet Caitlin rather enjoyed the simple life at South Leigh, which was the only place in England where Dylan found the sort of tranquil routine he needed to concentrate on his work. They were fortunate with some of their friends in the village, especially one couple, Harry and Cordelia Locke. Harry Locke was a music-hall comedian who had an immense fund of funny stories, which he told extremely well. One favourite routine Dylan enjoyed was when Harry would sit in a pub for hours talking in an imaginary foreign language. They would also play shove-ha'penny together in the village or at pubs like The Turf in Oxford.

Not far away from South Leigh lived another couple the Thomases got on well with, and whom they had met through Alan and Margaret Taylor: Ernst and Kay Stahl. Ernst Stahl was a

German lecturer at Christ Church and both he and his wife sometimes attended what Kay Stahl considered to be the rather grim literary salons which Margaret Taylor held at Holywell Ford. The room there was often too cold to be comfortable, and there was never enough to drink. Big jugs of cold hare stood in the kitchen, to which guests had to help themselves with spoons. A. J. P. Taylor would briefly look in on his wife's salons, then disappear into his study where he kept a personal supply of drink.[22]

Dylan still travelled up to London regularly. Between August 1947 and January 1948, he did some twenty broadcasts for the BBC, produced variously by John Arlott, Roy Campbell and Douglas Cleverdon. Cleverdon produced Dylan in the most substantial of these, which was a weekly serialization of Milton's *Paradise Lost*. This ran from 19 October to 14 December 1947. Dylan played the role of Satan, apparently standing in for the actor Paul Scofield at the last minute. Dylan received a devastating review for this in *The Listener* from Martin Armstrong, who complained that he had clearly resolved to outboom Milton. 'In the most literal sense of the expression,' Armstrong wrote, 'there was a Hell of a row. It swamped Milton, it swamped *Paradise Lost*. It occasionally swamped even the sense, for the louder Dylan Thomas shouts the more his articulation deteriorates.'[23]

The public did not necessarily agree, as Dylan's reputation as a radio performer grew steadily. But far more exciting for him, as 1947 drew to its close, was the sudden prospect of new, serious work in feature films for the following year.

10

THE BOAT HOUSE

(1948–1950)

Dylan went into 1948 as a man full of worries. He was haunted by the fact that lurking off-stage, like some monster which could devour him at any moment, was the Inland Revenue. Thanks to his peripatetic existence, his refusal to confront unpleasant realities and his habit of spending money as fast as he could get his hands on it, Dylan had so far managed to avoid having many dealings with the taxmen. But he knew it could not last. Now that he was doing so much freelance work for the BBC and becoming something of a household name, they were on to him.

Margaret Taylor was deeply concerned about the implications. It was not just that she feared she might be expected to stump up hundreds of pounds to bail Dylan out, which she could ill-afford; she was nowhere near as well-off as Dylan liked to make out. More worrying was the danger that tax demands that he could not meet would be the final straw for Dylan, which would stop him writing poetry completely, or maybe even encourage him to consider suicide seriously, rather than just talking about it, as he sometimes did. Accordingly, Margaret went up to London to see David Higham, who had returned from war duties to run his literary agency again, to discuss what could be sorted out.

The first and most important step was for Dylan to get a good accountant, and on David Higham's recommendation, Leslie Andrews was appointed. Dylan's financial year, as a freelance writer and broadcaster, was deemed to run from October, that being the month in 1946 when he had ceased to be an employee of Gryphon Films. Caitlin would not have been the only person who would have been astounded to see the figures that Andrews produced for the Inland Revenue. In the financial year 1947–8, for example, Dylan earned £2,482 in fees from radio, film work, book royalties and lectures,[1] which in 1993 equivalent purchasing power would be worth about £41,000.[2] Even allowing for the fact that professional expenses accounted for £612 of his gross earnings, this left Dylan with a comfortable disposable income, well above what many professional people enjoyed, let alone fellow-writers. Higham and Andrews both realized that the only way for Dylan to avoid financial Armageddon at the hands of the taxmen was to keep sufficient money back at source for past and future tax demands, which is what happened from 1948.

Even so, the question needs to be addressed: what did Dylan do with his money? The rent Margaret Taylor charged the Thomases for the Manor House at South Leigh was a mere £1 a week, and even that Dylan often failed to pay. He certainly was not giving much to Caitlin, who sometimes had to scrounge from friends and neighbours (including Margaret Taylor, which was the ultimate humiliation) to pay household bills. Dylan went through the roof when she once spent £5 on a new dress. It is true that there were sometimes medical expenses to be paid for Llewelyn, and from the autumn term of 1948, the boy's school fees. Moreover, Dylan was undoubtedly free and easy with his money when out pubbing. Yet there is a limit to how much one can spend on beer and taxis. Nor did he seem to have been helping out friends. When John Davenport, who had fallen on hard times, contacted him in the autumn of 1948 for a loan of £10, Dylan pleaded grounds of poverty and turned him down, despite all the hundreds of pounds' worth of gifts and hospitality that he had had from Davenport over the years. He was himself still sending out begging letters, and asking old chums like Mervyn Levy if they knew anyone who would be an easy 'touch'. There is no evidence to suggest that Dylan had expensive habits, like drugs or prostitutes. Nor was any great secret store of cash found when he died. The only plausible explanation is that he just frittered the money away, but as he hardly ever seems to have bought anything, this begs the question: on what?

One minor extravagance, which illustrates another side to Dylan's complex character, and a residual hankering after a certain bourgeois respectability, was his membership of London gentlemen's clubs. In 1947 he joined the National Liberal Club in Whitehall Place, the choice being made presumably because it was popular with Liberal-leaning professional men from Wales. Dylan tended to refer to the establishment as the 'National Lavatory Club', in tribute to the palatial gentlemen's toilets on the ground floor (no longer extant). Dylan relished the well-known story about the Conservative lawyer and statesman Lord Birkenhead (the former F. E. Smith), who used regularly to call into the National Liberal Club to make use of those splendid loos. Once challenged by a hall porter as to whether he was actually a member of the Club, Lord Birkenhead is reputed to have responded in mock innocence: 'You mean it's a Club as well?' Dylan would often end up there when he had tired of pubs, or they were closed, and he tended to be accompanied by a group of rowdy friends. The more sedate members of the NLC were not amused. Their suffering was shortlived, however. In 1949 his membership lapsed, for non-payment of dues.

In the meantime, Dylan had defected to the more literary-oriented Savage Club, which was then in Carlton House Terrace. As he explained to John Davenport, who proposed him for membership there, that way he could 'abandon the National Lavatory and be bad in worse company'.[3] Dylan was elected to the Savage in March 1949, and within a few months the Club Secretary was having to return cheques of his that had bounced.

Dylan's frequent stays in London, often of unpredictable length, were a major source of tension with Caitlin. During the ensuing rows she increasingly threatened to bring their relationship to an end. Dylan would then send her whining letters, begging her forgiveness and protesting his love. As he wrote to her from his parents' at Blaen Cwm, probably in February 1948, he couldn't understand 'how I can behave to you senselessly, foully, brutally, as though you were not the most beautiful person on earth and the one I love forever'.[4] Caitlin grew more bitter as she registered the fact that the remorse, if genuine, was always shortlived.

Dylan was at his parents' home – which he now dubbed 'Misery Cottage' – at the beginning of 1948 because both of them were in a poor state. D. J. had become a shadow of his former self. He had shrunk physically, the pot-belly of his middle age had gone, and his eyesight was starting to fail. The fire of his temper and his literary enthusiasms had been reduced to a faint flicker. He trembled and moaned and, as Dylan reported to Caitlin, cried out loud when the dog barked.

Dylan's sister Nancy was at Blaen Cwm too, having travelled over from her new home in Brixham in Devon, where she was living with her second husband Gordon Summersby, in order to look after D. J. Florence Thomas was laid up in Carmarthen Infirmary, flat on her back, having broken her leg in a bad fall. Dylan's old antagonism towards Nancy had not faded. He was still irritated by her jolly hockey-sticks manner. Mentally, Florence had not changed much either, even while strapped to her hospital bed with a great weight hanging down from a pulley over her steel-splinted leg. When Dylan went to visit her, she regaled him with information about the removed ovaries, dropped wombs and amputated breasts of her fellow-patients in the women's surgical ward. She was obviously going to be out of action for several months, though, and it was therefore agreed that D. J. would go to stay with Nancy and her husband in Brixham for a while. As Nancy's house was very small, however, and she had a Labrador dog of her own, there was talk of having to put the Thomases' mongrel Mably down, but Dylan took Mably back with him to South Leigh instead.

A couple of months later, D. J. and Florence followed. Florence was discharged from hospital in the third week of April, but clearly was not in any position to look after D. J. properly on her own. Nancy and her husband could not have both D. J. and Florence for more than a very short stay, not least because they were planning to return to India. Nancy had been a Field Army nurse during the war and had married Gordon Summersby out there. Accordingly, Dylan travelled down to Brixham by train on 22 April to arrange for D. J. and Florence to be ferried to South Leigh in an ambulance the following week. As there were not the facilities to accommodate his parents comfortably at the Manor House, Dylan had arranged for them to have Cordelia Locke's cottage in the village, which she and Harry were not using, at a rent of 3 guineas a week.

Domestic help would be provided by Mary, a woman from the village, who already worked as a daily at the Manor House and who seemed to have fallen under Caitlin's spell, as nothing could be too much trouble for her.

Against such a backdrop of domestic upheaval, it is perhaps surprising that Dylan was managing to write anything at all. As far as poetry was concerned, he was not. The poem 'In Country Sleep' that he had written in Italy was meant to form part of a grand sequence to be called *In Country Heaven*, which in principle he ought to have been working on at this time. Two later and rather different poems, 'Over Sir John's Hill' and 'In the White Giant's Thighs', were also said to be destined to form part of *In Country Heaven*, but Dylan never managed to finalize a coherent framework for this sequence, let alone write all its constituent parts. Similarly, J. M. Dent's plans to bring out a volume of Dylan's collected verse for the years 1934–47 were abandoned because two promised new long poems did not materialize.

Radio kept the wolves from the door. Dylan did nearly thirty recordings or live broadcasts for the BBC Home Service and Light Programme during 1948. These included recordings of several episodes each time of a serialization of W. H. Davies's *The Autobiography of a Super-Tramp*, which was produced by Roy Campbell. This went out weekly during the first four months of the year. In *The Listener*, Martin Armstrong, who had been so offended by Dylan's Satan, thought that *The Autobiography of a Super-Tramp*, in contrast, was 'good stuff'.[5]

Whereas radio broadcasts brought in tens of pounds, however, film scripts could bring in hundreds. This was probably the main reason Dylan was so keen to get work in the film industry. In 1947 Donald Taylor had finally managed to sell his project for *The Doctor and the Devils*, using Dylan's script, to the Rank Organization. This meant that Dylan received a fee of £365, paid in twelve instalments over 1947 and 1948, even though Rank decided that the subject matter of the film was too horrific for it to be made for the time being.[6] Having emerged from such a long and unpleasant war, the logic went, people on both sides of the Atlantic needed gentler entertainment.

The British film industry was enjoying something of a renaissance during this period, not least through support from the Government, which introduced a quota system to control the number of foreign films being imported. This was partly to stop British cinemas being swamped with products from Hollywood but it was also, more prosaically, a means of conserving foreign exchange. There was therefore a rush to churn out easily made – and preferably cheap – British films. Dylan got some freelance work with one company, the patriotically named British National, to do rewrite work on the scripts of two films aimed at the popular market: *Three Weird Sisters* and *No Room at the Inn*.

In the late spring of 1948, Dylan was approached by the actor Clifford Evans with an idea for a comedy film, to be set in Wales, for which he wanted Dylan to do the script. Dylan went to the film studios at Ealing for various meetings about the film, but seems to have had strong disagreements with the people who would be making it. These concerned both the movie's content and his fee. They were offering £250, while Dylan was holding out for £1,000, which is what he had been told by Sydney Box at Gainsborough Films was an appropriate script fee for a writer of his standing. The contract for the Ealing project was then awarded to someone else. This had the advantage that Dylan was therefore free to accept an offer from Sydney Box to work for Gainsborough Films instead, starting on 1 September.

Dylan worked on three films for Gainsborough, none of which was actually made. The first was based on a storyline which he had been pondering for some months, called *Me and My Bike*. This was conceived as a light-hearted cinematic operetta, in which the main character would cycle through his life (on a variety of machines) before pedalling up to Heaven to a chorus of bicycle bells. As Sydney Box gave Dylan *carte blanche* to let his fancy take free rein, he was initially very excited about the project. Unfortunately, it then collapsed, in the way that so many film projects do. Meanwhile, Dylan had been sidetracked on to another film, based on a story by Robert Louis Stevenson, entitled *The Beach at Falesa* and set in the South Seas. This would have cost a small fortune to make. The third, *Rebecca's Daughters*, was nearer to home, being the story of a gang of male highwaymen who dressed as women and made a series of raids on tollgates in South Wales in the 1840s. Gainsborough Films had already obtained a first draft script from somebody else, and this was passed on to Dylan in November by the scenario editor, Jan Read, for a complete rewrite.

Jan Read found Dylan charming and without side or pretensions, though maddeningly unreliable when it came to attending script conferences, which were held at Lime Grove in London. Sometimes he would turn up one or even two days late, armed with a feeble excuse, for example that he had only just heard from his agent David Higham when he should be there. He invariably wore his blue serge suit, which was by now extremely tatty. Dylan liked to keep the business discussions down to a minimum, so that everyone could then retire to the bar of the Shepherd's Bush Hotel, where he would amuse them with stories of Wales.

It was Jan Read's task to try to ensure that Dylan handed in his work on time. This was far from easy, as Dylan was forever coming up with pretexts for not having the next instalment ready. These invariably hinged on money. Read noticed that Dylan spent every penny of any advance he received before beginning work. Then he would send an avalanche of messages and letters begging for more money to be paid against future dues, so that insistent local tradesmen could be paid off, or Christmas presents bought for the children. Otherwise, not another word could be written. According to Jan Read, he was 'the wonder and despair of the studio accountants'.[7] None the less, when Dylan did get down to work, he wrote with great speed and fluency, demonstrating a fine ear for the way people actually talk.

At South Leigh, Dylan's domestic environment was turning into a cross between a Greek tragedy and an Ealing comedy. D. J. sat in the Lockes' cottage, cursing God and waiting for death, while Florence seemed increasingly blinkered by her own perception of reality. To Caitlin's intense annoyance, Florence stubbornly refused to acknowledge that her son was drinking to excess, or that there was anything at all unusual about a grown man of thirty-three lying in bed for hours in the morning after a hard evening's drinking, moaning horribly and calling out for bowls of bread and milk.

In the summer, Caitlin decided to get away for a while and took the children to Hampshire to stay with her mother. Margaret Taylor, abandoning her obligations at home in Oxford, stayed in South Leigh to help look after Dylan and his parents. Presumably to allay Caitlin's jealousy, Dylan wrote to her that the bitch (*sic*) was driving D. J. mad, patronizingly lecturing him on art and music, while letting the Manor House get filthy. She was wandering around red-eyed, Dylan wrote, alternately 'duckeying and weeping'.[8] Somewhat over-icing the cake, he maintained that even the daily help Mary hated Margaret. When Alan Taylor cycled over from Oxford to try to persuade her to go back and look after her own family, they had a terrible scene in the road. Alan Taylor went home despondent and defeated, realizing that their marriage could not last.

At the beginning of September, Dylan was in Edinburgh, speaking at the Festival, for which he had to hire a suit, as he had nothing decent to wear – or so he told John Davenport.[9] The event was meant to be a tribute to Hugh MacDiarmid (alias Christopher Murray Grieve), the eccentric poet-pioneer of the Scottish literary renaissance, who managed to be both a founder of the Scottish National Party and an intermittent communist. In his talk, Dylan defensively underplayed his own Celtic credentials, claiming that he was a Welshman who didn't live in his own country because he still wanted 'to eat and drink, be rigged and roofed, and no Welsh writer can hunt his bread and butter in Wales unless he pulls his forelock to the *Western Mail*, Bethesdas on Sunday, and enters public houses by the back door, and reads Caradoc Evans only when alone, and by candlelight'.[10]

Yet in reality Dylan was now pining for his homeland and Margaret Taylor was working hard to try to find somewhere at Laugharne for him to live, even though she knew that would put him further out of her reach. For a while it looked as though the Thomases might get the Castle House, where Richard and Frances Hughes used to live, but nothing came of it. In the meantime, life at South Leigh was enlivened by the arrival of Bill and Helen McAlpine, who had decided they wanted to live there too, to be near the Thomases. Caitlin believed that Bill worshipped Dylan and she considered that Bill's own poetry was hopelessly imitative of her husband's. But as she got on so well with Helen and they made an unusually harmonious foursome of friends, this did not matter.

Shortly before Christmas, Dylan and Bill cycled over to Witney, to buy various seasonal provisions for their wives. They had several beers there, and on the way back to South Leigh Dylan collided with a lorry. The nuts he had in his cycle-basket spilled all over the road. He broke a tooth, and an arm, as well as bruising his ribs, and he had to be carted off to the Radcliffe Infirmary in

Oxford. He was taken back to South Leigh in an ambulance, but typically managed to persuade the ambulancemen to stop at various pubs on the way. When eventually he was brought into the Manor House, Caitlin took one look at his arm in plaster and spat out: 'Play-acting!'[11]

Dylan inflated his injuries to 'a broken shoulder and ribs' when he wrote in early January 1949 to the head of BBC television drama, Robert MacDermot, explaining why he had failed to respond to a letter from MacDermot the previous month asking him if he would be interested in doing an adaptation for television of Henrik Ibsen's *Peer Gynt*. Wystan Auden had apparently been approached first, but had turned down the commission. Television was still very much in its infancy, as far as the British public was concerned, and Dylan confessed he had not actually ever seen any. He was interested in doing the adaptation, though, as *Peer Gynt* was one of his favourite plays. However, he said it would be impossible for him to finish the script by the end of February, as the BBC wanted. He therefore asked Robert MacDermot if the BBC would be prepared to put back the programme from its original slot of March or April to the autumn, which would give him time to do it properly. MacDermot agreed. The idea was that Dylan would work from a literal English translation of Ibsen's original Norwegian. He accepted a revised deadline of the end of May, despite the fact that he was still working on material for Gainsborough Films and had agreed to do a radio treatment of William Wycherley's *The Plain Dealer* simultaneously. He never did learn how to say no.

A further distraction intervened in the form of an invitation from the Czechoslovak legation in London to go to Prague at the beginning of March. Communists had seized control of the government there the year before and one of their efforts to acquire a spurious kind of international respectability was to hold a congress to launch the Czechoslovak Writers' Union. Numerous foreign guests were invited, not least from the other Soviet satellite states. Louis MacNeice was the other Briton selected for an invitation by the cultural attaché at the Legation, who knew both him and Dylan personally. But MacNeice, for all his leftist sympathies in the 1930s, would have nothing to do with an event that he considered to be organized by a Stalinist front. According to Dylan's report back to Aneirin Talfan Davies, when he got to the

Prague Congress he found he was the only non-communist present.[12]

The weather was bitterly cold and the food was awful, but Prague itself was lovely, the people were friendly and there seemed to be efficient central heating everywhere. The hosts had laid on a busy programme of banquets, receptions and cultural outings, including a performance of a Smetana opera. The congress itself was fairly brief and its content was predictable. Dylan made a short and platitudinous speech, saying how pleased he was to be in Czechoslovakia and conveying the fraternal greetings of English and Welsh writers. The final paragraph of his speech, as published in Czechoslovakia, remarked on how the faces of the people in a documentary film he had been shown the previous evening about the events of 1948 showed their 'delight and pride' in the birth of the new People's Republic. This sounds suspiciously as if it had been added later by some communist official, or at least reworked from whatever Dylan had really said. It illustrates clearly why Louis MacNeice had thought it better not to attend.

The Czech translator Jirina Haukova, who was then working for the Ministry of Information in Prague, met Dylan unofficially and took him on a tour of the old city. Dylan was enthusiastic about the historic buildings and threw his arms up to catch the falling snow, saying he would like to take some of it back to England in a bag. He was even more thrilled when he started to spot Pilsner signs, and each time this happened he dragged his guide into the attached tavern for a beer. But she did not see Dylan the abusive drunkard. The Dylan who visited Prague was like a precocious, naughty child on holiday: friendly and sincere and open. The day after the walk in the snow, Jirina Haukova invited a number of local poets to meet him, including the eminent Vladimir Holan. Despite the language barrier, Holan and Dylan talked non-stop, showing by hand-gestures who they ranked above whom among fellow-writers.[13]

April was spent in eager anticipation of the move back to Wales. Margaret Taylor had finally managed to acquire a house for Dylan and Caitlin, which she bought and then rented to them for a nominal sum. This was The Boat House, which Dylan and Caitlin had long loved from a distance. It was to be Dylan's last home and the one most intimately associated with his memory. By the time the Thomases moved there in May 1949, with Aeronwy (Llewellyn stayed on at his boarding-school in Oxford), Caitlin was seven months pregnant with their third child. Fortunately they soon found a willing local lass, Dolly Long, to help them settle in and survive. Margaret Taylor had given the Thomases quite a lot of basic furniture while they were at South Leigh, and this was brought over to Laugharne in a furniture van. It was the first and only time in their lives that they had had anything resembling a normal move.

The Boat House is an isolated dwelling, a little out of the town, on one bank of a broad estuary where the Rivers Taf, Towy and Gwendraeth meet. The house is reached by a narrow lane, not wide enough for any vehicle, which is now called Dylan's Walk. There are steps down from the lane into the front garden of The Boat House and then a steep path to the front door. This opens into the second of three floors, which are linked by tight, sheer stairs. Each floor has two main rooms, and there is an outside loo. When the Thomases were there, there was a big coal-burning stove, on which Caitlin would brew her famous stews. What Americans would call a 'deck' runs round the second floor of The Boat House, affording fine views over the estuary to the fields around Pentowin, Sir John's Hill and the sea. At low tide, waders and herons and other birds share the mudflats with the local cockle-pickers, moving smartly away when the tide rushes in and the sea comes up to lap at the property's wall.

Though much rougher in 1949 than it is now in its restored form as a Dylan Thomas museum, The Boat House seemed almost designed with a poet in mind. Yet Dylan did not do any of his writing there. Just as he had had the caravan in South Leigh and the little farm cottage near the villa outside Florence as a kind of studio, away from the noise and distracting presence of the family, so now he converted a tiny former garage a little way back up the lane towards the centre of Laugharne into a workshed. A simple writing-table was placed in front of the large window at the back of the shed, overlooking the bay. Portraits of favourite writers like Auden, Blake, Hardy and D. H. Lawrence, as well as reproductions of various paintings torn from magazines, were pinned to the walls.

D. J. and Florence had gone to Laugharne ahead of Dylan and Caitlin and were already settled in a house called Pelican, which Dylan rented for them. This is in Laugharne's main street, almost

opposite Brown's Hotel. Dylan quickly adopted a routine of spending his mornings at Pelican, doing crosswords with D. J., or
reading, then going over to Brown's for a natter with Ivy Williams.
After lunch, he would write or just think in his workshed, staring
out over the estuary or throwing little chunks of bread to the birds,
particularly the herons, who reminded him of Edith Sitwell.

Through Roy Campbell, Dylan was commissioned, rather bizarre-
ly, to write a piece for the BBC Scottish Region radio series,
'Scottish Life and Letters', on why he had gone back to live in
Wales. This was recorded in London in June 1949 and sent on to
Aberdeen. Its tone was very different from that of the talk he had
given at the Edinburgh Festival less than a year before. In the radio
broadcast, Dylan pictured himself in a train travelling from
Oxford to London, looking on his fellow, oh-so-English passen-
gers with contempt. He suddenly realized – or so he maintained –
that he didn't want to be in England at all, that 'dark and savage
country whose customs and tribal rites I shall never understand,
breathing an alien air, hearing, everywhere, the snobcalls, the
prigchants, the mating cries, the tom-toms of a curious, and maybe
cannibal, race'. Instead, he wanted to be in Wales. The very word
'Wales' rolled round his tongue 'like a gobstopper of magical
properties, ringing the word like a bell, making it rise and fall,
whisper and thunder like the Welsh sea whose fish are great
Liberals, fond of laver-bread and broth, and who always, on
Sundays, attend their green and watery chapels'.[14]

Certainly, the move to Laugharne temporarily removed Dylan's
poetic block, as almost immediately he got down to work on a new
poem, 'Over Sir John's Hill'. This is pre-eminently a place-poem,
celebrating the view from the workshed and the birds that Dylan
watched, particularly one heron. Vernon Watkins thought it was
perhaps the best poem Dylan ever wrote.

The move and the new burst of poetic creativity meant that the
deadline for the television adaptation of *Peer Gynt* came and went
without anything being produced. Doubtless feeling somewhat
guilty, Dylan went on the defensive with the BBC, complaining
that it was unreasonable of them to expect him to undertake such a
major piece of work in such a short space of time. He pointed out
that Louis MacNeice (who, unlike Dylan, was a salaried member of
the BBC staff) had been given a whole year on full pay, plus an
extra fee, to do a similar adaptation of Goethe's *Faust*. Dylan, in

contrast, had been offered 250 guineas, half of which was paid in advance, and he had been expected to complete the whole thing in less than six months. The deadline for his submission of the *Peer Gynt* script kept on being put back until finally, not long before his death, the BBC gave up hope. Similarly, Dylan's radio adaptation of Wycherley's *The Plain Dealer*, for which he had signed a contract for a 100-guinea fee, never materialized. The BBC sent a series of increasingly agonized letters and telegrams to The Boat House, to which Dylan failed to respond. Sometimes when he was lying in bed and he heard the postman coming down the path, he would bury his head under the blankets.

Predictably, Dylan disappeared when the new baby's birth was imminent, probably to Swansea. Caitlin had been swimming at the beach at Pendine, not far from Laugharne, on 24 July, and when she got home she went for a walk along the bank of the estuary. Suddenly birthpains came on fast, and she called Ebie Williams at Brown's Hotel to take her quickly in his car to Carmarthen Infirmary. She lost her temper with the admission staff there when they insisted that before she went up to the labour ward, she would have to fill in various forms and produce her ration card (rationing still being in force for certain foods in Britain four years after the end of the war). 'For God's sake,' she screamed, 'let me have this baby!'[15]

It was a boy, to whom Dylan and Caitlin gave the Irish name Colm (which Dylan often spelled as it is pronounced, 'Colum'), and the Welsh name Garan, which means 'heron'. He was an easy, sweet baby, full of charm, and he became Dylan's favourite child. Caitlin considered that first summer back at Laugharne, with the new baby, to be amongst the happiest times in her marriage.

None the less, Dylan was deeply preoccupied by creditors. He owed money to the milkman, the coalman and a builder, and started writing round friends and wealthy acquaintances once more, trying to rustle up some funds. The most loyal, like Margaret Taylor, bailed him out yet again.

A new lady patron materialized in the form of the Princess Caetani, a sixty-nine-year-old American from Connecticut, who had married an Italian aristocrat, Roffredo Caetani (also known as Prince Bassiano) and settled in Rome. There she edited an important avant-garde literary magazine called *Botteghe Oscure* (which means 'dark little shops'). Dylan managed to get a commission from her for a piece for her magazine, with payment in advance. Princess Caetani was luckier than most of the editors who dealt with Dylan at this time, in that he was indeed able to send her something not too long after receiving her cheque: the poem 'Over Sir John's Hill'. This did not stop Dylan harassing Princess Caetani over the next few months for more money, allegedly for a story that he would write for *Botteghe Oscure*.

However, the most exciting foreign development for Dylan came from the land of the mythical pot of gold on the other side of the Atlantic. Not long after the Thomases moved into The Boat House, Dylan received a letter out of the blue from John Malcolm Brinnin, an American poet two years his junior, who had recently been appointed Director of the Poetry Centre of the Young Men's and Young Women's Hebrew Association in New York. Brinnin had long been a fan of Dylan's poetry and it had been a dream of his to be able to ask Dylan to go to the United States, so that his work could become better known there. Now he could. Virtually the first thing Brinnin did when he took up his new job was to invite Dylan over to lecture at his Poetry Centre for a fee of $500 plus his return fare from Britain.

Dylan replied enthusiastically to Brinnin's offer, saying he would like to go to America for about three months, from January or February 1950. In his very first letter to Brinnin,[16] he explained that as his financial position was precarious he would need to start earning some money almost from the moment he arrived in New York. Ideally, he would also like to earn enough while in the United States to be able to bring a reasonable amount back home to Wales. Obviously that meant he would have to do far more than just address the Poetry Centre of the YM & YWHA. Initially, Dylan hoped that David Higham's American associate in New York, Ann Watkins Ltd, would be able to fix up a lucrative lecture tour for him, but the firm protested that it was essentially a literary agency, without the necessary expertise and contacts. Accordingly, John Malcolm Brinnin rashly offered to take on the job himself, for a set fee of 15 per cent of the proceeds, far less than a professional lecture agency would have charged.

This gave Dylan a little over six months to try to finish off various outstanding commitments and to get his affairs in order. Despite all the disappointments and shocks David Higham had experienced with Dylan, he still had great faith in his client's ability to earn a substantial living as a freelance writer and broadcaster, so he was prepared to put in a considerable amount of work to disentangle some of the knots Dylan had tied himself up in. Higham was able to arrange to buy back the rights to Dylan's first collection of verse, *18 Poems*, which Dylan had foolishly sold independently for a pittance in 1942 to the Fortune Press, who had then reissued the book. Higham's idea was that J. M. Dent should be able to acquire the rights for book publication of all Dylan's poems, to make him a more attractive long-term prospect for them.

At the beginning of October, David Higham sat down with Dylan and drew up a workplan for the next eighteen months, in the hope that Dylan might manage to honour more of his obligations if these were set out clearly within a reasonable framework. According to this plan, Dylan's first task was to finish a film treatment commissioned by Gainsborough Films for a Technicolor version of William Makepeace Thackeray's novel *Vanity Fair*, which was to star Margaret Lockwood. Dylan had begun work on this project in early July and was confident now that he could finish it off within ten days. Then he was to concentrate on the radio script of *The Plain Dealer* for a month, followed by the television script of *Peer Gynt*. Dylan estimated that that could be ready by the end of the year. That would enable him to go off to America with a clear conscience at the beginning of 1950. On his return, according to Higham's plan, he would then spend a year finishing his abandoned novel *Adventures in the Skin Trade*, putting together a little more material so there would be sufficient to bring out a new book with Dent, and writing a radio play for the BBC. This all looked wonderfully sensible on paper, but that is as far as most of it got.[17]

Dylan was doing some work, however. Although his radio commissions diminished considerably in the second half of 1949, after his move to Laugharne, he honoured four BBC commitments during that period, apart from the already mentioned broadcast for Scotland, 'Living in Wales'. These were a piece on the poet Edward Thomas, for the Welsh Service; a scripted studio discussion in Swansea on 'Swansea and the Arts', with Vernon Watkins, John Prichard, Alfred Janes and Daniel Jones; a reading of his own poems for the Third Programme; and a role in Louis MacNeice's radio play *The Dark Tower*, which was actually broadcast on the Home Service at the end of January 1950.[18]

Despite their different temperaments, Dylan and Louis Mac-Neice got on well, whether they were working together in the BBC studios or joking over a beer in a pub or at Lord's cricket ground (where a lot of BBC business seemed to take place during the summer). Moreover, when Louis MacNeice decided that he wanted to give up his BBC job as a radio producer, in order to take up a British Council posting in Athens, he recommended Dylan to succeed him. As they both envisaged it, Dylan could take on the job when he came back from America, and they believed that some of the work involved could realistically be done from Wales. However, the BBC had had its fingers burned too often with Dylan to even begin to take that proposition seriously.

Besides, Dylan's mind was increasingly focused on the American trip and where this might lead. He had been encouraged by an approach from Columbia Records in New York earlier in the year, contracting him to record five minutes' worth of his poetry for one of their albums of poets reading their own work, brought out under the series title *Pleasure Dome*. For a natural performer like Dylan, such recordings were an easy way of earning money, and they were an activity which was later to prove extremely lucrative to his estate. Furthermore, Dylan's American publisher, James Laughlin, had promised that he would do what he could to make Dylan's visit a success by introducing him to as many useful contacts as possible.

On 12 November, the celebrated Soho photographer and explosive character John Deakin came to Laugharne to photograph Dylan for a new glossy American magazine which he thought was going to be called *Flair*. Dylan dressed up in his best jacket and a bow-tie, and let Deakin place him among the graves in Laugharne's overgrown cemetery, up to his waist in weeds, with his hair 'uncut for months . . . blown up like a great, dancing, mousey busby'.[19] The resultant photograph, which later appeared in *Vogue* (and is on the back cover of this book) is one of the most enduring images of Dylan. It seems light years away from the studio portrait of the full-lipped young innocent that he had sent to Pamela Hansford Johnson only fifteen years or so before – the 'fucking cherub', as the mature Dylan characteristically described it (and which appears on the front cover of this book).

Equally characteristically, Dylan ended the 1940s with a fall at Laugharne, which left him with several broken ribs. At least, that was the excuse he gave shortly before Christmas for backing out of an arranged radio broadcast at the BBC's Cardiff studios, where he was due to be interviewed by his old friend Glyn Jones for a series called *How I Write*. Those 'chicken bones' of Dylan's had let him down again. Yet the injury, however serious in reality, was not going to stop him flying off to America in February.

11

THE POT OF GOLD

(1950–1951)

Dylan's original intention had been to take Caitlin along with him on his first visit to the United States, but as the day of his departure approached it became obvious that that was not feasible. A hectic programme of over forty engagements across North America had been arranged for him, and the Thomases could hardly expect the organizers of each event to cover Caitlin's expenses as well as Dylan's. Moreover, as one of the aims of the trip was to make a sizeable profit, Caitlin's presence would have defeated the object. Besides, having parked Llewellyn on her mother for so long during and immediately after the war, she doubted the wisdom of falling into the same pattern with Aeronwy and the six-month-old Colm.

There was a boisterous farewell party in London for Dylan before he left for the airport on the afternoon of 20 February. The flight to New York took seventeen hours, with stops in Dublin, 'somewhere in Canada'[1] – the normal refuelling stage of Gander in Newfoundland being iced over – and Boston. Dylan thought his two dozen or so fellow-passengers looked a nasty lot, but as he was feeling hungover from the London party he wasn't in the mood to communicate with them anyway. He found he couldn't sleep or read on the plane, so he spent a lot of the flight drinking alone in the lounge-bar beneath the main cabin.

This gave Dylan plenty of time to fret about what would be waiting for him in America, knowing only that it would be quite unlike any experience he had had up till then, and that he would be facing it on his own. He also had to decide which Dylan of his wide repertoire he would show to the Americans. It couldn't be the husband within a bickering bohemian couple, because Caitlin wasn't there. It couldn't even be the working writer, as there was never any suggestion that he would do any serious writing while he was in the United States. Consciously or unconsciously, therefore, Dylan opted for the poet-performer and pub-clown as his principal role: the talented shocker who could amuse, and who – in the spirit of Oscar Wilde – would give those funny Yanks a show that would make them feel they had got their money's worth.

Dylan's plane landed at Idlewild Airport, New York, before dawn on one of the coldest days of that winter; the temperature was down to about -15° Centigrade. When Dylan emerged in his duffel-coat, carrying suitcases secured with string, John Malcolm Brinnin was there to meet him: smartly dressed in East Coast fashion and immaculately groomed, he was feeling distinctly nervous about what he had let himself in for. According to the highly subjective but entertaining book Brinnin wrote about Dylan in America – which was for a long time taken as gospel by Thomas devotees – he led the new arrival straight to the airport bar for a breakfast of a double Scotch and soda.[2] Suitably fortified, they then drove in Brinnin's car through the icy early morning light to the Beekman Tower Hotel in Manhattan, on the corner of First Avenue and 49th Street. Dylan's room was at least twenty storeys up. For a while he just stood by the window, stunned, staring down at what looked like toy cars on the streets below. Room service was summoned to bring up iced beer.

Dylan had actually wanted to stay in an apartment in New York, rather than a hotel. As Brinnin himself lived well out of town, various people had been approached to see if they would be willing to put him up. It was explained to them that this was an undertaking not be accepted lightly, so most refused. The British poet Ruthven Todd, who had known Dylan in England before the war, and who was now based in America, even asked the overtly gay poet Harold Norse (whose close chum Chester Kallman had been Wystan Auden's lover for the past ten years) if he could cope with

Dylan. Norse agreed, but heard no more. Perhaps Brinnin thought it would be safer for everyone concerned if Dylan were installed in a hotel, though the wisdom of that decision was quickly brought into question.

At first glance, New York was all that Dylan had expected, only more so. The skyscrapers and the traffic and the noise left him dazed. Instead of suggesting Dylan get some sleep on this first morning, however, Brinnin waited while he shaved and changed and then took him down to the nearest Irish neighbourhood bar. With typical American hospitality, Brinnin thought he ought to steer Dylan somewhere where he would feel at home. Having heard of Dylan's fondness for drink, he obviously felt it was his obligation as a host to keep him well supplied. From Brinnin's book, one gets the impression that Dylan spent most of his time in New York moving from bar to bar or pouncing on every passing female, until he was incapable of moving any further. Yet Dylan's letters home to Caitlin and to his parents, as well as the observations of other friends and acquaintances in America, present a much less simple picture. The fact that many of the American reminiscences of Dylan flatly contradict each other is as much a reflection of his chameleon-like nature as of their authors' powers of invention.

What is certain is that Dylan's first three days in New York were hectic, and that he probably drank more spirits in those three days than he normally did over a period of months, with predictable effects on his digestion and his sobriety. Brinnin took him walking down the canyon-like streets and drove him round in the car sightseeing. They went up to the top of the Empire State Building, and frequented the bars and restaurants of Greenwich Village. Dylan took a liking to that part of southern Manhattan, because of its more human, almost European scale. Brinnin was worried his guest wasn't eating properly, and he would coax him to eat a pastrami sandwich or a light Italian meal. Yet Dylan wrote to his parents that one of his strongest earliest impressions of New York was the wonderful food. He claimed to have stuffed himself with milk-shakes, fried shrimps, fried chicken and 'a T-bone steak the size of a month's ration for an English family'.[3] He told them he thought Brinnin was a 'terribly nice man', yet if Harold Norse's *Memoirs* have more than a grain of truth, then Dylan quickly found Brinnin overwhelming.

Apparently Norse phoned Dylan at the Beekman Tower Hotel on the first day he was there, having heard from Ruthven Todd that he had arrived. When Norse mentioned he was a friend of Todd's, Dylan told him to come on over. According to Norse, he found Dylan in the penthouse bar with Brinnin, who bristled when Norse entered the room. Dylan allegedly beckoned Norse over and whispered into his ear, loud enough to be overheard: 'How can I get rid of this bastard?' Brinnin excused himself for half an hour, and Dylan held Norse enthralled, displaying the easy informality and concentrated attention that could quickly convert strangers into loyal fans. He spoke of not being able to write the good poems of his youth any more and how he had come to America with the clear intention of earning money while he was still able to cash in on his fame. Norse found him 'entirely natural, ineffably sad, a sorrowful, tragic clown . . . He spoke with the intimacy of an old friend – with no sign of drunkenness.'[4] Apart from pinching the cocktail waitress's bottom as she went past, Dylan did not behave in the least bit oddly.

As soon as Brinnin came back, however (according to Norse), Dylan started speaking loudly and acting with drunken abandon. It was the sort of sea-change he had perfected when he was out in Chelsea with Mervyn Levy fifteen years earlier, emerging from a pub apparently sober only to turn himself into an instant drunk when he saw someone he wanted to impress. Brinnin, Norse and Dylan got into the hotel lift, along with an unknown, distinguished-looking grey-haired man and two elderly women in evening dress. On the long descent down to the ground floor, in a scene straight out of a Marx Brothers film, Dylan suddenly switched into his Cat-and-Dog routine, bearing fangs and growling loudly. As the two women looked on in alarm, he bit the strange man's back several times. Brinnin tried to maintain his composure, shepherding Dylan out of the lift when it reached the ground floor, across the hotel lobby and into his car. Brinnin informed Harold Norse in no uncertain terms that he was not invited to accompany them for the rest of the evening.

When Brinnin called at the Beekman Tower the following morning, Dylan had already gone out. Brinnin tracked him down at Murphy's Bar and took him to Costello's restaurant where they were due to meet Harvey Breit of the *New York Times* for an interview over lunch. Ruthven Todd and two other old friends of

Dylan's, Len Lye and his wife Jane, joined them. When Jane Lye walked in and set eyes on Dylan – for the first time in about a decade – she took in his bloated figure, his matted, wild hair and his broken and tobacco-stained teeth, then exclaimed in dismay, 'Oh, Dylan, the last time I saw you, you were an *angel*!'[5] He looked pained. But the conversation soon became a riot of London reminiscences, with Dylan recounting a string of alleged near run-ins with the police, enraged husbands and literary grandees. The stories were painted in broad, bold strokes. Harvey Breit wrote a few notes, knowing that most of what he was hearing was unpublishable, until at last he managed to get Dylan to give a few anodyne first impressions of New York. When he was asked why he had come to the Big Apple, though, Dylan replied: 'to continue my lifelong search for naked women in wet mackintoshes'.[6] The image of women so clad was, like French letters, one which recurred repeatedly in Dylan's conversation and correspondence. Needless to say, it did not appear in the piece on Dylan that Harvey Breit wrote for the *Sunday Times Book Review*.

That evening, after a refreshing nap, Dylan went with Brinnin to a dinner party at the 12th Street apartment of a serious young academic critic called Marshall Stearns. Various university professors and other members of New York's strait-laced literary high society were waiting there to inspect the Celtic curiosity. Everything was going reasonably smoothly until someone asked Dylan to explain the meaning of his poem 'Ballad of the Long-legged Bait'. Dylan couldn't bear such impromptu questions, especially from total strangers, and replied tartly: 'It's a description of a gigantic fuck.'[7] That remark would have won him a laugh and a cheer and a free pint of beer from the regular crowd in 'The French' in London's Soho, but in these refined surroundings it merely provoked scandalized, silent embarrassment.

Worse was to come. Brinnin took Dylan on to a more laid-back party at Harvey Breit's apartment, where a large group of writers, critics and actors had gathered, including James Agee, Wystan Auden, Ruth Ford, Katherine Anne Porter, Lionel and Diana Trilling and James and Tania Stern. Ruth Ford had come on from the theatre where she was appearing at the time and she charmed Dylan by informing him that she had a picture of him pinned up in her dressing-room. He seems to have interpreted this as a come-on, as, according to Brinnin, he then lunged at her, unsuccessfully.

As the evening wore on, and Dylan got steadily drunker, people started looking imploringly at Brinnin, to encourage him to take his wayward charge home. When Katherine Anne Porter, then aged nearly sixty, tried to leave, Dylan suddenly took hold of her and lifted her up until her head was almost touching the ceiling. With great aplomb, she calmly said goodnight and waited to be let down. Dylan stumbled out of the party after her and followed her down the stairs, which enabled Brinnin to steer him back to the car.

When they arrived at the Beekman Tower Hotel, Brinnin wanted to show Dylan up to his room, but Dylan insisted he would be all right. Brinnin never found out exactly what happened next, but the hotel management (who had presumably already been informed of their guest's dog antics in the lift the previous evening) suggested firmly that it would be better if Dylan found somewhere else to stay. Subsequently he was moved to Midston House, on 38th Street, where his friend the New Zealand poet Allen Curnow – who was also on a visit to New York – was already installed.

In contrast to this débâcle, Dylan's first reading at the Kaufmann Auditorium at the Poetry Center of the YM & YWHA on 92nd Street was a triumph. He'd been sick a few times during the day, and just a few minutes before he was due to go on stage, he had a fit of coughing that almost knocked him off his feet. Then he retched into a nearby basin. Yet when the moment to perform arrived, he marched confidently on to the stage and gave a reading that held the thousand or so people crammed inside the hall spellbound. In a pattern that was to be repeated across the country, he first read a selection of work by other poets, including Auden, Hardy, Lawrence, MacNeice and Edith Sitwell. Then he turned to his own verse, delivering it with a force that won him a standing ovation. Outside the hall, however, Dylan crumpled again, vomiting into the gutter. With some difficulty, Brinnin persuaded him to give a party they had both been invited to after the reading a miss, and to get to bed back at the hotel instead.

Following a second successful reading at the YM & YWHA Poetry Center, Dylan travelled out of New York with John Malcolm Brinnin for a short stay at Brinnin's home at Westport. On the slow journey along the traffic-clogged freeway, Dylan explained how he had been attacked in the British press for signing the Stockholm Peace Petition the year before. This had confirmed many people's suspicions that Dylan was a 'fellow traveller', whereas in fact his signing was little more than another example of his gullibility. The attendant rumpus had meant there were some tough questions to be answered when he applied for his American visa in London. However, it had not taken his interrogator long to decide that Dylan was politically harmless. As Brinnin put it in his summary of the discussion he had with Dylan in the car on the way to Westport, Dylan's 'socialism' was essentially Tolstoyian: 'the attempt of the spiritual aristocrat to hold in one embrace the good heart of mankind, a gesture and a purpose uncontaminated by the *realpolitik* of the twentieth century'.[8]

At Westport, Brinnin's poodle bitch was on heat. The house was surrounded by a posse of male dogs standing as if on sentry duty, waiting for the canine temptress to appear. As Dylan had just received a letter from Caitlin, he went outside to sit on a large stone in the snowy garden and read it undisturbed. As Brinnin witnessed from the window, Dylan then started lecturing the dogs that were stationed around him, telling them he knew exactly how they felt. Back in the house, he read out passages of Caitlin's letter to Brinnin and mimicked the way she scolded him, declaring – as other friends have testified that she often did – that she hadn't understood a word he had said to her since the day they married, because of the way he mumbled. Dylan told Brinnin, as he told everyone else in America when the subject of his wife came up, that 'she's the only one for me'.[9]

This did not stop Dylan making a clumsy pass at the novelist Shirley Jackson when Brinnin and he went over to her house in nearby Saugatuck the following evening. As Shirley Jackson's husband, the critic Stanley Edgar Hyman, sat watching a boxing match on television, Dylan allegedly pursued Ms Jackson round the house. According to one version of the story, related secondhand by Brendan Gill of the *New Yorker*, Hyman got so fed up at having his TV-viewing interrupted by the figure of his wife rushing repeatedly through the room with Dylan in hot pursuit that he grabbed at Dylan's belt when he came within reach, bringing him crashing down on the floor. However embroidered that account may be, it is certain that everyone, including John Malcolm Brinnin, had had far too much to drink. But Brinnin's last sight of Dylan that night was of him sitting up in bed back at Brinnin's house, contentedly reading a cheap mystery paperback, while all around him on the bedcovers was an array of Tootsie Rolls, Milky Ways, Baby Ruths and other chocolate bars and sweets. This constant passion for candy made several people wonder whether Dylan might be slightly diabetic, or having thyroid problems.

From Westport Dylan went with Brinnin to Yale University at New Haven, where he seemed extremely uneasy. He embarrassed some of the faculty members at dinner after his reading to the student body was over by pathetically musing about how he could have gone to university himself if he had really wanted to. He then launched into a series of scurrilous anecdotes about the British Royal Family, as usual in such situations making liberal use of four-letter words. When he got down to the fine detail of what he claimed Oscar Wilde had done with a jockey, his hosts decided it was time the evening was brought to an end. It was with considerable relief that Brinnin put Dylan on a train for Boston the following day.

A reading at Harvard University in Cambridge, Massachusetts, seems to have passed without undue incident, and from there Dylan was driven by car 100 miles or so to Mount Holyoke College, at South Hadley. This was one of the most venerable academic institutions for women in the United States. Dylan persuaded his driver to stop several times along the way, calling in at bars for beers and games on the pin-ball machines. They arrived so late at Mount Holyoke that dinner was already over. The audience that had been kept waiting in the lecture hall was starting to get restless. Clearly inebriated, Dylan tottered to the lectern. Some of the students giggled as he tried to pour himself a glass of water from a jug that was evidently empty. 'That's right,' he said, 'laugh at an old ham.'[10] Yet when he began his reading it was as if he went on to auto-pilot, delivering another resonant and memorable performance that struck even the most experienced members of the English faculty as being like nothing else they had ever heard.

The quality of these readings helped Dylan's reputation spread ahead of him across the United States. The fact that the testimonies to his talent were accompanied by stories of outrageous behaviour at social events after the performances only strengthened people's desire to see him for themselves. At Mount Holyoke there was a small party for some of the teaching staff after Dylan's reading and he proceeded to flirt with the lady professors there, irrespective of their age and looks. According to one of the women present, Marianne Brock, Dylan gave a loud and crude enumeration of her and her colleagues' physical attributes, starting with their feet and working up. Some were offended, but most thought it ridiculously funny. Dylan made a few fumbled attempts at pinching one or two female bottoms, then said he wanted to put his hands up to someone's warm bosom. But his meandering progress around the room was interrupted when he fell over a coffee table and then had to be escorted gently off to bed. One of Dylan's hosts in the English Department at the college, Joseph Bottkol, went home afterwards and laughed out loud for twenty minutes.[11]

By 9 March Dylan's tour had taken him as far as Washington, DC, where he had a letter of introduction to Princess Caetani's half-sister Katherine Biddle, herself a modest poet. Mrs Biddle's husband Francis had been US Attorney-General during the war and both of them had a philanthropic interest in the arts. They insisted that Dylan stay in their luxurious house rather than at a hotel, but when Dylan wrote to Caitlin from there he said that it was hell on earth. He claimed to be totally sick of America already, with its driving lust for success and its adulation of power, although the major part of his 'pilgrimage of the damned' was yet to come.[12] The Biddles had to fly off to Bermuda, but left Dylan alone in the house with the servants. This gave him plenty of time to rifle his hosts' wardrobes and drawers until he found a selection of shirts that suited him. He made no secret of the theft when John Malcolm Brinnin came to pick him up in his car, to drive him back to New York. When Francis Biddle returned from Bermuda he was not particularly upset by the loss of his shirts, but he was dismayed to discover a bundle of Dylan's dirty laundry screwed up into a ball and stuffed under his bed.

On 14 March Dylan began a five-week sweep across the country, travelling alone by plane and train or being driven in other people's cars. He was armed with a fistful of tickets and a simpleton's diary, prepared by John Malcolm Brinnin, telling him where to go, when he had to be there and – as far as possible – who would be looking after him when he arrived. It was a punishing schedule of journeys and lectures, that took in upstate New York, Ohio, Illinois (including Chicago, where he was fascinated by Skid Row), Indiana and Iowa. On 21 March he arrived in Iowa City, where his host, a university lecturer called Ray West, was rather taken aback to discover that Dylan was planning to stay for almost two weeks, as he didn't have to be at his next stop – Berkeley, California – until 4 April. John Malcolm Brinnin had suggested that Dylan make use of this extended break to get an American dentist to do something about his awful teeth. However, so much work needed doing to them that the dentists he approached recommended he get things sorted out back home instead.

The poet Robert Lowell was teaching at the State University of Iowa, where Dylan gave a reading at the beginning of his stay. On one occasion, Dylan stood in for Lowell at his Writers' Workshop class. Lowell was surprised to note that Dylan used the same booming, declamatory voice for every poem he read, even those which would have been much more effective if they had been delivered more quietly. However, when some of Lowell's colleagues suggested that it might also be a good idea for Dylan's art if he stayed off spirits, Lowell stood up for him, saying he should be allowed to drink what he liked, as his boisterous behaviour might liven up Iowa City. None the less, it is clear from an article written over twenty years later by Ray West[13] that Dylan's conduct in Iowa City was far from reprehensible. For example, he caused amusement, rather than offence, when a girl student asked how she could support herself while she tried to be a poet and Dylan replied that she should try going on to the streets. Moreover, most of West's colleagues and friends took Dylan's far-fetched anecdotes for what they really were: flights of fancy.

Several of the people who had to look after Dylan during this first US tour were convinced that he had no idea where he was half the time, but they probably did not realize that he switched off from places that he considered of little or no interest. In contrast, when he got to San Francisco, his enthusiasm was boundless. He wrote to Caitlin that the city 'is and has everything . . . The wonderful sunlight . . . the hills, the great bridges, the Pacific at your shoes. Beautiful Chinatown. Every race in the world. The sardine fleets sailing out. The little cable cars whizzing down the city hills. The lobsters, clams, & crabs.'[14] He had been very lucky in that he had fallen on his feet in San Francisco. He had arrived with a letter of introduction to Ruth Witt-Diamant, an English litera-ture lecturer at San Francisco State College, who insisted that he move out of the hotel into which he had checked and go to stay at her house. She proved to be a good friend both to him and to

Caitlin. Moreover, the teaching staff at Berkeley, who were more liberal than some of their colleagues in the mid-West, took to Dylan and wanted him to be given an appointment in their Speech Department the following year. The prospect was immensely appealing, not just for the financial security that the salary would bring, but also because Dylan could see himself living in San Francisco with Caitlin and the infant Colm. It was the only city outside Britain with which he felt such a rapport. The teaching opportunity came to nothing, however, as the conservative Dean of Studies did not share his staff's tolerant attitude to Dylan's lifestyle, and he vetoed any firm offer being made.

Compared to San Francisco, Vancouver in Canada, which was next on Dylan's itinerary, was disturbingly provincial; it reminded him unpleasingly of Cheltenham. He winced when he went on to the platform of the University of British Columbia and found himself standing in front of two Union Jacks. In the hotel where he was staying, men and women were not even allowed to drink in the same bar. The only saving grace in Vancouver was a visit from the novelist Malcolm Lowry, whom Dylan had known in England. Lowry was then living in a hut up in the mountains of British Columbia. Having stayed with Henry Miller, his pretty young Polish wife and their two small children in *his* hut at Big Sur in California only a week before, Dylan was starting to get extremely nostalgic for his own little workshed in Laugharne.

Nothing would have made him miss Hollywood, however, as Tinsel Town held an almost mythical fascination for him, just as it did for so many other writers with a keen interest in the cinema. He travelled to Los Angeles from Vancouver – via Seattle and Montana – and was put up by the novelist Christopher Isherwood. Isherwood was at a turning point in his own career, having spent the previous few years dividing his time between the Vedanta Centre in Hollywood (trying to be a monk), and a boisterous, boozy relationship with the young Irish-American photographer Bill Caskey. Dylan's main link to Isherwood was through the film director Ivan Moffat, who had returned home to America after training in England. Despite their very different characters, Dylan and Isherwood got on well.

When Isherwood had first arrived in America from China, before the war, the writer and magazine editor George Davis had asked him in New York if there was anything in particular he wanted. Isherwood had replied: a blond boy with sexy legs, and George Davis had come up with exactly that. The young man concerned was a major reason for Isherwood's return to the United States soon afterwards to live. Now, twelve years later, in Los Angeles, Isherwood in turn asked Dylan if there was anything *he* wanted and Dylan replied: a short blonde girl with big boobs. Isherwood obliged by introducing him to the young actress Shelley Winters. Over dinner with Isherwood and Ivan Moffat, Dylan told Miss Winters – who had no idea who he was – that one of his greatest fantasies was 'to touch the titties of a beautiful blonde starlet'. Amused by the situation, she decided to acquiesce. Ivan Moffat produced a bottle of champagne and Dylan dipped his finger into a glass of it before delicately brushing it over each of the breasts that Shelley Winters had exposed. 'Oh, God!' he uttered, 'Nirvana!'[15]

Dylan's other major Hollywood fantasy was to meet Charlie Chaplin, and Shelley Winters said she could arrange this. At the time she was sharing a small apartment with Marilyn Monroe. She invited Dylan for dinner there the following Sunday, along with a journalist, Sidney Skolsky, after which they would all go to one of the Chaplins' famous evening parties. On the Sunday, Marilyn Monroe gathered wild flowers on a nearby vacant lot to decorate the apartment, and then mixed martini cocktails in a milk-bottle, while Shelley Winters prepared the meal. As she recalled in her memoirs, 'Mr Thomas drank most of his dinner', polishing off not only the lion's share of the martini, but also most of a bottle of red wine, and then a bottle of white wine, and finally a six-pack of beer he had picked up at a supermarket on the way over. The net result was one very drunk, singing Welshman, who had to be bundled into Shelley Winters's car. He suddenly grabbed hold of the steering-wheel as they drove into the Chaplins' drive, with the result that the vehicle ended up in the middle of the tennis court.

Initially, Charlie Chaplin played the courteous host and even charmingly sent off a telegram to Caitlin in Laugharne when Dylan said that she (and the rest of the town) would never believe he had been with Charlie Chaplin. But Chaplin's good humour quickly turned sour as he realized just how sozzled Dylan was. According to Shelley Winters, she sat on Dylan's lap for a while in the hopes of restraining him from creating too much havoc among the other guests, who included Greta Garbo, Lotte Lenya, Marlene Dietrich and Thomas Mann. However, when Charlie Chaplin's son started singing a song that his father was playing at the piano, Dylan pushed Shelley Winters off on to the floor, took hold of Charlie Junior's hands and started dancing round the room with him. Charlie Senior abruptly stopped playing, knocked Dylan's hands away from his son and hissed: 'Even great poetry cannot excuse such rude, drunken behaviour.' Summoning up as much dignity as he could muster, Dylan made his way out of the house, peeing into one of the potted plants as he left.

Despite all the home hospitality Dylan received in America and the fact that he was usually getting at least $100 for each reading he gave, plus expenses, it became obvious when he returned to New York on 24 April that this trip to the land of the pot of gold was not going to be the great money-spinner he had hoped for. John Malcolm Brinnin had tried in vain to persuade Dylan to allow him to transfer most of his earnings to a bank in Carmarthen, and to aim to live on a reasonable allowance, but Dylan insisted on receiving his fees and expenses in cash or cashable cheques instead, so that he could use the money as he wished. He did send a number of small cheques to Caitlin in Laugharne, none of which appears to have been for more than $50. He also despatched nylon stockings to her and to his friend Ivy Williams at Brown's Hotel, as well as sweets to Llewellyn at Magdalen College School. He caused great offence in his son's case by failing to enclose any note with the present. Brinnin realized with a sense of growing despair that far from returning to Britain with $3,000 or more, as he had originally calculated, Dylan was likely to have nothing at all left, given the rate at which the money was slipping through his fingers.

Typically, Dylan began to blame Brinnin for this, rather than his own carelessness. He accused Brinnin of having failed to arrange sufficiently generous expenses to cover all his air and rail travel adequately. He also criticized him for allegedly not organizing enough profitable engagements for the final part of the tour, although in fact his diary for the three and a half weeks from his arrival back in New York included no fewer than fourteen readings, eight of which were outside the State of New York, in places as varied as Gainesville, Florida, Ann Arbor, Michigan and Bloomington, Indiana. Brinnin's last failing, according to Dylan, was not arranging for him to get away from America as early as he should. But this too was Dylan's own fault, as he insisted on returning to

Europe by ship, and no passage was available on the *Queen Elizabeth* until the end of May.

In order to get a sailing permit, Dylan had to get clearance from the US tax authorities. Brinnin accompanied him, of course, and derived considerable satisfaction from being able to produce the immaculate accounts he had been keeping during Dylan's stay in America and negotiating a lower amount of tax to be paid than he had feared. Despite the bad vibes he was starting to feel from Dylan, Brinnin at least felt vindicated.

Meanwhile, Dylan was enjoying himself in New York, for all his protestations in letters to Caitlin that he was homesick. He was staying at the Hotel Earle in Waverly Place, on Washington Square, which was much cheaper than the grander accommodation he had had at the outset of his visit. It was also very convenient for the bars and restaurants of Greenwich Village that he liked so much. He was still getting invited to lots of parties and he was being made to feel loved and wanted in other ways. For example, after a reading of extracts from *Portrait of the Artist as a Young Dog* at the Kaufmann Auditorium in New York on 15 May – the only such prose reading Dylan gave on this tour – John Malcolm Brinnin was contacted by the popular writer Anita Loos asking whether Dylan would be interested in appearing in a leading role in a new comedy by Garson Kanin, *The Rat Race*, which was due to open on Broadway in the autumn. It was hardly a feasible suggestion, but the idea of being a well-paid New York actor certainly had its attractions.

Dylan also took advantage of his last few weeks in New York to have a couple of affairs with women. One of them, at least, was serious. 'Pearl' was a highly intelligent lady who had gone on from teaching at a top women's college to become a powerful figure in the world of magazine publishing. It is highly likely that she first met Dylan through her job, as he was trying to get a number of commissions for pieces in American magazines. Indeed, he sold a reworked version of his childhood Christmas memories to *Harper's Bazaar* for $300. Dylan and 'Pearl' could only have seen each other a few times in the last fortnight or so that Dylan was in New York, but she had long been an admirer of his poetry and their affair seems to have been intense. For once it was far more than just a case of Dylan allowing an interested female to mother him, or of accepting a convenient bed for the night.

'Pearl' saw Dylan off when he sailed on the *Queen Elizabeth* at midnight on 3 May, as did John Malcolm Brinnin. Brinnin himself was feeling rather emotional about Dylan's departure. Though one part of him was relieved at having such a difficult charge off his hands, he also felt a great sense of personal loss. He had the satisfaction of knowing that he had secreted $800 in cash in a leather handbag that he had given Dylan to take back as a present for Caitlin, which would be a welcome surprise. But like many of Dylan's new friends in America, Brinnin wondered just how the errant poet was going to survive.

Caitlin was in London to welcome Dylan. She insisted that they stay on in the capital for a few days, as she needed a break away from the numbing domestic existence at Laugharne. Dylan, in contrast, was tired, even after his leisurely journey across the Atlantic, and he thought only of getting home. His reunion with Caitlin was passionate and he was genuinely pleased to see Aeronwy and Colm after such a long break. Yet home life in Laugharne was far from the idyll that he had romanticized about in his letters home while he had been away. His old ambivalence to his native land soon resurfaced. By mid-July he was writing to two friends he had made at the University of Nôtre Dame in Indiana of 'this arsehole of the universe, this hymnal blob, this pretty, sick, sad, fond Wales'.[16]

One cause of Dylan's renewed dissatisfaction was the return to a life of worry over money. The $800 Brinnin had put in Caitlin's bag were immediately used up paying off outstanding debts. New bills quickly accumulated. Moreover, Dylan once more seemed incapable of taking advantage of the money-earning opportunities available. He failed to deliver articles requested by magazines such as *Vogue*, or to write up his American experiences for British outlets. Between his return to Britain and the end of 1950, he made only seven recordings and broadcasts for the BBC.

There was one magical afternoon that summer when worries were put to one side. Alfred Janes and his wife drove Dylan and Caitlin over to Pennard to visit Vernon and Gwen Watkins. Daniel Jones and his wife joined them, then everyone went for a long walk along the cliffs. Caitlin and the others were keen to have a swim, but Dylan suddenly threw himself down on the grass, saying he couldn't walk any more. Gwen Watkins felt she had to stay with him, so she took him back home to her garden, where they sat on the lawn talking. Revived by a glass of lager, Dylan switched into brilliant form, recounting the terrors and fascinations of America, and how embarrassed he had felt about his teeth in such a country of perfect smiles. They quoted favourite bits of Dickens to each other. When the others returned from the beach, Dylan and Dan Jones, like in the old Swansea days, put on an impromptu dramatic entertainment, in which Dan played the role of an Egyptian Pharaoh, mummified in an old zinc bath stood upright on its flat end. Dylan was an Egyptologist exploring the tomb. Vernon Watkins was roped in as a grave-robber and when he appeared on the scene, the mummified Pharaoh Dan arose from the dead. Later, Dylan scoffed a high tea of prawns, ice-cream and chocolate biscuits, and squealed like a delighted child when he was pushed higher and higher on a swing in the garden. It was the last time Gwen Watkins saw him alive, and it was one of the last truly happy days he spent with Caitlin.[17]

Caitlin had her suspicions about what Dylan had got up to with other women in America, though she did not know how seriously to take his pub stories about being set upon by nymphomaniacs from coast to coast. One day, however, while she was going through the pockets of one of Dylan's jackets, in the hope of finding some money, she came across some love letters from 'Pearl' instead. These sent her into a wild fury of jealousy. When Dylan came home from drinking at Brown's Hotel, Caitlin confronted him with the evidence of his infidelity, but he shrugged it off, saying all women were like that in America. Caitlin wrote a vituperative letter to 'Pearl', telling her to leave her husband alone.

Early in September, Dylan travelled up to London to see John Malcolm Brinnin, who had come over on a brief holiday. While he was away, Caitlin got a phone call at The Boat House from Margaret Taylor, who said she had to come to Laugharne to see Caitlin at once. A few hours later, Margaret arrived by taxi from Carmarthen station, put her arms round Caitlin and followed her down into the kitchen. There Margaret told her that 'Pearl' had turned up in London and Dylan was taking her round all the pubs he habitually frequented, introducing her to his friends. Margaret described her as 'dark-haired, with dangling, jingling bracelets'[18] and insisted that she was a real threat. 'Pearl' had invited Dylan to go away with her to France, Margaret reported, but Dylan had declined.

According to John Malcolm Brinnin, Dylan, 'Pearl' and he went on a Thames river trip to Greenwich, where Dylan told Brinnin he was in a terrible dilemma because he loved both 'Pearl' and his wife. But Margaret Taylor seems to have successfully put a stop to the affair by somehow intercepting the letters 'Pearl' sent to Dylan care of the Savage Club in London.

Caitlin recorded in her memoirs that she would have been capable of knifing 'Pearl' or strangling her if she had met her, but she resisted the temptation to rush off to London to have a showdown with Dylan and instead waited until he came back to Laugharne. They had a terrible fight that night, of a kind that would become a regular occurrence, with Caitlin pummelling Dylan with her fists on the floor, until sometimes he would pass out. In bed, later, they would make up and be tender to each other, but Caitlin knew their relationship could never be the same again.[19]

One night, during one of these fights, Caitlin snatched up the manuscript of a poem that Dylan had just finished polishing, 'In the White Giant's Thigh', and tore it to pieces, throwing them out of the window. When her temper had abated, though, she began feeling terribly guilty, and shortly before dawn crept out in her nightdress on to the mudflats of the estuary and gathered up the pieces of manuscript that had not yet been swept away by the tide, then laid them out on the kitchen table in repentance.

Dylan read 'In the White Giant's Thigh' on the BBC Third Programme (along with 'Over Sir John's Hill' and 'In Country Sleep') on 25 September. He also interested the BBC producer Douglas Cleverdon in a project that had been turning over in his mind for several years: a radio play, provisionally entitled *The Town That Was Mad*, which would evolve into *Under Milk Wood*. Dylan sent Cleverdon almost forty pages of a draft script towards the end of 1950. He also confidently wrote to Princess Caetani that he was hoping to finish the play in the New Year. As she was always keen to have material for her magazine, he promised he would send it to her when it was ready. In return she would send some money as an advance.

As so often, though, Dylan's concentration was broken by the pressure of creditors at his door. Once again he approached the Royal Literary Fund for a grant to see him through. Thanks largely to the efforts of the writer and politician Harold Nicolson,

Dylan was successful again, being awarded £300. In his letter of support for the application, Harold Nicolson told the Secretary of the Fund that he was aware that Dylan was a heavy drinker and that his wife was 'equally unreliable'.[20] The Fund seems not to have paid the money directly to the Thomases, fearing that it might be swallowed down in drink. Instead, almost half was sent directly to Magdalen College School, to pay Llewellyn's outstanding school fees, £18 went to Aeronwy's school, £15 to the Savage Club, and £50 to the Laugharne Pharmacy, which supplied The Boat House not only with medicines but also with booze.[21]

Dylan got what at first appeared to be a welcome respite from domestic pressures in January 1951, when the film producer 'Bunny' Keene took him to Persia to work on a documentary film sponsored by Anglo-Iranian Oil (a precursor of BP). Dylan was contracted by Green Films, for a fee of £250 plus expenses, to do the script for a propaganda piece which would highlight the great advantages British enterprise was bringing to Iran. He was in the country for about five weeks, first in the capital Teheran and then in Abadan and Isfahan.

Dylan thought Teheran ugly, dirty and noisy and full of disease. The poverty he encountered upset him, as did the horrible British oil-men who were forever running down the 'wops' in their conversation. He wrote to Caitlin about seeing a local man pissing into the gutter and then cupping his hands a few yards further down the road and drinking water from the same drain. Only in the big hotels or the company guesthouses could Dylan get an alcoholic drink – and beer was an outrageous 6 shillings a bottle. In a hospital in Teheran, Dylan saw wide-eyed, malnourished children, with bloated bellies, matchstick arms and blue, wrinkled flesh. One child had an arm and all his toes missing, having fallen into the fire at home while his mother went out begging.

Abadan was better, Dylan told Caitlin, with its balmy winter weather, tall palm trees and buzzards circling overhead. When crowds of bright-eyed, smiling children came running up, asking for pieces of bread or sweets or a coin, he happily handed over his lunch, which was gobbled up in seconds. To 'Pearl', Dylan wrote more surreally of young British oil-men allegedly going crazy from the heat and lack of sex, howling in the night like maddened jackals. In the next room to his, Dylan claimed, the Egyptian Deputy Minister of Education was galumphing drunkenly with a thin, hairy secretary, while under his own bed, pleading dervishes lay.[22]

There was no such frivolity in Dylan's last letter to his wife from Iran, in response to a curt missive from Caitlin informing him that as far as she was concerned the marriage was finished. He replied that he wanted to die. He was wandering round Isfahan in 'a kind of dumb, blind despair', or sitting in his room 'in a strange town in a benighted country, crying like a fool'.[23] He assumed now that she would not be in London to meet him when he returned in mid-February, but he begged her that this should not be the end.

12

BEAST, ANGEL, MADMAN

(1951–1952)

While Dylan was in Persia, Caitlin thought of leaving Laugharne and going back to live with her mother. Yet to do so would have meant accepting a humiliating defeat. She had no money with which she could have made a clean break on her own. Nor did she want to go off with another man. Yet she had started retaliating against Dylan's infidelity and long absences by sometimes taking men home from Brown's Hotel bar, just for an hour or so, while Dylan was away.[1] When Ivy Williams told Dylan this was going on, he refused to believe it. The truth was that for all the pain and disappointment Caitlin felt, she needed Dylan, just as he needed her. He called her his 'cattle-anchor'. His sanity and creativity depended as much on the essential stability of his marital life – with all its rows and fights and debt-drudgery – as on the freedom to perform, to travel and to commit all the sins condemned by his Welsh Non-conformist ancestry.

Consequently, Caitlin had not moved out after all by the time Dylan returned to Laugharne from Teheran and there was a reconciliation of sorts. In the weeks that followed his Iranian visit, Caitlin became pregnant for the fourth time. Dylan settled back into his routine of morning chats with Ivy Williams, daily visits to his parents over the road at Pelican, and afternoons spent in the workshed. After she had got Aeronwy ready for school, Caitlin would go up to the shed early on the winter mornings to light its little coal-fired stove for Dylan. She prepared his meals at The Boat House, which he usually ate alone, to be away from the children. He would push the food into his mouth with one hand and use the other to hold up comics or detective novels or copies of the *New Yorker* which friends in America sent over for him to read.

A new source of irritation for Caitlin was provided by frequent telephone calls at all times of the day and night from another lady admirer of Dylan's who had appeared on the scene: Marged Howard-Stepney. She was a cousin of Frances Hughes, and it was probably through Frances and Richard Hughes that she met Dylan. One year older than him, Marged was the only daughter of Sir Stafford Howard and his Carmarthenshire heiress wife Catherine Stepney, from whom Marged inherited large estates. Impulsive and attractive, in a rather upper-class way, she lived in a substantial house in Llanelli and had had two broken marriages. As her son put it later, she became a saviour of lost souls.[2] Marged had a huge capacity for alcohol, and tended to travel around with a case of gin in the boot of her car. On one occasion when she stayed at The Boat House, she brought the bottles in with her and stored them under the bed, so they would be within easy reach. She also had a minder, who tried to prevent her from doing herself any serious harm. Much of her money was tied up in trusts, in the hope that this would stop her spending or giving it all away.

Marged Howard-Stepney never became as hopelessly infatuated with Dylan as Margaret Taylor, who bought a holiday cottage in Laugharne in the spring of 1951 so that she could see more of her idol. But Marged did fulfil a similar role to Margaret's as a faithful patroness of Dylan and his household for the last three years of his life. Caitlin would lie in bed, fuming inwardly, as she heard Dylan murmuring into the telephone downstairs when Marged rang. As with all his sponsors, Dylan was prepared to butter Marged up to keep the contributions flowing. Caitlin did not think there was anything sexual going on between Dylan and Marged, but none the less she felt marginalized and abused by their relationship. On one occasion, when the Thomases had been invited to dinner at the big house in Llanelli, Caitlin became so exasperated at being ignored as her husband and Marged sat huddled together, in deep conversation, that she seized a torch from the mantelpiece and hit

Dylan over the head with it as hard as she could, knocking him out. Marged screamed: 'My God! You may have killed him! Don't you realize he's a genius?'[3]

Thanks partly to the encouragement of such friends, and Caitlin's own bizarre brand of domestic support, Dylan wrote two important poems in 1951. The first, 'Lament', is suffused with the bitterness of a dying poet whose life and sexual energy are spent; Dylan himself referred to it as 'coarse and violent'.[4] Its power stems from the poet's evocation of frustration and disgust. One of Dylan's most explicit poems, it leaves the listener or reader feeling deeply uneasy.

The second poem, 'Do Not Go Gentle into That Good Night', is charged with a different and even more unsettling anger: rage in the face of imminent death. Though he rarely let such emotions show, Dylan was deeply distressed by the slow, ugly disintegration of his father, D. J., to whose ailments had been added heart trouble. The poem is in many ways a rebuke to the God in whom D. J. did not believe for the sordid cruelty of mortality, as well as an encouragement to D. J. not to lose his fire in this final days. Perfect in its brevity and the unity of its thought, 'Do Not Go Gentle into That Good Night' is for many people, including the present author, Dylan's most memorable work.

At the end of April, Swansea University College English Society invited Dylan to give a reading at the Students' Union – the first time he had performed on his home territory since the infamous evening in 1934 when he had behaved so extravagantly at the John O'London's literary group. Among the audience was the young university lecturer and future novelist Kingsley Amis. One of Amis's pupils was the Secretary of the English Society and he invited Amis to join a small party with Dylan in a local pub before the reading. Dylan was already sitting there, with a pint of light ale on the table in front of him. He was rather balefully making conversation with half a dozen students, and trying out some of his scatological limericks on them. He turned to Amis and slowly declaimed a well-practised epigram: 'I've just come back from Persia, where I've been pouring water on troubled oil.'[5]

Dylan filled his pockets with bottles of beer before heading up the hill with his entourage for the reading. About fifty people had gathered in a scruffy basement room, which was normally used for ping-pong. As Amis recalled six years later, in an article in the

Spectator, the event started badly. Dylan pulled out a dog-eared manuscript that had served him on his American tour and cracked one of the little jokes that had raised a laugh on the other side of the Atlantic: 'I can't manage a proper talk. I might just manage an improper one.' The Swansea students responded to this opening with a stony silence and a few of them exchanged apprehensive looks. Things improved when Dylan started reading the poems; Amis particularly recalled Auden's 'The Unknown Citizen' and Dylan's own 'Fern Hill'. Amis acknowledged that Dylan's voice was magnificent, but he felt that some of his lengthy pauses were shamelessly overdone, not least in his rendition of Yeats.

Back at the pub afterwards, Dylan was morose. He had been rattled by some of the students' questions, which he felt were designed to turn him into an Aunt Sally. Various people claiming friendship with Dylan prior to his becoming famous hogged the limelight in the bar, so that the students who were genuinely interested in talking to their guest quickly drifted away. He complained later that they had abandoned him.

Dylan perked up considerably when he learned that John Malcolm Brinnin was going to make a second visit to Europe, this time in the company of his friend Bill Read. For all his criticisms of Brinnin, Dylan knew that he was the key to America as far as he was concerned. Having forgotten, or conveniently pushed aside, his supposed dislike for so much about the United States, Dylan was now keen to get back there. He was also hopeful that on a second visit he would be able to retain more of the money he earned, especially if Caitlin were with him.

Brinnin and Bill Read arrived in Britain in July. In Cardiff, Brinnin arranged with Aneirin Talfan Davies at the BBC Welsh Home Service to write a talk on Dylan, which he would put together in Laugharne. Brinnin and Read then took the train to Carmarthen, where Dylan was waiting for them with Billy Williams's taxi. To Brinnin's surprise, Dylan was looking smart in a new tweed suit and a rakishly angled cap. He was smoking a cigar with all the nonchalance of a country host welcoming visitors down for the weekend. The 13 miles or so to Laugharne took well over two hours, as they stopped at more than half a dozen pubs on the way. The last was The Cross House in Laugharne itself, where Dylan had arranged for Caitlin to join them.

Nothing Dylan had told Brinnin about Caitlin in America had prepared him for her wild beauty. He was fascinated by her, but he sensed considerable suspicion on her part. This may have been partly because she was convinced (as she tended to be with all Dylan's admirers) that Brinnin was in love with her husband. However, her wariness also reflected her conviction that America and Americans could fatally corrupt Dylan.

The following day, Dylan took Brinnin and Read to see Laugharne Castle and introduced them to Ivy Williams at Brown's Hotel. They sat listening to Ivy's tales and playing nap while Dylan popped over to see Florence and D. J. before finalizing arrangements for an excursion around West Wales that afternoon in Billy Williams's taxi. When Billy came to pick them up, Dylan sat in the front with him, while Caitlin went into the back with the two visitors. As they drove down narrow country lanes Caitlin started quizzing Brinnin about 'Pearl': what she was like, whether she was still in touch with Dylan, and if she had any plans to come back to Britain. Acutely embarrassed, Brinnin tried to change the subject, but Caitlin kept coming back to it, like a cat worrying a mouse. Finally, he gave her a few anodyne details about her rival, but he could see she was not satisfied.

There was some forced gaiety during the afternoon, notably at St David's Head, where, for the benefit of Bill Read's camera, Dylan marched up and down the ruins of a monastery in a grotesque imitation of Mussolini. But the atmosphere in the car got more thunderous as Dylan insisted that they press on ever further to Fishguard, where they could have a magnificent lobster dinner. This itself proved to be something of a wash-out, as they were the only customers in the restaurant, which had only one lobster left to share between them. Hardly a word was spoken over the meal. Dylan fell fast asleep in the car on the journey home and it was past eleven when the by now thoroughly miserable little party got back to The Boat House. As Caitlin swept past John Malcolm Brinnin on the stairs she said angrily, 'Now you can see what I mean. America is out!'[6] Brinnin and Bill Read wondered if it wouldn't be better if they left immediately, but as there was nowhere they could go so late at night, they had no choice but to stay.

The morning brought a totally different mood, as Caitlin gaily cooked a fish breakfast on the house's deck and called to the two

Americans to come down and eat. Dylan said Brinnin could use the workshed to write his BBC script, which gave the visitor ample opportunity to note its contents. At this time these included portraits of Walt Whitman, Marianne Moore and Edith Sitwell, and a Cartier-Bresson photograph of a Mexican mother and child. The floor of the workshed was littered with rolled-up pieces of discarded worksheets, old cigarette packets, unanswered letters, tradesmen's bills and empty beer bottles.

At dinner that evening, in the tiny dining-room of The Boat House, the conversation turned to sex-fiends and brutal murders. Dylan relished recounting all the gory details of a man who had disembowelled a young virgin and then rearranged her entrails in fancy patterns. As the conversation progressed, however, Caitlin started contesting many of the things Dylan was saying. Suddenly, he flicked an empty matchbox that he had been holding in his hand in her direction; she picked it up and threw it straight at his face. Then she grabbed his hair and pulled him from his chair down on to the floor. As Brinnin and Read looked on helplessly, dishes were knocked from the table and chairs crashed over as their hosts fought like cat and dog. Finally Dylan broke away and fled upstairs. For the next hour Caitlin poured out all her grievances against Dylan and America to her house-guests.

Yet the following morning everything was calm once more. Brinnin finished off his radio script in the workshed while Dylan stayed in the house studying the racing results in the newspaper. When Brinnin's rather pretentious and flattering piece on Dylan was completed, he read it out loud to everyone at the house. At the end Dylan looked up and declared in the tones of someone reading a newspaper headline: 'Randy-dandy Curly-girly Poet Leaps into Sea from Overdose of Praise', and then made as if to throw himself over the sea wall.[7]

Whatever Dylan thought of the quality of Brinnin's piece, he must have been envious of the facility with which it was written. Apart from a short broadcast on the Festival of Britain, which Dylan recorded for Aneirin Talfan Davies in Cardiff on 5 June, he completed no work at all for the BBC between late April and the beginning of November. Nor was the BBC prepared to advance him money on any of the projects he suggested. From now on, the arrangement would be strictly cash on delivery.

Dylan wrote frantic notes to various friends and patrons, claiming that the pressure of debt would once again oblige him to flee the creditors of Laugharne. A few, including T. S. Eliot, took pity and paid up. In at least one case, Dylan said he would have to sell The Boat House, though in fact it was not his to dispose of, as it still belonged to Margaret Taylor. She, meanwhile, was searching for a new house in London, with the express purpose of giving Dylan and Caitlin a home-base there. Dylan would joke with those friends from whom he was not trying to extract any money that he would soon, in true gentleman's style, have a town and a country residence.

Once John Malcolm Brinnin was back in the United States, plans began to crystallize for Dylan's second reading tour in America, which would start in late January 1952. Caitlin made up her mind definitely that she did want to go as well, but as the new baby grew inside her, she realized that it could get in the way. As she did not really want another child anyway, she decided to have it aborted. She discovered that this could be done quite easily, and legally, in London, for a fee of £100. This she acquired from Marged Howard-Stepney, despite the fact that Marged tried repeatedly to persuade her to keep the child. Dylan did not express any opinion either way. He travelled with Caitlin to London for the abortion and made sure she got safely to the clinic. Then he disappeared exactly as he had done with her other pregnancies.

In her memoirs, Caitlin went into gruesome detail about this first abortion of hers. She had drunk a great deal of whisky beforehand, but she was only given a local anaesthetic at the clinic and therefore remained fully conscious throughout. As the foetus was about six months old, it was already well developed and had to be cut into chunks before it could be extracted. The nurses refused to answer when Caitlin asked them whether it was a girl, as she had hoped it would be when she thought she was going to have the baby. Far from emerging upset from this ordeal, however, Caitlin left the clinic feeling 'strong and positively gay'.[8]

Not that the rows with Dylan abated. In October, Elisabeth Lutyens, the composer, came to stay with the Thomases at Laugharne and witnessed another instance of Caitlin ripping up one of Dylan's manuscripts, this time in front of him. He merely chuckled and said he had plenty of other copies. But the atmosphere then disintegrated so rapidly that he took himself off to Swansea, saying he was leaving for good. From there he phoned home to say he was going to commit suicide. Caitlin summoned Billy Williams, who drove her and Lizzie Lutyens to Swansea, where they found Dylan roaring drunk in a pub. Caitlin and he had another blazing argument and she went for him with her fists flying. Lizzie Lutyens dodged to the sidelines, while Dylan whined and grovelled on the floor as Caitlin pummelled him. Later she said she would happily have killed him.[9] When they all got back to The Boat House, they found little Colm, who was not yet three years old, wandering around the house on his own. Then Caitlin felt guilty.

The resilience of both Dylan and Caitlin was remarkable. It was as if they had come to feed off their violent confrontations. In the calm between the storms, Dylan got on with his radio play, which he had now retitled *Llareggub*, resurrecting the joke-name of his adolescence. The play focused on the comic side to the foibles of the people (real and imaginary) of a community closely based on Laugharne. Dylan told a number of friends, including John Malcolm Brinnin, that from now on he only wanted to write happy things. It is clear from a letter he wrote to Princess Caetani in October, asking for money to enable him to continue with the project, that the nature and shape of what was to become *Under Milk Wood* were now very clear, although he had only written the opening scenes. Princess Caetani sent him £100.

One of the reasons why Dylan had been unable to give the play his full creative attention was that he had been finishing a new poem called 'Poem on His Birthday'. This would be the last complete free-standing poem he wrote. In it the poet (all of thirty-seven) approaches death singing the praises of the natural world. Aneirin Talfan Davies and several other critics saw this as yet another example of Dylan's growing religious sensibility. Oscar Williams, who was still faithfully fulfilling his role as an unofficial, unpaid literary agent in America, placed 'Poem on His Birthday' with the *Atlantic* magazine for the unusually large fee of $200.

By the end of the month, Dylan and Caitlin were able to take possession of the basement flat in the new London house that Margaret Taylor had bought at 54 Delancey Street in Camden Town. The gypsy caravan that Dylan had used as a workroom at South Leigh was brought up to London and parked in the garden. There was no real chance to settle in, however, as arrangements for going to America took up most of Dylan's time. David Higham (whom Caitlin had dubbed 'the lavatory brush' because of his thick, bristly hair and beard) succeeded in negotiating a contract for Dylan with the publishers Allan Wingate for a 60,000-word American travel diary. This was meant to be delivered by the end of June 1952, and Dylan was given £100 as a partial advance on signature. The book was never written.

Over the other side of the Atlantic, John Malcolm Brinnin was working hard organizing another busy schedule of readings, which this time would include a much wider range of English literature, from Shakespeare on. There was a last-minute panic when it looked as if the American Embassy might refuse to grant Dylan a visa, because of the trip he had made to Czechoslovakia in 1949, even though he had been to the United States in the interim. But on 15 January 1952, having left Aeronwy in Margaret Taylor's care, and Colm with Dolly Long, the daily help who looked after The Boat House in Laugharne, the Thomases boarded the *Queen Mary* bound for New York.

Five days later, Brinnin was waiting for them on the quayside, with a box of Dylan's favourite cigars, gardenias for Caitlin and a tiny square of symbolic red carpet. He drove them out of the city to Millbrook, New York, for a couple of days' break at the home of the photographer Rollie McKenna. There Dylan ignored the biting winter wind and obediently posed among the tortured bare branches of a climbing vine as Rollie McKenna took a series of deeply unsettling pictures in which he looks in deep anguish. On the second evening, two old friends of the photographer's, a married couple who were both university professors, came by for dinner. During the meal, Caitlin interrupted many of Dylan's stories, correcting him or capping his remarks. When the male professor started answering a serious query from Dylan about the rest of the teaching staff at his college, Caitlin butted in: 'And are they all stuffed shirts like yourself?'[10] This set the tone for her stay in America.

After a couple of nights at the Hotel Earle in New York, Dylan and Caitlin moved into a one-room kitchenette apartment in the Hotel Chelsea. This was an old-fashioned building on West 23rd Street at Seventh Avenue that was popular with bohemian writers and artists because of its moderate prices and the management's tolerant attitude. It was convenient for the bars in Greenwich Village that Dylan liked to patronize, notably The White Horse

Tavern on Hudson Street. This was run by an elderly German and was the nearest thing to a British pub Dylan ever found in America. He became as faithful to it as he was to Brown's Hotel in Laugharne, and friends and acquaintances in New York who wanted to track him down would often start by looking for him there. After his death, The White Horse Tavern became a major stop on the Dylan Thomas trail for the thousands of fans who wanted to have a beer in a place where the poet had got drunk.

According to Caitlin, he would go off to The White Horse early in the morning for light ale, while she explored the city's big department stores. All good intentions about being careful with money evaporated when she saw the vast array of clothes and other desirable goods on offer. John Malcolm Brinnin, who was acting as banker for the Thomases, very quickly became alarmed at their joint capacity to spend. On a single day, Caitlin bought $400-worth of clothes and presents. Soon Brinnin found himself having to borrow money to satisfy their demands. This particularly rankled as he knew that Dylan was earning two or three times his own salary.

Apart from very brief side trips to Washington, Burlington, Vermont and Montreal, Dylan spent the whole of February giving readings in and around New York in such venues as the Museum of Modern Art, Columbia University, New York University and the YM & YWHA Poetry Center. The Thomases were taken up in a big way by the more social elements of New York's literary society, which meant that they usually had one or two parties every night, as well as brunches, lunches and dinners. These were usually accompanied by large amounts of alcohol, Caitlin's favourite tipple being rye. She acquired several new friends of her own, notably Rose Slivka, the wife of the sculptor David Slivka. Caitlin would go off to the ballet with Rose or spend hours gossiping and wandering the streets. But when she was with Dylan she was frequently cantankerous. At his readings she would ridicule the adulation he received, especially when it came from young girls. At parties she was constantly putting him down.

Brinnin sat in on a bizarre example of the Thomases' continual low-level warfare when a young lady from *Time* magazine took the three of them out for lunch. Dylan had oysters and whisky. The journalist wanted to interview him for the magazine's book pages, as New Directions was about to bring out a tiny volume of the six major poems he had written since 1946. Each serious question she put was parried by Dylan with a flippant remark or a blatant untruth, until Caitlin started contradicting him and angrily telling him to stop fooling around. As the journalist became more and more bewildered, Brinnin hid his head in a railway timetable, wondering what on earth she would write. The more the Thomases drank, the louder their arguments got, until other diners in the restaurant started glaring at them because of the noise. The journalist eventually abandoned the interview. At least on this occasion no one got hit. At one New York evening party in the Thomases' honour, which was again witnessed by Brinnin, an hysterical hostess was left surveying the wreckage of broken glasses, overturned tables, smashed *objets d'art* and a hole in her bedroom wall.[11]

In Cambridge, Massachusetts, early in March, Dylan had an appointment with a wealthy young woman patron of the arts whom he was hoping to touch for $1,000. Although he was receiving generous payment for most of his speaking engagements, he needed a lump sum to send to England as Llewelyn's school fees were overdue and Magdalen College School was getting impatient. The potential benefactor invited Dylan to lunch at the Ritz Hotel. Caitlin timed a walk round town with John Malcolm Brinnin's mother – who had become another good friend – so that she would be able to spy on the lunch to see what her husband was up to. Caitlin seems to have taken a particular dislike to the woman concerned because she had reportedly told Dylan that he ought to stop drinking. According to Caitlin's memoirs, when she got to the hotel she found Dylan almost huddled over the lunch table, listening attentively to everything the woman was saying. Enraged, Caitlin went for her calling her a 'bloody bitch' and telling her to 'bugger off'.[12] When Dylan remonstrated with Caitlin later that she had just lost them $1,000, she said she didn't care and that she would do it again.

Brinnin was relieved to see the Thomases off the following week, as they left for Pennsylvania, Arizona and California. He gave them their tickets through to San Francisco and $400 in cash to tide them over until they got to the coast. Just four days later he received a frantic telegram saying they had already spent the lot and needed more money urgently. In the meantime, they were stuck at the Arizona home of the painters Max Ernst and Dorothea

Tanning who, Caitlin claimed, had such a reputation for stinginess that for once she and Dylan did not dare ask their hosts to bail them out. More charitably, in a letter to John Malcolm Brinnin, Dylan reported that Max Ernst and his wife were 'lovely, charming and hospitable', but broke.[13]

The Thomases also stayed with Ruth Witt-Diamant in San Francisco. A letter from Magdalen College School was waiting for them at her house. This stated that unless Dylan sent £100 immediately, they would be unable to keep the boy at the school. As Dylan had apparently told Caitlin before leaving England that he had made arrangements for Llewelyn's fees to be paid while they were away, she was furious. Dylan calmed her down by saying that he would arrange for David Higham to send the school some money straight away.

The sort of pressure Dylan was under on this North American trip was graphically illustrated in Vancouver, in the second week of April. A group of local newspaper reporters attended one of his readings there and wanted to get him photographed as drunk as possible, knowing that this would make a good story. They tipped the waiters at a function after the reading to set up a table in another room, and to cover it with dozens of full glasses of beer. Dylan was then lured into the room on the false pretence that he was wanted on the telephone. The cameras started clicking as soon as he was standing in front of the backdrop the photographers wanted. It didn't take much persuasion to get him to pose with a glass in his hand. Then the press gang urged him on to drink as many of the glasses as he could, as the photographers' bulbs continued to flash.[14] Dylan was incapable of turning down even such cynical hospitality, just as the passive side of his nature made him easy prey for the female poetry 'groupies' in North America who talked their way into his company or his bed. Sometimes in the mornings he could stand back and see the shallowness and danger of fitting into the pattern of his own growing legend, but in the evenings, tired from a reading and softened by drink, he found it difficult not to succumb.

It had been Dylan's vulnerability that originally attracted Caitlin, blended as it was with humour and a rare talent with words. Yet that same vulnerability had now grown to exasperate her, as increasingly she felt not protectiveness towards him but pity, even contempt.

By the end of April Dylan was so weary of life on the lecture circuit that he phoned John Malcolm Brinnin saying he wanted to back out of one of his engagements. This was at Tulane University in New Orleans, which was the last stop on his scheduled sweep across the country back to New York. This surprised Brinnin, as he knew that Dylan particularly wanted to see the French quarter in New Orleans, which he imagined he might like as much as San Francisco. More important, Brinnin was worried about the bad publicity that would inevitably be generated by Dylan's cancelling a long-arranged commitment at the last minute.

When Dylan was adamant that he could not go through with the reading, Brinnin insisted that he telephone Tulane University personally to explain his indisposition. Dylan said he would. On the day of the reading, however, Brinnin was summoned to the phone once again. This time it was Tulane University, concerned that they had not had any confirmation of Dylan's arrival. Brinnin's heart sank when he realized that Dylan had not been in touch with them and that he would have to make inadequate excuses on Dylan's behalf instead. Although Dylan was sometimes late for other performances, this was the only occasion that he missed one, in more than 150 different engagements spread over four separate trips to the United States. However, this lapse was sufficient to win him a damning reputation for being unreliable.

Brinnin was dismayed. But he was also angry with himself for assuming that Dylan would be capable of cancelling the New Orleans booking properly. When he next joined up with Dylan, though, on May Day at the Hotel Chelsea in New York, the incident had been completely eclipsed by a new crisis: the arrival of a telegram informing the Thomases that Llewelyn had been sent away from his school because of the non-payment of his fees. One can imagine the humiliation this must have caused the thirteen-year-old boy. It transpired that Dylan had not after all made the necessary arrangements for the money to be sent while he was in San Francisco.

Caitlin exploded, calling Dylan 'a bastard . . . the lowest form of scum, a congenital liar'.[15] She said she was going to leave Dylan for good. She asked John Malcolm Brinnin if he could get her enough money so she could buy a passage to London, as there was no way she was going to stay on in New York. Dylan persuaded Brinnin to go out with him to a bar, where he sat with his head in his hands, unable to speak. Caitlin came by and said she was going out to make her travel arrangements. After an hour or so, Brinnin took Dylan back up to his room at the Chelsea and stayed with him while he slept for a while. When Dylan woke he was curiously revitalized, as if he knew that this was yet another storm in a tea-cup that would soon blow over. He went ahead with an afternoon engagement at the Gotham Book Mart, a famous New York second-hand book-store that was also a centre for literary events. He signed copies of his books and recordings of his work that had recently been made, and chatted amiably with writers and fans present. Brinnin mar-velled at his resilience, but Dylan's optimism was well founded. News of Llewellyn's reinstatement at school, following the des-patch there of the necessary funds, came before Caitlin managed to organize her departure, and so she stayed. When the two of them left on the *Nieuw Amsterdam* on 16 May, however, after a number of further readings on the East Coast and in Washington, Caitlin felt that as far as she was concerned, this visit to America had been a great mistake.

The proofs of Dylan's *Collected Poems 1934–1952* were waiting for him when he got back to Laugharne. His publishers, J. M. Dent, thought the book would consolidate his reputation and open up a new chapter in his career, but they wanted a preface to the volume. Dylan had failed to write this preface while he was in America, despite a cabled offer of an extra £100 if he did. Now he told E. F. Bozman, the editor-in-chief at Dent's, that it would take him about a week to do. But sitting watching cricket at Lord's one day, Dylan got sun-stroke, which turned into pleurisy (or so he said) as June and then July slipped by. His next delaying tactic was to suggest that instead of writing a prose prologue it would be more fitting to do it in verse; E. F. Bozman acquiesced.

Dylan was in London again in the middle of July to record a selection of poems by Theodore Roethke and Robert Lowell for Peter Duval Smith at the BBC Third Programme; some of these had to be re-recorded a fortnight later as they were considered unsatisfactory. In the meantime, Dylan had an urgent summons to meet up with his accountant Leslie Andrews in Carmarthen for a session with Dylan's local Tax Commissioners, who were insisting on taxing him on £1,907 he had earned during his trip to America in 1950. An appeal against this assessment failed. To make matters worse, a few days later a National Insurance inspector called at

The Boat House in Laugharne to draw Dylan's attention to the fact that he had only completed one card of insurance stamps since the National Health scheme began. Unless he paid for just over another £50 worth of stamps by 22 July, he would face prosecution. Dylan turned to his agent David Higham, begging him to save him from a legal case by sending £50 to his bank account in Chelsea.

At the same time, though, Dylan was going behind Higham's back to persuade Douglas Cleverdon at the BBC to arrange direct payment to himself, without any deduction of agent's commission or income tax, for a new project. This was to be a radio programme based on a book of poems called *Spoon River Anthology* by the American Edgar Lee Masters. Though the sum of money involved was relatively small, Dylan felt that in his desperate situation every extra penny would count. Cleverdon, who had enormous faith in Dylan's talent, made the necessary arrangements. According to his recollections of their collaboration, the script for *Spoon River Anthology* was only completed because Dylan was (voluntarily) locked into the BBC Reference Library overnight, away from all distractions and drink.[16]

Cleverdon was especially keen that Dylan should finish his much more ambitious play for voices, *Llareggub*, whose unsteady progress he had been following closely. Princess Caetani had published the first part in the May 1952 issue of *Botteghe Oscure*, but Dylan had then failed to produce more than a few lines of the rest. Cleverdon came up with what he hoped would be an incentive for Dylan to press on by arranging for the BBC to pay him £5 each time he submitted another 3,000 words. Even this proved an insufficient impetus. In October Cleverdon went to Laugharne to stay for a week to try to encourage Dylan to write. Instead, he found himself spending endless hours drinking with the poet in Brown's Hotel. When closing time came and Cleverdon thought they would at last get back to The Boat House for some supper and some work, Dylan would instead wander round to the back of the hotel, knock on the kitchen door and then be invited in by Ivy Williams for a couple more hours' drinking inside. Very little progress on the manuscript was made.

To add to Dylan's worries, Margaret Taylor's finances were running low. For a while, she thought she might have to sell The Boat House, and apparently Marged Howard-Stepney was approached to see if she would be willing to buy it, which would enable the Thomases to remain living there. In the end, though, Margaret Taylor did not need to dispose of it until after Dylan's death.

At about this time, Dylan drafted a begging poem to Marged Howard-Stepney, headed: 'You told me, once, to call on you/When I was beaten down . . . ' In it, Dylan appealed almost romantically to its intended recipient to rescue him in his hour of need. It seems doubtful that the poem was ever sent. Instead, Caitlin found a copy of the draft on the floor of Dylan's workshed. This was cause for yet another grand row, and a grovelling note of apology from Dylan to Caitlin, in which he claimed that the content of the poem was 'foul, sponging lies'. He begged his wife's forgiveness for his 'callous attempt at mock-literature of the slimiest kind'.[17] The two of them alternated between periods of bickering and barely speaking to each other. When Dylan escaped to give readings in North Wales and Gloucester, in order to raise a few pounds, Caitlin complained that he was merely finding ways of avoiding serious work.

It took Dylan nearly four months following his return to Wales to complete his preface to the *Collected Poems*, by which time E. F. Bozman at Dent's was beginning to tear his hair out. None the less, Dent's managed to bring the book out on 10 November, in a first edition of nearly 5,000 copies, as well as a de luxe signed collectors' edition of just 65 copies. Reprints soon had to be ordered, and the book sold over 30,000 copies in hardback in Britain over the next two years.

The *Collected Poems* were dedicated to Caitlin. Apart from the six new poems Dylan had written since 1946, the volume contained all the work that had appeared in his previous three books of verse, with the single exception of 'Paper and Sticks' (from *Deaths and Entrances*), which he had come to hate. The collection was greeted by the critics with all the acclaim due to a major literary event. Philip Toynbee in the *Observer* declared that Dylan was the 'greatest living poet in the English language'. Cyril Connolly in the *Sunday Times* wrote that Dylan at his best was unique, 'for he distils an exquisite, mysterious, moving quality which defies analysis as supreme lyrical poetry always has and – let us hope – always will'. An anonymous reviewer in the *Times Literary Supplement* expressed the opinion that if Shelley was right in claiming that poetry '"creates anew the universe, after it has been annihilated in our

minds by the recurrence of impressions blunted by reiteration",
then Mr Thomas is a poet of poets'. Stephen Spender in the
Spectator hailed Dylan as a 'romantic revolting against a thin
contemporary classical tendency' and said that in his poetry 'the
reader feels very close to what Keats yearned for – a "life of
sensations" without opinions and thoughts'. Dylan wrote to
Spender to thank him for the review, but pulled him up on his
contention that Dylan must have been influenced by Welsh bardic
poetry, pointing out that he could not speak Welsh.

The rapturous welcome given to the *Collected Poems* was a great
comfort to Dylan's father, who was now in great pain and almost
blind. On 15 December, the day before he died at the age of
seventy-six, D. J. suddenly wanted to get up and go into the
kitchen, as he thought his mother was in there cooking onion soup.
Later, his delusion passed and he said simply: 'It's full circle now.'[18]
In those final months of daily contact while Dylan was in Laugharne, he felt closer to his father than at any time in his life. He was
the man who had opened the door to creative literary expression
for Dylan, having failed to walk through it himself. His death was a
bitter blow.

13

THE GATES OF HELL

(1953)

In accordance with D. J.'s wishes, there was no religious funeral service for him. His body was cremated and his ashes were buried alongside those of his brother Arthur, who had died in 1947. Dylan could not bring himself to go into the crematorium, but a friend who did claimed later that he had seen D. J.'s skull crack open in the heat of the furnace. The friend added ghoulishly that they might at that very moment be breathing in particles of D. J. from the smoke coming out of the crematorium chimney. Dylan turned away abruptly and was violently sick. Later he hit the bottle hard.

In contrast, Florence was remarkably self-controlled. Caitlin did not see her cry. In a letter to Charles Fry at the publishers Allan Wingate[1] Dylan described his mother as being a 'permanent invalid' now, for whose care he had the sole responsibility. This was just another pretext, however, for not delivering the contracted travel book on America. In reality, Florence was astonishingly robust, displaying the same talent for survival that had kept her cheerful during the long and difficult years of her marriage to D. J. This was all the more surprising as Florence did not just have D. J.'s death to cope with. Her daughter Nancy was terminally ill with cancer in Bombay, where she was living with her husband

233

Gordon Summersby. Nancy had been in Britain for hospital treatment in the summer of 1952, but she was too ill to travel back again now to mourn her father, even if she had wanted to. She died in India four months later.

Barely a month after D. J.'s cremation, Marged Howard-Stepney was found dead in her London house, kneeling on the floor with her head in a cushion. The autopsy showed that although she had taken an overdose of a sleeping draught, she had died of asphyxiation. The verdict at her inquest was death by misadventure. Dylan took Marged's death as a personal slight. He maintained that she had intended to leave him a substantial amount of money in her will, but there was no written record of this, and her son and heir understandably saw no reason to honour a commitment he could not be sure had ever been made. To Dylan, though, it appeared that the Fates were against him, determined to rob him of the peace of mind that would allow him to write.

To complicate matters, Caitlin was pregnant again. She did not know for certain that Dylan was the father, but she was convinced they could not afford another child. Once more she opted for a termination, which this time was carried out at a friend's house in Hammersmith by a 'back-street' abortionist, who was well known in the Soho pubs. He executed the task by poking around inside Caitlin with a pair of rubber gloves. Dylan told some people that he paid for this second abortion out of the £250 he received for the Foyle's Literary Prize he had just been awarded for his *Collected Poems*. To others he claimed that the money came from a number of BBC radio recordings he did in Swansea in the first six weeks of 1953. But in her memoirs, Caitlin denied that Dylan had paid for the abortion, though she did not reveal who did.[2]

The BBC recordings Dylan made in Swansea were all produced by Aneirin Talfan Davies. They included a reading of poems by Vernon Watkins and a series of four personal verse anthologies, the first of which was broadcast on St David's Day. Dylan put an immense amount of time and effort into these anthologies, spending whole days in Aneirin Talfan Davies's office poring over all the books the producer had brought in from home or which Dylan had brought back with him from America. Occasionally he would phone Vernon Watkins at the bank where he was still working, to get more advice and suggestions.[3] There were six or seven poems in each broadcast, and the choice showed that Dylan's tastes had remained constant in recent years. The poets he selected included W. H. Auden, D. H. Lawrence, Wilfred Owen, Edith Sitwell and Vernon Watkins himself.

A first attempt at recording some of the poems, on 2 and 3 February, had to be abandoned because Dylan's voice broke down. He explained to Aneirin Talfan Davies that he was suffering from flu and bronchitis and he arranged to come back to Swansea the following week to try again. One can never be quite sure what to believe about Dylan's illnesses, not least because he hardly ever went to the family doctor in St Clears, except when his bones were broken. He was not a hypochondriac as such, though he regularly used illness, both real and fictitious, for dramatic effect. There was no doubt, however, that by 1953 he was genuinely suffering quite badly from chest ailments. The cold, damp atmosphere in Laugharne in winter did not help. Dylan would often spend hours in the morning lying in bed coughing and wheezing; nearly thirty years of heavy smoking had taken their toll. His puffy face and sallow skin betrayed his heavy drinking and his eyes showed the signs of someone who seldom had a full night's sleep. By now Dylan rarely slept for three or four hours at a stretch. He would wake up suddenly in the middle of the night, beset with what he tended to refer to as 'the terrors'. Sometimes these were worries over debt, but on occasions they seemed to be a more generalized despair and panic about life.

Dylan had also developed gout. This gave him quite a lot of pain and meant that he could not bear the children bumping into him, an added reason for keeping well away from them. The two older ones, at least, were aware that he found their company irritatingly distracting except when he was in the mood to play with them. Aeronwy considered it especially hurtful that on the rare occasions when the whole family travelled by train Dylan would sit in a carriage on his own, reading a cowboy story or a cheap detective novel, while Caitlin stayed in another with the children.[4]

Towards the end of February 1953 David Higham decided it was time he took even closer control of Dylan's affairs than before, otherwise Dylan might never manage to complete any more work. They had lunch together in London, after which Dylan sent Higham a complete list of all his debts in Laugharne, which he agreed to settle directly out of Dylan's retained earnings. The most substantial of these debts was back rent on Pelican, however, where

Florence was still living. This amounted to £165. The owner of Pelican, however, was Ebie Williams, the landlord of Brown's Hotel, and Dylan thought Ebie wouldn't mind waiting a little longer for most of the outstanding money, if something could be paid on account. Fortunately, Dylan's brother-in-law Gordon Summersby then offered to pay Florence's rent in future, which was one weight off Dylan's mind.

If Higham had not had to retain so much of Dylan's income to pay outstanding debts and back tax, the Thomases would, in theory, have been quite prosperous in 1953. Dylan was certainly earning much more than most British writers, which was why yet another financial appeal on his behalf, launched by Stephen Spender, failed to get a positive response. Instead, money started to come in from the US edition of the *Collected Poems*, which were published in America in March and sold even more copies there than in Britain. Then J. M. Dent in London decided to publish the film-script, *The Doctor and the Devils*, that Dylan had done with Donald Taylor years before. Dent's were also keen to bring out a new book of Dylan's short stories and radio broadcasts. This was intended to include many of the earlier pieces that had never appeared in book form in Britain. Dylan had not kept copies of them, but by a lucky coincidence he had recently been contacted by a man called John Alexander Rolph, who wanted to compile a complete bibliography of Dylan's work. Dylan readily agreed and in return got Rolph's cooperation in tracking down the texts of long-lost stories in magazines. The collection was not ready until after Dylan's death and some of the more daring early stories were in fact removed because they were considered 'too raw' for publication. The report submitted by the publisher's reader denounced 'The Burning Baby' as 'a horrible fantasy'. He thought the 'Prologue to an Adventure' was 'a welter of pornographic filth' and he considered 'The Horse's Ha' 'disgustingly obscene'.[5] Dent's produced two volumes from the remaining material: *Quite Early One Morning* (published in 1954) and *A Prospect of the Sea* (1955).

On 9 April Dylan made his television debut in a programme called 'Home Town: Swansea', which was broadcast live from the BBC TV studios in Cardiff. It was presented by Wynford Vaughan-Thomas and the other participants were Dylan's old chums, Fred Janes, Dan Jones and Vernon Watkins. As Dan Jones recalled in his memoir of Dylan, they were all rather nervous about this new experience and indulged in more than their usual intake of liquid refreshment in one of the Cardiff pubs beforehand.

Rather than have a general discussion among the participants, the producer wanted each of them to speak for a few minutes about his life. Prior to the broadcast, Dylan sat chuckling to himself and scribbling notes on the back of several envelopes, while the others chatted and tried to relax, having decided to talk off the cuff. When the programme began, Fred, Dan and Vernon got through the ordeal reasonably comfortably, and then the camera turned to Dylan, who had been kept till last as the star turn. He sat on the studio table, swinging his legs, and as his swollen face got redder and redder under the studio lights, he launched into a convoluted but amusing tale about a landlady called Mrs Parsnip. Unfortunately, he had not memorized properly whatever it was that he had written on the back of the envelopes, and by some quirk suddenly found himself back at the beginning of his story, which he then started to tell all over again. As Dan Jones recalled: 'The studio manager began to make frantic rotary gestures, but instead of winding up, Dylan wound round. Towards the end of the third repeat, "I had a landlady called Mrs Par . . . " Snip! Dylan's camera light went out.' A wincing announcer then brought the programme to an end.[6]

One reason Dylan may not have prepared adequately for the broadcast was that he was trying to get everything sorted out before leaving for another American tour the following week. This had meant some hurried and intensive work on *Under Milk Wood*, as he was now calling his play for voices, having tried the title out on John Malcolm Brinnin. The idea was that there would be some concert performances of this in the States, as well as his more usual poetry readings.

Caitlin was firmly opposed to this third transatlantic trip, accusing Dylan of wanting to go to America for 'flattery, idleness and infidelity'. Rather feebly he countered that his true motives were 'appreciation, dramatic work and friends'.[7] Caitlin was also worried about his health. It was partly to assuage her fears that Dylan arranged with Brinnin that this time he would only spend six weeks in America, and that he would restrict his travels to the eastern seaboard, Washington and North Carolina. None the less, he hoped to earn enough from the trip to be able to spend most of the winter of 1953–1954 with Caitlin in Portugal, which he had heard was sunny and cheap.

John Malcolm Brinnin was waiting for Dylan on the pier in New York when he sailed in on the SS *United States* on 21 April. Brinnin was relieved to see that he was looking sober and relaxed after five days at sea. Dylan joked that he had been so bored by his fellow-passengers that he had shut himself in his cabin wardrobe one day, for a change of perspective. Brinnin checked him in to the Hotel Chelsea, where he had been allocated a particularly nice room, and the staff were enthusiastic with their welcome. There were similar warm greetings at The White Horse Tavern, where the proprietor sent a bottle of whisky over to their table. Brinnin did not want to spoil the atmosphere by getting down to discussion about Dylan's lecture tour immediately. But he did have his suspicions confirmed that *Under Milk Wood*, which was due to have its première in the Kaufmann Auditorium in New York on 14 May, was not actually finished. Dylan assured him everything would be ready in time.

That first day, as Dylan and Brinnin progressed round the bars of Greenwich Village and then went on to the Algonquin Hotel to join Howard Moss, the poetry editor of the *New Yorker*, for more drinks, Brinnin could not fail to notice the turned heads and whispered conversations wherever they went, as people recognized his companion. When this was pointed out to Dylan, he laughed it off, but Brinnin could see he was pleased to be a talking-point in celebrity-conscious New York. One irony of this was that his sudden fame was partly due to a vivid piece that had appeared in the 6 April issue of *Time* magazine. In that article it was stated that when Dylan 'settles down to guzzle beer, which is most of the time, his incredible yarns tumble over each other in a wild Welsh dithyramb in which truth and fact become hopelessly smothered in boozy invention. He borrows with no thought of returning what is lent, seldom shows up on time, is a trial to his friends and a worry to his family.'

Dylan had been so angered by this caricature that he instructed his solicitor and old schoolfriend in Swansea, Stuart Thomas, to issue a writ for libel. In response, Time-Life International hired a private detective to follow Dylan round New York on his last visit to the city in the autumn, noting down where he went and what he did. The accumulated material would have been more than enough to enable *Time* to put up a spirited defence had the libel case ever come to court. Dylan's death meant that it never did.[8]

It was at the Algonquin that evening in April that Dylan first met Elizabeth Reitell, who had a few months previously been appointed assistant to John Malcolm Brinnin in his duties as Director of the YM & YWHA Poetry Center. Nearly six years younger than Dylan, Liz Reitell was a tall, bright and efficient woman, attractive in a rather stern but striking way. She had a powerful personality of the kind that gets noticed in a room full of strangers. Liz had studied theatre design at Bennington College, a well-known liberal establishment in Vermont. Twice married, she had been an officer in the Women's Army Corps during the war, and had gone on to develop her talents as an artist and a dancer. As Brinnin had to be out of town a lot of the time, because he had a teaching post in Connecticut, it had fallen to Liz to find a cast of actors for the reading of *Under Milk Wood*, not an easy task as nobody in New York knew exactly what the play was about. Her first meeting with Dylan was hardly auspicious. He felt intimidated by this brisk, cool American female who was going to act as midwife to his theatrical baby; her opening line on meeting him was to ask where the script was. As she confessed later to Brinnin, Liz looked at the boozy and simpering poet she was going to have to work with and asked herself: 'Why all this fuss over this fool?'[9]

Brinnin was determined not to act as nursemaid to Dylan on this tour so he left him on his own in New York later that evening and went off to Connecticut. He next saw him the following Saturday afternoon in Cambridge, Massachusetts, when Dylan came to speak at Boston University in nearby Boston. Brinnin had an apartment in Cambridge, which became a home base for Dylan as he fulfilled various engagements in New England. He quickly found a favourite spot in the apartment, in a chair by a picture-window that looked out over the Charles River towards Beacon Hill. For hours every day he would sit there writing additions and corrections to the manuscript of *Under Milk Wood*, keeping a supply of cigarettes and beer-cans at his side. Liz Reitell would ring every so often from New York to see how he was getting on, as she became increasingly nervous about whether the play really would be ready for its première.

On the evening of 3 May Dylan gave a solo reading of most of the still unfinished *Under Milk Wood* at the Fogg Museum lecture hall at Harvard University. He had been busy on the text all day

and turned down the suggestion of dinner before the performance. He threw all his actor's skills into the reading, which was
punctuated by extended bursts of laughter from the audience.
Dylan's gratification was obvious. But at the end he was exhausted,
and as he came off the platform, he told Brinnin that he needed a
drink.

Brinnin was puzzled to note during Dylan's stay in America this
time that his need for drink seemed to vary day to day, according
to his mood. There were evenings when he got completely plas-
tered, especially when he was at a convivial party and downing
whisky or martini rather than beer. Yet at other times he seemed
content with only the occasional lager. His state of health also
fluctuated violently. On occasions he appeared to be almost on the
verge of collapse, then only hours later he was functioning perfectly normally again.

Dylan was similarly vacillating in his emotions. He sent a number
of passionate letters home to Caitlin, yet when his old flame 'Pearl'
got in touch with him in New York, he readily agreed to see her
again and seems to have spent at least one night with her at
another friend's apartment in Cambridge. Since their affair on
Dylan's first American trip in 1950 'Pearl' had married and spent
some time in Mexico before she realized that neither her husband
nor Mexico was for her. Gossip was rife at a party in Cambridge
after Dylan's reading at the Massachusetts Institute of Technology
on 11 May, as Dylan and 'Pearl' wandered among the other guests
with the conspiratorial camaraderie of lovers. Yet at other social
occasions, and after readings, Dylan was ready to accept the
fawning attention of star-struck girls whose names he barely
remembered.

Moreover, Dylan and Liz Reitell found themselves being drawn
to each other in the intense hours of collaboration trying to finish
Under Milk Wood for its New York premiere. Much of this writing
and reworking was carried out in Rollie McKenna's apartment,
with two typists on hand to prepare a readable script from Dylan's
handwritten notes. Until almost the last moment Liz feared that
the first performance might have to be cancelled. John Malcolm
Brinnin had in his pocket two alternative scripts for the short
opening speech he had prepared: one presenting Dylan and the
work that was about to be performed, the other apologizing for the
fact that it had had to be cancelled. Three hours before the play

was due to begin, the last third of the script was still in a disorganized state, and Dylan was so tired he didn't think he would manage to write another word. In the event, largely at Liz's urging, he suddenly got a second wind. Twenty minutes before the curtain went up at the Kaufmann Auditorium, last-minute additions to the script were still being handed to the actors.

Dylan himself read the part of the First Voice who sets the scene, and there was a deep hush around the packed hall as he intoned: 'To begin at the beginning . . . ' The first few minutes were agony for Dylan and the actors, as no reaction came from the packed hall. Then the reverential silence was broken by a few titters, as members of the audience started to realize that this was no solemn piece of formal poetry but a joyous, bawdy celebration of eccentric humanity. The titters soon turned to guffaws. At the end of the play the audience sat as if stunned for a moment and then rose to their feet in wild acclaim, recognizing that they had witnessed the birth of something excitingly original. The actors themselves, semi-professionals for the most part, as the Poetry Center was operating within a tight budget, were convinced that Dylan was a genius.

The excitement created by this airing of *Under Milk Wood* gave Dylan a short new burst of creative confidence. He knew there were a few minor alterations to make to *Under Milk Wood* before its second performance, in the same hall, a fortnight later. Yet already he was planning another play for voices, to be called *Two Streets*. This was to be a more serious work for just two players. a boy and a girl who grow up in a Welsh industrial town (based on Swansea) are each searching for fulfilment. The audience gradually suspects they could find that in each other. They only meet at the end of the piece, however, when it is too late for them to become the lovers they might have been. As Dylan planned it, the audience would be plunged immediately into the intensity of the piece by the opening screams of a woman in labour.[10]

Before Dylan could think any more about this new play, however, he received an unexpected message at Brinnin's apartment in Cambridge from the Russian composer Igor Stravinsky, who wanted to talk to him about a possible collaboration. Stravinsky was in Boston for a production of his opera *The Rake's Progress* by Sarah Caldwell's Opera Workshop at Boston University. Only one performance of this had originally been planned; the tickets were sold out and the composer was delighted with it. A second performance was then hastily arranged, with a different cast of singers – mainly music students – who sadly were inadequately rehearsed. Stravinsky thought the result was so awful that he retired violently ill to his suite at the Sheraton Plaza Hotel.

It was there that Dylan visited him a few days later. Stravinsky was lying in bed, with a beret on his head and a thermometer in his mouth. His wife Vera and his faithful amanuensis Robert Craft were in attendance. Stravinsky proffered Dylan a glass of whisky, apologizing that he could not join him in a drink, as his doctor had put him on a teetotal regime.

Stravinsky had first heard of Dylan from Wystan Auden, during Dylan's 1950 American tour, when Auden arrived late for an appointment in New York, saying he had been helping to extricate Dylan from some scrape. Stravinsky then familiarized himself with some of Dylan's poems and Vera went to hear the poet read at the University of Illinois at Urbana. Then, in early 1952, the British film director Michael Powell contacted Stravinsky, asking if he would write some incidental music for a film he wanted to make based on an episode in Homer's *Odyssey*, for which Powell wanted Dylan to do the script. It did not look as though this film project would come to anything, however, as the producer was unable to raise sufficient funds.

Now Boston University wanted to commission a new short operatic piece from Stravinsky, and Robert Craft suggested that Dylan do the libretto. It is possible that Aldous Huxley, who was a close friend of the Stravinskys in their adopted home of Los Angeles, had also sown the seed of a possible collaboration with Dylan in the composer's mind. Dylan was intrigued by the prospect and said he had heard *The Rake's Progress* broadcast from Venice. Wystan Auden and his lover Chester Kallman had done the libretto for that, and Dylan said he knew the text well, commenting, 'Auden is the most skilful of us all.'[11] When asked what theme he would be interested in working on, Dylan replied that he would like to examine the rediscovery of love and language in a world devastated by the dropping of an atomic bomb. There would be no abstractions or conceits, he said, only people, objects and words. Stravinsky approved of the idea.

The composer was also attracted to the personality of Dylan himself, despite his chain-smoking, his drinker's red nose, his large, protuberant behind and belly, and his moaning about suffering from gout. As Stravinsky confided later to Robert Craft, 'As soon as I saw him I knew that the only thing to do was to love him.'[12] They parted agreeing that the project would go ahead: Stravinsky would have an extra room built on to his Los Angeles home, where Dylan could stay and work. As Dylan envisaged it, he would go back to England, make arrangements for the children to be looked after and then travel to Los Angeles with Caitlin for the whole of the month of July. He informed his wife that the arrangement was that he would be paid £500 in advance, plus first-class sea-passages to America, another £500 on completion, and then 'royalties until we die'.[13]

Another reason for Dylan's high spirits was that he and Liz Reitell had become lovers. He had penetrated her defensive armour by disconcertingly informing her that he knew that her often extravagant public behaviour was just a mask behind which a vulnerable personality was hiding. Moreover, as so often in the past with his friends and lovers, Dylan brought out the protective side of Liz's nature by playing the lost little boy. Liz was genuinely worried about his health, and with good reason. Apart from his problems with gout, Dylan succeeded in fracturing an arm again, by falling downstairs at a dinner before a performance of Arthur Miller's play *The Crucible*. At first Dylan did not realize what had happened, but during the play he started to feel more pain and complained so loudly that he was asked to leave the theatre. Liz summoned her doctor, Milton Feltenstein, who dealt with the arm, gave Dylan injections for his gout and lectured him about moderating his drinking. Unusually, Dylan seems to have taken the doctor's words to heart and he quickly grew to trust Dr Feltenstein with his 'winking needle and his witty wild way'.[14]

Despite the inconvenience of having his arm in a sling, Dylan was on good form at the second performance of *Under Milk Wood* at the Kaufmann Auditorium on 28 May. But the strain took its toll. His face turned deathly pale almost as soon as he came off stage, and Liz Reitell and John Malcolm Brinnin had to take him back to the Hotel Chelsea to lie down. The following day, Dylan promised Dr Feltenstein that he would consult a doctor back home in Britain to arrange a comprehensive programme to restore his health. Brinnin noticed that Dylan hardly drank in the following days. Yet when Barbara Holdridge and Marianne Mantell from

Caedmon Records came to collect him from the hotel, to record some of his poems the evening before he was due to leave for London, they were shocked by his bloated appearance and the fact that his suit seemed to be smeared with vomit. The recording session took much of the night. Some of the poems Dylan read with ease, but others he kept fluffing until he lost his temper and started to swear into the microphone. Afterwards Barbara Holdridge erased the tapes of everything except the material that would appear on the record Caedmon was planning to make, to ensure that Dylan's mistakes and obscenities could not be retrieved and turned into a party piece.[15]

Dylan flew to London on 2 June, the day of the Coronation of Queen Elizabeth II, arriving in the early hours of the following morning. In a letter to Oscar Williams, Dylan reported that

> queasy, purple, maggoty, scalped, I weak-wormed through fes-toons, bunting, flags, great roses, sad spangles, paste and tinsel, the million cardboard simpers and ogrish plaster statuettes of the nincompoop queen, I crawled as early as sin in the chilly weeping morning through the city's hushed hangover and all those miles of cock-deep orange-peel, nibbled sandwiches, broken bottles, dis-carded vests, vomit and condoms, lollipops, senile fish, blood lips, old towels, teeth, turds, soiled blowing newspapers by the unread mountain, all the spatter and bloody gravy and giant mousemess that go to show how a loyal and phlegmatic people – 'London can break it!' – enjoyed themselves like hell the day before.[16]

When he turned up at Margaret Taylor's house, where he was going to stay, a party that had started two days before was still in full swing.

Back at Laugharne, Dylan set about making further revisions to the manuscript of *Under Milk Wood*. There were amendments both to the structure of the piece and to the text (notably passages relating to the old sea-dog, Captain Cat). Dylan was polishing the play for publication and for several further profitable public performances that John Malcolm Brinnin had promised to arrange in America when Dylan returned there. Typically, the publication arrangements were becoming rather complicated. Allan Wingate had threatened to sue Dylan for the return of the advance they had paid for the American travel book he never wrote, but David Higham bought them off with an option on *Under Milk Wood* instead. They were not impressed with what they saw of the manuscript, however, and short-sightedly sold the option on to J. M. Dent.

As ever, Dylan was worried about money. Caitlin was finding it increasingly difficult to handle Aeronwy who, in her mother's phrase, had at the age of nine or ten turned from a spoilt but loving child into a fiend. She was so stubborn and naughty that Caitlin sometimes hit her in anger. When some fellow-passengers on a train once remonstrated with Caitlin, saying that one could not do that to a child, she shot back: 'You would if you had this one!'[17] The Thomases decided to send Aeronwy away to the Arts Educational School at Tring in Hertfordshire from September, which meant that there would now be two lots of boarding-school fees to be paid, on top of their own living expenses and accumulated debts.

Dylan took Caitlin and Aeronwy with him to the International Eistedfodd in Llangollen in early July, as Aneirin Talfan Davies had commissioned him to do a radio portrait of it for the BBC. The weather was unpleasantly windy and Talfan Davies said later that Dylan wandered around in a bewildered haze. The resultant script makes much of the incongruity of Javanese percussionists, pigtailed Alpine angels and Ukrainians with Manchester accents wandering the streets of the dull little Welsh town. But the piece fails to come alive, unlike Dylan's earlier radio scripts.

Similarly, the BBC hierarchy was dissatisfied with the one and only solo television broadcast Dylan made, on 10 August. Entitled 'Personally Speaking', and broadcast from the Dean's Library at St Asaph, this showed Dylan reading a new story (later known as 'The Outing', and published in the American magazine *Harper's Bazaar*). The programme got a glowing review in *The Listener*, but the Controller of TV programmes in London sent a stiff memo to Cardiff complaining that it had made appalling television as Thomas kept on having to consult his script, as if he had not learned it properly. In fact, he only completed writing the story in the studio itself, just before the broadcast began. Caitlin watched the programme on the TV set in Brown's Hotel, keeping up a running commentary of sardonic comments.[18]

Domestic tension was undoubtedly partly to blame for Dylan's diminished skills. The fights with Caitlin were becoming more frequent and violent. As Dylan wrote, only half tongue-in-cheek, to his old friend Dan Jones: 'Last week I hit Caitlin with a plate of beetroot, and I'm still bleeding.'[19] When John Malcolm Brinnin and Rollie McKenna came over from America to Wales on a visit at the beginning of September, they were disturbed to see that Dylan had a deep, livid gash over his right eye. He claimed this had been caused in a fall, but later in New York he told the actor Roy Poole that the real cause of the injury was Caitlin's hitting him with a coffee-pot.[20]

Brinnin and McKenna had been commissioned to do an illustrated profile of Dylan's life in Laugharne for the American magazine *Mademoiselle*, which had bought serialization rights for *Under Milk Wood*. Caitlin invited them round to The Boat House for dinner, for which she prepared wild duck. She had read in a French cookbook that it was most important that wild duck should not be overcooked. But when John Malcolm Brinnin started carving the bird at Caitlin's request, blood spurted out of the rubbery flesh. Llewelyn, who was home for the summer holidays and had been granted the rare privilege of eating with the adults, started pulling faces and making disgusting noises as portions of blatantly underdone meat were handed round. Caitlin insisted that it was absolutely delicious, until Dylan ordered her to 'take the bloody thing off the table'.[21]

Brinnin thought the atmosphere at The Boat House was so unbearable that Dylan was looking for any excuse to get away. Brinnin tried to dissuade him from undertaking another American tour in the foreseeable future, however, as he believed that this would stop him writing and would damage his health further. But Dylan was determined to press ahead. Financial problems at Boston University meant the opera project with Stravinsky had had to be postponed, but the composer still wanted to proceed and was trying to find alternative funding elsewhere. Dylan had also opened negotiations with a lecture agent in America, Felix Gerstman, in the hope of getting on a lecture circuit of women's clubs and professional bodies that would be much more lucrative than the college audiences Brinnin had lined up on his three previous US tours. That way, he argued, he could earn thousands of dollars in a matter of weeks, and then take things easy for the winter, perhaps in Majorca. Reluctantly, Brinnin agreed to do what he could to facilitate a short fourth US visit, to begin in October.

However, this left unresolved the problem of how to settle outstanding debts in Laugharne. David Higham managed to negotiate a contract for the publication of the still unfinished novel *Adventures in the Skin Trade*, which Dylan promised faithfully he would now complete. But Dylan then took the highly unethical step of directly approaching E. F. Bozman at Dent's, asking him without Higham's knowledge if the firm could advance him some extra money on royalties to come. Bozman replied politely but firmly that that was out of the question. He tried to reassure Dylan that in the not too distant future he would be a great commercial as well as a critical success; all he needed was patience and a little discipline. But as Bozman recalled in a magazine piece after Dylan's death, he was his own worst enemy when it came to furthering his best interests:

> Courteous in manner, soft-spoken and persuasive in conversation, apparently business-like, without any sign of self-importance and grateful for, and mildly surprised at, anything that was done for him commercially, he could nevertheless be counted on to miss every opportunity that came his way for making a practical success of his authorship and to set at naught every effort that was made to persuade him to help himself.[22]

Dylan's last full day in Laugharne was 8 October. Fred Janes came over to say farewell, and to introduce Dylan to the artist Ceri Richards, whose work was greatly inspired by Dylan's poetry. The two men got on well, but their conversation was terminated abruptly when another row between Dylan and Caitlin blew up and Fred thought it was better that they leave. In the evening, Dylan and Caitlin went to the cinema in Carmarthen, where Dylan had a blackout. By coincidence, the family doctor from St Clears was sitting just in front of them. Caitlin arranged with him to take Dylan round for an examination after the film, but they failed to keep the appointment.

The following morning the two of them left Laugharne. Dylan went three times to Pelican to kiss his mother goodbye, as if he knew he would never see her again. Then, despite Caitlin's protestations, he insisted on taking a taxi to Swansea to look up Dan Jones. Jones was working hard to try to finish an urgent musical commission, but Dylan dragged him away from his desk and inveigled him into a drinking session that continued for the next three days. Convinced by this time that Dylan was subconsciously trying to evade departure for the United States, Dan Jones managed to get him and Caitlin and their suitcases to the bookshop run by their mutual friend Ralph Wishart, who cashed a post-dated cheque for Dylan, enabling the Thomases to proceed at last to London.

There, on the evening of Monday, 12 October, David Higham and Douglas Cleverdon from the BBC waited in vain at Simpsons in the Strand for Dylan to join them for dinner, when he was meant to hand over the script of *Under Milk Wood*, which Cleverdon needed to copy for a broadcast performance. It must be a matter of conjecture whether Dylan had actually finished the script, as he had told Cleverdon on the phone from Laugharne, or whether he had deliberately missed the dinner appointment by lingering in Wales because he still had some work to do on it. His official excuse, when he rang Douglas Cleverdon to apologize for not turning up at the restaurant, was that he had not had enough money to buy a train ticket from Carmarthen – a rather feeble lie by Dylan's standards. They agreed to meet on the Thursday instead, when Dylan would deliver the script in person to Broadcasting House.

This time he did keep his word. When he presented Douglas Cleverdon with the handwritten manuscript, he pointed out that it was the only copy in existence; he would therefore call by to pick it up again on the Saturday morning, as he needed to take it with him to New York on the following Monday. This gave Cleverdon's secretary less than forty-eight hours to type it out on duplicating stencils, from which other copies could be run off.

On his way out of the building, Dylan ran into Constantine FitzGibbon and they went off for a drink, not at The George or any of the other pubs frequented by the BBC crowd, but somewhere quiet where they could have a proper talk. Dylan seemed subdued and sad. He told FitzGibbon that he didn't really want to go to the United States so soon again at all, though he was looking forward to the possibility of working with Stravinsky. He outlined his synopsis for their opera to his friend. After a while, though, FitzGibbon sensed that Dylan was getting restless, and they moved on to a livelier pub. There Dylan was soon swallowed up by a crowd of admirers and he quickly brightened, launching into his role as bar entertainer. It was a classic case of what his friends had come to term 'instant Dylan'.[23]

Dylan duly collected the original manuscript from the BBC on the Saturday, but then phoned Douglas Cleverdon in a panic later in the weekend to say that he had lost it. He was pretty sure he had left it in a pub somewhere in Soho, but he couldn't be certain which. He told Cleverdon he was very welcome to keep it if he could find it, so long as he got one of the BBC typescripts to him in time. Cleverdon did indeed track the manuscript down a few days later, at The Helvetia pub in Old Compton Street. Years later he sold it to a rare book dealer, though not before a law suit over its rightful ownership.

During the last few days in London, Dylan seems to have been very confused. His good humour had not been helped by the fact that Brinnin had sent his air-ticket to Laugharne, not realizing he had already left for London. By the time the ticket caught up with him, he had missed the original departure date; Monday the 19th was a rearrangement. On the day, as promised, Douglas Cleverdon brought a copy of the typescript of *Under Milk Wood* to Victoria Air Terminal, where Dylan was drinking with Caitlin, Harry and Cordelia Locke (with whom the Thomases had been staying), and Margaret Taylor. Only Harry Locke accompanied Dylan to the airport bus itself. He was dismayed when instead of waving, Dylan gave a thumbs-down sign through the window.

Liz Reitell was at the airport in New York to meet him and was even more perturbed by his mood. Dylan had a habit of making up or embroidering stories about his fellow-passengers on planes and boats, but this time he seemed genuinely shaken by an encounter he described with an Irish priest, who had got so drunk and abusive on the flight that he had had to be locked in the lavatory until he could be taken off the plane at the fuel-stop in Newfoundland. Far from greeting Liz enthusiastically, Dylan mumbled that he needed to go to the airport bar for a drink. When they got there, they found it was being picketed by striking workers and Liz refused to cross the picket-line.

Disgruntled, Dylan arrived at the Hotel Chelsea to find that the charming old Hungarian management there had reassigned to someone else the large, bright room overlooking 23rd Street that had been booked for him, as he had not arrived on the day he was due. They said they would move him into a similar room as soon as one became available in a few days' time, but in the meantime he would have to make do with a smaller room facing the back. Knowing how indifferent Dylan usually was to his surroundings, Liz was concerned when he made a terrible fuss about not getting a room like the one he had had before. To make things worse, on the second night in the smaller room, Dylan announced to her in anxious tones that he had just seen the most gigantic cockroach in the world – with teeth.

Dylan's spirits rose towards the end of the week, when he joined rehearsals for *Under Milk Wood* at the Kaufmann Auditorium, with the half-dozen actors he had so enjoyed working with before. Two performances were scheduled, for the Saturday evening and Sunday afternoon, 24 and 25 October. Dylan had been disturbed to discover several mistakes in the typescript Douglas Cleverdon's secretary had prepared, some of which were the result of his confusing handwritten alterations. Some passages that he had bracketed to be left out of a one-man performance of the play that he had given in Tenby, West Wales, earlier in the month had been omitted by the typist. Remembering and reinstating them was more of a nuisance than a major problem, however.

Liz Reitell wanted to keep Dylan to herself as much as possible during that first week of his last visit to New York. This was partly in the hope of strengthening their relationship, but also in order to stop him being made too tired or too drunk by people who wanted to experience Dylan the Roaring Boy. Liz decided it would be good for him if they took walks together round Greenwich Village, and sampled different restaurants. At one seafood place, however, Dylan suddenly declared that the fish was inedible and flew into a tantrum. There was nothing for it but to take him back to the hotel. Unfortunately, at the hotel there were constant interruptions from friends and fans ringing in to wish Dylan well, or to invite him out to parties. One evening, Liz returned from her office at the Poetry Center to find him almost paralytically drunk in his room with a group of film buffs from an organization called Cinema 16. They had arrived with several bottles of whisky and beer. Alarmed to see that Dylan was not talking sense, Liz immediately ordered his guests to leave. She had not expected to have to be Dylan's nanny as well as his girlfriend, but it dawned on her that he needed this if he was to survive, both physically and psychologically. As far as was possible, she dropped her other responsibilities at the Poetry Center and took full-time charge of the poet.

At one of the last rehearsals of *Under Milk Wood*, Dylan was too ill to play a major part, and instead sat in the Green Room of the

Kaufman Auditorium with Liz Reitell's good friend Herbert Hannum (who five years later became her third husband). Dylan's temperature seemed to be fluctuating violently, and Herb Hannum covered him with overcoats borrowed from people at the Poetry Center. He had food and hot-water bottles brought in, and for a while Dylan seemed to recover. He insisted on sitting in on the last twenty minutes or so of the rehearsal. But afterwards his state worsened again, and he vomited on the Green Room floor. As Herb Hannum moved Dylan on to a couch, Dylan grabbed him by his jacket lapel and whispered: 'I've seen the gates of Hell tonight.'[24]

The following morning, over breakfast at a chop-house near the Hotel Chelsea, Dylan told Hannum that the events of the previous evening had made him realize how far his health had deteriorated. He said he knew he ought to stay clear of spirits and stick to beer, and that he should eat properly and regularly. But somehow he lacked the necessary willpower. Hannum tentatively asked whether he had thought of consulting a psychiatrist, but Dylan pooh-poohed the idea. When Liz joined the two of them a little later, however, she and Hannum both urged Dylan at least to see a doctor. He capitulated under their joint pressure and was taken off to see Dr Feltenstein, who had treated him in the spring.

It was obvious at first glance to Dr Feltenstein that Dylan had not heeded the warnings he had given him about taking better care of himself. However, as everyone's immediate concern was that he should be able to get through the two performances of *Under Milk Wood*, Dr Feltenstein decided to give his patient a shot of the cortisone-based drug ACTH, which would give his system a boost that should see him through the following few days. The injection swiftly took effect. Very shortly after leaving the doctor's surgery, Dylan said he wanted to go into an Army and Navy Stores to buy some shirts. The crisis had apparently passed.

Even so, when John Malcolm Brinnin came to New York later that day to join Dylan at the Poetry Center, he was shocked by his friend's appearance, indeed he could barely stop himself gasping aloud. As he recalled later, Dylan's face 'was lime-white, his lips loose and twisted, his eyes dulled and gelid and sunk in his head. He showed the countenance of a man who has been appalled by something beyond comprehension.'[25] Liz Reitell identified this 'something' as an ineffable loneliness from which Dylan was unable to escape. An appalling feature of that loneliness was that as the horrors closed in on him in his mind, he was incapable of sharing his fears with even those people who were close to him, just as his friends were incapable of bringing him sustained relief.

Astonishingly, Dylan was able to go through with the performance of *Under Milk Wood* on the Saturday night. John Malcolm Brinnin thought it went all right, but not as well as the two in May. Afterwards there was a party for the cast and friends at Rollie McKenna's apartment. Dylan was subdued and refused alcoholic drink throughout the evening. It was only when all the guests except John Malcolm Brinnin and Liz Reitell had gone that Dylan suddenly brightened up. As Liz Reitell told Rob Gittins years later, Dylan 'had a tremendous ability in the absolute worst of times . . . to flip himself over as though he were a coin and suddenly be joyous and brisk and full of fun'.[26] This brought only temporary respite for her own complex fears about Dylan, though. His dependency on her, mixed with a growing emotional coldness, left her feeling exhausted and perplexed.

John Malcolm Brinnin, who also loved Dylan, in a different way, was similarly distraught. Dylan joined him at his hotel the day after the party at Rollie McKenna's and immediately started talking about money. Dispassionately, Dylan started berating Brinnin because this American trip was not going to earn him as much as he would have liked. At first Brinnin listened in disbelief and then the awful suspicion implanted itself in his mind that Dylan had only ever seen him as a means of acquiring money. It was as if all Brinnin's friendship and countless hours of devoted activity on Dylan's behalf were forgotten. In short, he felt he had been used. He was so devastated that he could not face the matinée performance of *Under Milk Wood*, which everyone who saw it acknowledged was the greatest. There was a huge and enthusiastic audience at the Kaufmann Auditorium, and they gave the piece a brilliant reception. But Brinnin spent the time being comforted by Rollie McKenna in her apartment. She managed to talk him out of leaving New York immediately.

Buoyed by the afternoon's performance, Dylan was keen to accept an invitation to a party given by a refugee countess who lived at Sutton Place, and whom he had been given to understand would be a willing lay. Reluctantly, Liz Reitell agreed to go with him, and was soon horrified, first to see Dylan drinking whisky by the tumblerful, then to see him disappear up the stairs with their hostess. When John Malcolm Brinnin arrived late at the party, having tracked Dylan down, there were only about nine or ten people left. By now Dylan had emerged from the countess's bedroom, and he, Liz and John sat together in a darkened room for a heart-to-heart talk, in which Dylan's two admirers laid bare their hurt feelings. John Brinnin was the first to break down in tears, followed shortly afterwards by Liz Reitell. Dylan then joined in, and after a cathartic few minutes' weeping, grasped Brinnin's hands and said, 'John, you know, don't you? This is forever?'[27] Brinnin was so moved by the force of this remark that it was not until he was travelling back to Boston by train hours later that he started to analyse what Dylan really meant. He never had another chance to ask him.

Dylan spent that night not with Liz but with another girl who had been arranged for him by an acquaintance. The following day, Monday, 26 October, he went on a drinking spree. When Liz Reitell tracked him down in the bar of the Algonquin Hotel, he was loudly regaling a group of strangers about his supposed horrific exploits in the Middle East during the war. As Liz described later, Dylan's talk became increasingly disconnected, violent and obscene. He ranted on about blood and mutilation and death. When Liz took hold of his hand in an attempt to calm him, he started to sob. She led him out into the street, where he began pulling faces at passers-by and swearing at them. Then suddenly he stopped at a crossroads, stood up straight and said to Liz, 'You hate me, don't you?' 'No,' she replied, 'but it's not for your want of trying.'[28]

Later, they went to Goody's Bar in Greenwich Village, where they had spent quiet evenings together in better days. Dylan got up to buy some cigarettes from a machine and when he returned he remarked vehemently on how filthy it was that the couple in the next booth to them were snogging. Astounded, Liz told him he was talking like a puritan. Speaking as if this was something he had thought of for the very first time, Dylan agreed that that was exactly what he was.

The following day was his thirty-ninth birthday. Ever since he was a boy at school, Dylan had maintained that he would not live to see forty. Now it was as if the bell had tolled. Yet he was remarkably chirpy that morning. It was possibly on that occasion that Wystan Auden spotted him going into the Hotel Chelsea, carrying a brown paper bag full of groceries, and looking neither drunk nor on the verge of death.[29] In the evening, Dave and Rose Slivka gave a party for him at their home in the Village. Dylan came on from The White Horse Tavern with Liz; both had been looking forward to the event enormously, as the Slivkas had invited a wide range of Dylan's friends. But his mood took a sudden downward turn. He wouldn't touch any of the food that had been prepared and he refused all drinks. After about an hour he declared that he had to leave immediately. Liz accompanied him back to the Hotel Chelsea, where he lay on his bed and whined self-pityingly about the awfulness of middle age and what a filthy and undignified creature he had become. Seeing him slide into deep depression, Liz started haranguing him about his apparent inability to do anything to help himself. He screamed at her to stop. Liz then made as if to leave, but Dylan begged her to stay.

Somehow he managed to get through his appointments the following day, which included taking part in a forum on film art organized by Cinema 16. When one of his fellow panelists talked about the 'vertical' nature of poetry and the 'horizontal' nature of drama, Dylan started making some suggestive up-and-down movements with his hands, which soon had the more irreverent members of the audience giggling. Encouraged by this response, Dylan then played the part of the philistine Welshman puncturing all the arty pretensions of the event. When the symposium's chairman, Willard Maas, tried to reinject a note of seriousness by pointing out that none of the panelists had mentioned the word 'love', Dylan fluttered his eyelashes at him and lisped: 'Oh, Willard! I didn't know you cared!'[30] This brought the house down.

The fillip this success gave Dylan lasted for a couple of days. He behaved well at parties, including one given by his old friend Ruthvan Todd, and to Liz's relief, he shook off the countess from Sutton Place, who seemed to want to expropriate him for herself. But on the third day, Dylan failed to keep an appointment with Liz and stayed out late drinking in bars with a rowdy group of friends. According to the private detective hired to follow him by Time-Life International, Dylan also took some Benzedrine that night, which, if true, was the first time such a thing had happened. Then on his way back to the Chelsea in the early hours of the morning, Dylan allegedly pushed an unknown woman out of his moving cab.

Liz Reitell was alarmed when Dylan recounted this story to her the following morning. For several days she had been worried that in his unstable condition he might do himself an injury, but until now it had not occurred to her that he could be a danger to anybody else. That evening, her fears were intensified. They were invited to a fairly sedate party along with Howard Moss, and Dylan took an instant fancy to a young girl who was dancing there. To the self-evident disgust of the other guests, he began to pursue the young lady with all the finesse of a lumbering bear. Then he pounced, bringing both of them crashing down to the floor and seriously injuring the girl. Liz Reitell was mortified. Howard Moss quickly spirited her and Dylan away to his apartment, where Dylan stiffened and exclaimed in anguish that he could see a mouse. To calm him down, Liz pretended that she could see it too. Then Howard Moss diverted Dylan's attention by getting him to read some poems of his choice; unhesitatingly, Dylan chose works by Auden.

November 3rd was election day, and Dylan received a stream of visitors to his room at the Hotel Chelsea. He voiced his cynicism about politics and even tried to dissuade Liz Reitell from going out to vote. As he was due in the late afternoon to see the agent who was meant to organize his future lecture tours, Liz shooed everyone out when she returned from the polls and then tried to moderate Dylan's drinking. She cleared away the dirty ashtrays and attempted to make both the room and Dylan look respectable. Her preparations paid off. When the lecture agent arrived, he declared that if Dylan would sign a contract with him, he would guarantee him a minimum income while on tour of $1,000 a week. In 1953, that was a sizeable sum.

This seemed at long last to be the break that Dylan had been awaiting for so many years, which would cure all his financial worries. Yet as soon as the lecture agent had left the room, Dylan lay down on the bed feeling inordinately depressed. It was as if the prospect of all the lectures to come was another form of trap that he had fallen into. As the evening wore on, he started reminiscing about Laugharne, then suddenly announced that he wanted to die. When Liz told him that he didn't have to die, if only he would take hold of himself, he started weeping uncontrollably.

Liz stayed with him as he slept fitfully until about 2 a.m. Then he suddenly sat up in bed and said he needed to go out for a drink and some fresh air. Too exhausted physically and emotionally to try to stop him going, Liz lay on the bed waiting for him to return. He was away about an hour and a half, and swayed at the door as he came in, declaring: 'I've had eighteen straight whiskies. I think that's a record.'[31] Most of Dylan's friends later thought this was just a typical piece of Welsh bravado, or one of Dylan's tall tales, but what was certain was that he had had too much to drink. He stumbled across the room, put his head in Liz's lap and fell sound asleep.

When he woke mid-morning, he said he couldn't breathe. He insisted on going out again, and this time Liz accompanied him. They walked all the way from the Chelsea to The White Horse Tavern. Dylan had only a couple of beers there before telling Liz that he was suffering agonies. She took him back to the Hotel Chelsea and summoned Dr Feltenstein. It was the first of three such visits during the course of the day. Despite the medication administered by the doctor, Dylan's condition was clearly not improving. By the time of the third visit, he was having wild hallucinations, which Liz was convinced were symptoms of delirium tremens. Dr Feltenstein gave Dylan a sedative, to calm his angry ravings against the creatures that were plaguing him. According to Paul Ferris's researches, the drug administered was morphine sulphate, a curious and incautious choice. Dr Feltenstein subsequently always refused to confirm or deny that that was indeed the case.

Before he left for the third time, Dr Feltenstein insisted that Liz find someone, preferably male, to come to stay with her and Dylan, as she was clearly getting near the end of her tether. The painter Jack Heliker obliged. Not long afterwards, Dylan woke and sat bolt upright, raving about the 'horrors' that were besetting him; these were now geometrical shapes that were tormenting him like devils. Liz then lay down on the bed by his side, holding his hand. She managed to get some sleep herself as Jack Heliker kept watch. Later Heliker claimed that Dylan woke shortly after midnight and said, 'After thirty-nine years, this is all I've done.'[32] Liz Reitell remembered things differently, maintaining that Dylan's last words were 'Yes, I believe you', after she told him that the horrors would go. Either way, she suddenly felt his grip tighten on her hand and Heliker saw his face turn blue. Dr Feltenstein was summoned yet again and arrived in a matter of minutes. He called for an ambulance which then ferried Dylan to St Vincent's Hospital, which was run by Roman Catholics. Just one of the many unanswered questions about this fateful day was why the doctor had waited so long before getting Dylan hospitalized.

Liz Reitell was almost hysterical, and phoned John Malcolm Brinnin in Cambridge to ask him to come at once. It was seven o'clock in the morning before Brinnin arrived, to find Liz and Ruthven Todd at St Vincent's waiting anxiously for more news from the doctors who had been analysing Dylan's condition all night. The various diagnoses included liver failure, diabetes and a rather indeterminate condition described as 'gross insult to the brain'. He was in a coma and was receiving oxygen and a blood transfusion, but did not seem in imminent danger of death. The longer he remained in a coma, however, the more likely it was that he would be severely impaired mentally if he ever emerged from it.

John Malcolm Brinnin set about informing those people who needed to know about Dylan's condition. He could not face phoning Caitlin in Laugharne, so he contacted David Higham in London instead, knowing that Higham would be able to make arrangements for Caitlin to travel to New York. By an uncanny coincidence, Higham's message got through to Caitlin as she was sitting with a group of friends and neighbours listening to a recorded broadcast that Dylan had made about their little town.

There were problems about getting a seat on a plane and Caitlin did not arrive in New York until Sunday morning. Thanks to the intervention of the British Embassy, she was spared the usual immigration procedures. Rose and Dave Slivka were at Idlewild Airport to meet her, and police motorcycles flanked the car that took her to St Vincent's. When she swept into the building, almost the first person she saw was John Malcolm Brinnin. 'Well,' she asked, 'is the bloody man dead or alive?'[33]

Liz Reitell had tactfully withdrawn from Dylan's bedside in advance of Caitlin's arrival. But she and John Malcolm Brinnin were astounded when Caitlin stayed only fifteen minutes in Dylan's room before re-emerging in a state of great agitation. She started banging her head hard against a window. The Slivkas then intervened and drove her home to their apartment for a few hours' rest. When she returned that afternoon, she dismayed the nurses by almost dislodging the tubes connected to Dylan's body in her attempts to embrace him, and by smoking in dangerous proximity to the oxygen tent. After friends gave her some whisky, her stressed state turned to violence, as she first attacked John Malcolm Brinnin, and then laid into the medical staff who tried to restrain her. She bit one orderly on the hand and tore at a nun's habit. When she had been subdued, she was placed in a strait-jacket and taken away. The doctors said she was too uncontrollable to be kept at St Vincent's and with a heavy heart John Malcolm Brinnin had to agree to her being temporarily committed to a mental institution for her own safety.

Acutely aware that the Thomases had no funds with which to meet the medical expenses that were being incurred, Brinnin spent the rest of Sunday and much of Monday morning, November 9, setting in motion a fundraising exercise which would cover these and, he hoped, leave something over for Caitlin and the children. On the Monday it was clear that Dylan's condition was entering a new and terminal phase. Brinnin sat for a while in the crowded hospital waiting-room with friends and fans of Dylan's whom he had never seen before. Then, as he stepped out into the corridor, the poet John Berryman came rushing up to him saying, 'He's dead! He's dead! Where were you?'[34]

Postscript

THE AFTERMATH

Newspapers in Britain were quick to eulogize Dylan when the news of his death came through. Both the *Daily Express* and the *Daily Mail* called him an 'absolute genius, a genius who loved life and talk and saloon bars'. The *Daily Herald* hailed him as 'the most prominent poet in our literary landscape'. The *Manchester Guardian* rhapsodized: 'He thought in images where lesser mortals were content with phrases.' Vernon Watkins was only one of Dylan's many literary friends who were asked to write obituaries; in Vernon's case the request distressingly arrived before Dylan was actually dead.

Caitlin was soon released from the Rivercrest Clinic in New York into the care of her friends Dave and Rose Slivka. She had calmed down considerably since her outbursts at St Vincent's Hospital and set about writing telegrams to Florence Thomas and her children, as well as to close friends. She went to view Dylan's body at the Manhattan funeral parlour where it was laid out. Much more daunting, though, was the prospect of a memorial service, which had been arranged at St Luke's Episcopal Church of Trinity Parish, on Friday, 13 November. Over 400 people attended. Caitlin took her rightful place with the principal mourners at the front of the church, possibly unaware that right at the back sat the huddled figure of Liz Reitell, feeling 'like the loneliest person in the world'.[1]

By chance, the SS *United States* was sailing for Southampton that afternoon and it was arranged that Caitlin would accompany Dylan's body back to Britain on the ship. She supervised the loading of the coffin into the hold. The Slivkas and other New York friends, armed with bottles of champagne, stayed with her in her cabin until the last possible moment before departure. As Caitlin recalled in her memoir *Leftover Life to Kill*, by the time they left she was mad, drunk and heartbroken. She went into the ship's bar and ordered five double whiskies, on the pretext that she was expecting friends. She sat down and drank them slowly, one after another, knowing that the alcohol would remove all her inhibitions. Then she leaped up and executed what she later described as a 'mad dance of destruction', sweeping glasses off tables and doing high-kicks, splits and cartwheels among the debris. The Captain arrived and got some seamen to take her down to a bunk in the hold, where she found that some of the sailors were playing cards on Dylan's coffin. 'Dylan would have liked that,' she thought.[2]

Billy Williams was waiting at Southampton docks with a vehicle to transport Caitlin and the coffin back to Laugharne. They stopped at several pubs on the way, and at some point must have taken a wrong turning, because they found themselves in Devon instead. When they eventually got home, Dylan's body was put on view in the front room at Pelican. Florence Thomas was stoically calm, encouraging people to go in to have a look at her son, saying, 'He's *nice*.'[3] Daniel Jones, who had appointed himself commander-in-chief of the funeral operations (as well as being Dylan's literary executor) thought the American morticians had turned the embalmed body into something entirely artificial.

The day of the funeral remains engrained in the memories of the older people of Laugharne. Caitlin was in a frenzy of grief, howling like a wolf, and Dylan's friends had gathered from far and wide. The Williams brothers carried the coffin to the graveyard of St Martin's Church, where a simple wooden cross would mark Dylan's grave. Afterwards Caitlin and many of the other mourners retired to Brown's Hotel. There Caitlin knocked a tray of drinks out of Fred Janes's hands, so that he was soaked in beer from head to foot. When someone else offered her a box of chocolates, she threw them at the ceiling in a rage. Fights broke out in different parts of town, while Louis MacNeice and some of the other more sober visitors reported back to Dan Jones what was going on elsewhere. Someone had tried to break into Dylan's workshed, doubtless on the hunt for valuable souvenirs. And one woman was wandering around town offering herself to any man who would have her. All in all, it was a scene of which the inhabitants of Llareggub would have been proud.

Caitlin knew she could never live in Laugharne without Dylan. She returned to the island of Elba, where she had once been so happy, and got involved with one of the miners she found so fascinating. She later married an Italian, who helped her through periods of alcoholism and emotional distress, some of which was caused by legal proceedings instituted against various people, including the Trustees of Dylan's estate. Caitlin and her second husband settled in Sicily, and had a child. Her children by Dylan went their separate ways. Of the three, Aeronwy was most consciously their father's child, taking an active role in the work of the Dylan Thomas Society, which still organizes a programme of regular events. Florence Thomas was left alone in Laugharne with The Boat House and her memories.

Dan Jones was worried that Caitlin and the children would be left in great financial difficulty after Dylan's death, but things didn't turn out half as badly as he feared. St Vincent's Hospital in New York magnanimously waived all its fees, and appeals on both sides of the Atlantic raised a tidy sum. Moreover, as Dan Jones worked through Dylan's chaotic papers, he came to realize that the income from his estate would be far from insignificant. Indeed, Dylan's popularity is still so high forty years after his death that the royalties on his poems, books and recordings exceed £100,000 a year.

A whole Dylan Thomas industry has grown up. His profile looms from the walls and windows not just of Brown's Hotel but also of half a dozen other hostelries in the Swansea area, in London and in New York. Over 35,000 pilgrims each year visit The Boat House, which is now a Dylan Thomas museum, where books, videos and souvenirs are on sale. Plaques have appeared on properties associated with him, from his childhood home at 5 Cwmdonkin Drive, Swansea to the house in Delancey Street, Camden Town, that he and Caitlin inhabited so briefly. Largely thanks to the former US President Jimmy Carter, who had asked why Dylan was not commemorated in Westminster Abbey, since 1982 he has his place in Poet's Corner there as well.

Though Dylan ought to be remembered primarily for his poetry, his most powerful and oddest legacy is his legend. He has become a stereotyped image of what a wild poet should be, though of course he was quite unique. His very complexity and contradictions make him a subject of great fascination, even for those who know little of his work. Researching into Dylan's life has made me realize how impossible it is to distinguish exactly what is true and what is false in that Dylan legend. But that in itself is strangely fitting. Dylan constructed his life with the same exhuberant creativity that he channeled into his verse.

NOTES

Abbreviations

CF Constantine FitzGibbon, *The Life of Dylan Thomas*
CL Dylan Thomas, *Collected Letters* (ed. Paul Ferris)
CT Caitlin Thomas (with George Tremlett), *Caitlin – Life with Dylan Thomas*
JMB John Malcolm Brinnin, *Dylan Thomas in America*
PF Paul Ferris, *Dylan Thomas*

Foreword
1. Quoted by Gwen Watkins in *Portrait of a Friend*, frontispiece.

Chapter 1: The Middle Room (1914–1925)
1. George Tremlett, *Dylan Thomas*, p. 22.
2. PF, p. 23.
3. Letter from Dylan to Pamela Hansford Johnson, 15 October 1933, CL, p. 25.
4. Author's interview with Haydn Thomas, 1991.
5. PF, p. 6.
6. 'The Hunchback in the Park', *Collected Poems 1934–1952*, p. 93.
7. CF, pp. 30–1.
8. Mervyn Levy, 'A Womb with a View', *John O'London's Magazine*, 29 November 1962.

Chapter 2: The Rimbaud of Cwmdonkin Drive (1925–1932)
1. CF, p. 50.
2. Letter from Dylan to Nancy Thomas, undated, CL, pp. 5–6.
3. 'Memories of Christmas', *Dylan Thomas: The Broadcasts*, p. 25.

4. PF, p. 50.
5. Author's interview with Haydn Taylor, 1991.
6. Daniel Jones, *My Friend Dylan Thomas*, p. 9.
7. Ibid.
8. Quoted in full in CF, pp. 55–8.
9. Interview with Paul Ferris in *Everybody's*, 21 April 1956.
10. Pamela Hansford Johnson, *Important to Me*, p. 141.
11. Quoted in Bill Read and Rollie McKenna, *The Days of Dylan Thomas*, p. 38.

Chapter 3: Thirties' Writer (1933–1934)

1. Letter from Dylan to Trevor Hughes, ? February 1933, CL, p. 13.
2. Letter from Bert Trick to Bill Read, quoted in Bill Read and Rollie McKenna, *The Days of Dylan Thomas*, p. 47.
3. PF, p. 87.
4. Ralph Maud, *Entrances to Dylan Thomas' Poetry*.
5. Letter from Dylan to Pamela Hansford Johnson, ? October 1933, CL, p. 30.
6. Letter from Dylan to Pamela Hansford Johnson, ? November 1933, CL, p. 55.
7. Letter from Dylan to Pamela Hansford Johnson, December 1933, CL, p. 59.
8. Pamela Hansford Johnson, *Important to Me*, p. 141.
9. PF, p. 111.

Chapter 4: The Vagabond (1934–1936)

1. PF, p. 112.
2. Quoted in Bill Read and Rollie McKenna, *The Days of Dylan Thomas*, pp. 67–8.
3. Letter from Dylan to Pamela Hansford Johnson, ? October 1934, CL, p. 172.
4. Dylan interviewed by Miron Grindea, *Adam*, no. 238, 1953.
5. Sheila Macleod, 'The Dylan I Knew', ibid.
6. Letter from Dylan to Pamela Hansford Johnson, ? October 1934, CL, p. 166.
7. Rayner Heppenstall, *Four Absentees*, pp. 44–5.
8. *Time and Tide*, 9 February 1935.
9. Derek Stanford, *Dylan Thomas*, p. 12.
10. Letter from Dylan to Bert Trick, ? February 1935, CL, p. 185.
11. A. J. P. Taylor, *A Personal History*, p. 130.
12. Geoffrey Grigson, *Recollections*, p. 85.
13. Letter from Dylan to Bert Trick, ? ? 1935, CL, p. 192.
14. Letter from Dylan to Daniel Jones, 14 August 1935, CL, p. 198.
15. Letter from Dylan to Haydn and Nancy Taylor, 27 October 1935, CL, p. 202.
16. Letter from Dylan to Glyn Jones, ? December 1934, CL, p. 180.
17. Quoted in PF, p. 140.
18. CT, p. 1.

Chapter 5: A Pleasant and Eccentric Marriage (1936–1938)

1. Nicolette Devas, *Two Flamboyant Fathers*, pp. 36–49.
2. CT, p. 10.
3. Ibid., p. 23.
4. Ibid., p. 27.
5. Ibid., p. 4.
6. Daniel Jones, *My Friend Dylan Thomas*, pp. 58–9.
7. Letter from Dylan to Nigel Henderson, 7 July 1936, CL, p. 233.
8. CT, pp. 8–9.

9.   *Sunday Times*, 15 November 1936.
10. Footnote in CL, p. 225.
11. Nicolette Devas, *Two Flamboyant Fathers*, p. 191.
12. CT, p. 39.
13. Letter from Dylan to Pamela Hansford Johnson, 6 August 1937, CL, p. 255.
14. Letter from Dylan to Geoffrey Grigson, 7 September 1937, CL, p. 259.
15. Nicolette Devas, *Two Flamboyant Fathers*, pp. 193–4.

Chapter 6: Poverty with Distinction (1938–1940)
1.   CT, p. 54
2.   Gwen Watkins, *Portrait of a Friend*, p. 19.
3.   Letter from Vernon Watkins to Francis Dufau-Labeyrie (undated).
4.   Gwen Watkins, *Portrait of a Friend*, p. 48.
5.   Letter from Dylan to James Laughlin, 1 May 1938, CL, p. 299.
6.   Letter from Dylan to Henry Treece, 23 March 1938, CL, pp. 280–1.
7.   Letter from Dylan to John Davenport, 14 October 1938, CL, p. 329
8.   CT, pp. 57–8.
9.   Letter from Dylan to Henry Treece, 23 March 1938, CL p. 282.
10. Letter from Dylan to Henry Treece, 7 July 1938, CL, p. 310.
11. Letter from Dylan to John Davenport, 14 October 1938, CL, p. 329.
12. Letter from Dylan to John Davenport, 4 November 1938, CL, p. 337.
13. Letter from Dylan to David Higham, 27 October 1938, CL, p. 335.
14. Letter from Dylan to Vernon Watkins, 20 December 1938, CL, p. 343.
15. CT, p. 61.
16. Gwen Watkins, *Portrait of a Friend*, p. 75.
17. Ibid., p. 78.
18. Letter from Dylan to John Davenport, 11 May 1939, CL, p. 378.
19. Letter from Dylan to David Higham, ? July 1939, CL, pp. 392–3.
20. Letter from Dylan to Desmond Hawkins, 3 September 1939, CL, p. 407.
21. Letter from Dylan to John Davenport, 14 September 1939, CL, p. 410.
22. Letter from Dylan to Desmond Hawkins, 14 September 1939, CL, p. 411.
23. Ibid.
24. CT, p. 72.

Chapter 7: Poetry, Guile and Beer (1940–1942)
1.   Letter from Dylan to Charles Fisher, 16 March 1938, CL, p. 275.
2.   Letter from Dylan to Archie Harding (BBC), 6 May 1941, CL, p. 484.
3.   Author's interview with Rupert Shephard, 1991.
4.   CT, p. 74.
5.   Letter from Dylan to Lord Howard de Walden, 24 December 1940, CL, p. 467.
6.   Quoted in PF, p. 184.
7.   Footnote to CL, p. 476.
8.   Letter from Dylan to Clement Davenport, 2 April 1941, CL, p. 478.
9.   PF, pp. 186–7.
10. Letter from Dylan to Vernon Watkins, CL, p. 490.
11. Letter from Dylan to Ruth Wynn Owen, CL, p. 496.
12. PF, p. 196.
13. Daniel Jones, *My Friend Dylan Thomas*, pp. 63–4.

Chapter 8: New Directions (1943–1945)

1. CT, pp. 83–7.
2. Quoted in PF, p. 184.
3. Julian Maclaren-Ross, *Memoirs of the Forties*, p. 121.
4. Ibid., p. 123.
5. Ibid., p. 201.
6. Ibid., p. 132.
7. Quoted from footnote to PF, p. 190.
8. Letter from Dylan to Caitlin, ? ? 1943, CL, p. 509.
9. Michael Luke, *David Tennant and the Gargoyle Years*, pp. 146–7.
10. Julian Maclaren-Ross, *Memoirs of the Forties*, p. 126.
11. Author's conversation with Ronald Harwood, 1992.
12. Quoted in CF, p. 296.
13. CF, p. 297.
14. Letter from Dylan to Vernon Watkins, 27 July 1944, CL, p. 517.
15. Letter from Dylan to Donald Taylor, 28 October 1944, CL, p. 530.
16. Gwen Watkins, *Portrait of a Friend*, pp. 110–14.
17. PF, p. 205.

Chapter 9: Chelsea, Oxford, Italy (1945–1948)

1. Letter from Dylan to Oscar Williams, 30 July 1945, CL, p. 559.
2. *Dylan Thomas: The Broadcasts*, p. 9.
3. CF, p. 132.
4. *Dylan Thomas: The Broadcasts*, p. 287–9.
5. CT, pp. 97–8.
6. Quoted in PF, p. 221.
7. *Dylan Thomas: The Broadcasts*, p. 287.
8. John Arlott, *Basingstoke Boy*, p. 111.
9. Letter from Dylan to James Laughlin, 24 November 1946, CL, p. 607.
10. Letter from Edith Sitwell to Maurice Bowra, 8 May 1946, *Edith Sitwell: Selected Letters*, p. 139.
11. Author's conversation with Dannie Abse, 1993.
12. Quoted in PF, p. 129.
13. PF, p. 220.
14. CT, p. 99.
15. Letter from Dylan to his parents, 11 April 1947, CL, p. 622.
16. *Dylan: Druid of the Broken Body*.
17. BBC broadcast, printed in *Dock Leaves*, spring 1954.
18. CT, p. 101.
19. Letter from Dylan to Ronald Bottrell, 20 June 1947, CL, p. 645.
20. CT, p. 102.
21. A. J. P. Taylor, *A Personal History*, p. 188.
22. Author's interview with Kay Stahl, 1991.
23. *The Listener*, 30 October 1947.

Chapter 10: The Boat House (1948–1950)

1. Quoted in PF, p. 231.
2. Information from Central Statistical Office.
3. Letter from Dylan to John Davenport, 26 August 1948, CL, p. 684.
4. Letter from Dylan to Caitlin, ? ? 1948, CL, p. 667.
5. Quoted in *Dylan Thomas: The Broadcasts*, p. 295.
6. PF, p. 230.

7. Jan Read's introduction to script of *The Beach of Falesa*.
8. Letter from Dylan to Caitlin, ? ? 1948, CL, p. 678.
9. Letter from Dylan to Caitlin, 26 August 1948, CL, p. 684.
10. Quoted in PF, p. 237.
11. Quoted in CF, p. 336.
12. CF, p. 343.
13. Ibid., p. 345.
14. 'Living in Wales', in *Dylan Thomas: The Broadcasts*, p. 203.
15. CT, p. 113.
16. Letter from Dylan to John Malcolm Brinnin, 28 May 1949, CL, pp. 708–9.
17. Footnote to CL, p. 719.
18. *Dylan Thomas: The Broadcasts*, p. 298.
19. Letter from Dylan to Bill and Helen McAlpine, 12 November 1949, CL, p. 727.

Chapter 11: The Pot of Gold (1950–1951)

1. Letter from Dylan to his parents, 26 February 1950, CL, p. 749.
2. JMB, p. 5.
3. Letter from Dylan to his parents, 26 February 1950, CL, p. 750.
4. Harold Norse, *Memoirs of a Bastard Angel*, p. 190.
5. JMB, p. 14.
6. Ibid., p. 15.
7. PF, p. 251.
8. JMB, p. 33.
9. Ibid., p. 35.
10. PF, p. 255.
11. Quoted in PF, p. 257.
12. Letter from Dylan to Caitlin, 11 March 1950, CL, p. 752.
13. Ray West in *San Francisco Fault*, 1972.
14. Letter from Dylan to Caitlin, April 1950, CL, p. 757.
15. Shelley Winters, *Best of Times, Worst of Times*, p. 31.
16. Letter from Dylan to Mr & Mrs John Nims, 17 July 1950, CL, p. 767.
17. Gwen Watkins, *Portrait of a Friend*, pp. 135–6.
18. CT, p. 145.
19. Ibid., p. 147.
20. Quoted in footnote to CL, p. 775.
21. Footnote to CL, p. 779.
22. Letter from Dylan to 'Pearl', 17 January 1951, CL, p. 786.
23. Letter from Dylan to Caitlin, ? January 1951, CL, p. 787.

Chapter 12: Beast, Angel, Madman (1951–1952)

1. CT, pp. 155–61.
2. Quoted in PF, p. 291.
3. CT, pp. 149–50.
4. Letter from Dylan to Princess Caetani, 20 March 1951, CL, p. 791.
5. Kingsley Amis, *Memoirs*, p. 134.
6. JMB, p. 110.
7. Ibid., pp. 123–4.
8. CT, p. 152.
9. Ibid., p. 161.
10. JMB, p. 141.
11. Ibid., p. 151.

12. CT, p. 166.
13. Letter from Dylan to John Malcolm Brinnin, 4 April 1952, CL, p. 827.
14. Earle Binney's recollections for BBC, quoted in CF, p. 352.
15. CT, p. 169.
16. Douglas Cleverdon, *The Growth of 'Milk Wood'*, p. 19.
17. CL, pp. 835–37.
18. Letter from Dylan to Alfred Janes, 5 January 1953, CL, p. 860.

Chapter 13: The Gates of Hell (1953)
1. Letter from Dylan to Charles Fry, 16 February 1953, CL, p. 868.
2. CT, pp. 172–3.
3. Aneirin Talfan Davies, 'The Golden Echo' in *Dock Leaves*, spring 1954.
4. Aeronwy Thomas-Ellis's unpublished recollections.
5. Footnote to CL, p. 882.
6. Daniel Jones, *My Friend Dylan Thomas*, pp. 79–80.
7. Letter from Dylan to John Malcolm Brinnin, 18 March 1953, CL, p. 879.
8. Author's telephone conversation with Stuart Thomas, 1993.
9. Quoted in PF, p. 318.
10. JMB, p. 212.
11. Robert Craft, *Stravinsky – Glimpses of a Life*, p. 55.
12. Robert Craft, *Conversations with Stravinsky*, quoted in CF, p. 386.
13. Letter from Dylan to Caitlin, ? May 1953, CL, p. 889.
14. Letter from Dylan to Liz Reitell, 16 June 1953, CL, p. 892.
15. Barbara Holdridge quoted in PF, p. 321.
16. Letter from Dylan to Oscar Williams, 22 June 1953, CL, p. 900.
17. CT, p. 86.
18. PF, p. 323.
19. Letter from Dylan to Daniel Jones, 24 August 1953, CL, p. 910.
20. Rob Gittins, *The Last Days of Dylan Thomas*, p. 17.
21. JMB, p. 226.
22. E. F. Bozman, 'Dylan Thomas' in *Books*, December 1953.
23. CF, pp. 390–1.
24. Rob Gittins, *The Last Days of Dylan Thomas*, p. 58.
25. JMB, p. 255.
26. Rob Gittins, *The Last Days of Dylan Thomas*, p. 77.
27. JMB, p. 259.
28. Ibid., p. 263.
29. Charles H. Miller, *Auden – an American Friendship*, p. 108.
30. JMB, p. 265.
31. Ibid., p. 272.
32. Rob Gittins, *The Last Days of Dylan Thomas*, p. 161.
33. JMB, p. 285.
34. Ibid., p. 293.

Postscript: The Aftermath
1. Quoted in Rob Gittins, *The Last Days of Dylan Thomas*, p. 197.
2. CT, p. 191.
3. Daniel Jones, *My Friend Dylan Thomas*, p. 1.

BIBLIOGRAPHY

The place of publication is London unless otherwise stated.

Books by Dylan Thomas
18 Poems (Sunday Referee and Parton Bookshop, 1934)
Twenty-five Poems (J. M. Dent, 1936)
The Map of Love (J. M. Dent, 1939)
Portrait of the Artist as a Young Dog (J. M. Dent, 1940)
Deaths and Entrances (J. M. Dent, 1946)
Collected Poems 1934–1952 (J. M. Dent, 1952)
The Doctor and the Devils (J. M. Dent, 1953)
Under Milk Wood (J. M. Dent, 1954)
Quite Early One Morning (J. M. Dent, 1954)
Adventures in the Skin Trade (Putnam, New York, 1955)
A Prospect of the Sea (J. M. Dent, 1955)
Letters to Vernon Watkins (J. M. Dent and Faber and Faber, 1957)
The Beach at Falesa (Jonathan Cape, 1964)
Twenty Years A-Growing (J. M. Dent, 1964)
Rebecca's Daughters (Triton, 1965)
Me and My Bike (Triton, 1965)
Poet in the Making: The Notebooks of Dylan Thomas (J. M. Dent, 1968)
Dylan Thomas: Early Prose Writings, ed. Walford Davies (J. M. Dent, 1971)
The Death of the King's Canary, with John Davenport (Hutchinson, 1976)
Collected Letters, ed. Paul Ferris (J. M. Dent, 1985)
Dylan Thomas: The Notebook Poems 1930–1934, ed. Ralph Maud (J. M. Dent, 1989)
Dylan Thomas: The Broadcasts, ed. Ralph Maud (J. M. Dent, 1991)

Other Works
Abse, Dannie, *A Poet in the Family* (Hutchinson, 1974)
Ackerman, John, *A Dylan Thomas Companion* (Macmillan, 1991)
   Dylan Thomas, His Life and Work (Macmillan, 1991)
Amis, Kingsley, *Memoirs* (Hutchinson, 1991)

BIBLIOGRAPHY

Arlott, John, *Basingstoke Boy* (Willow Books, 1990)
Brinnin, John Malcolm, *Dylan Thomas in America* (Arlington, 1988)
Cleverdon, Douglas, *The Growth of 'Milk Wood'* (J. M. Dent, 1969)
Craft, Robert, *Stravinsky – Glimpses of a Life* (Lime Tree, 1992)
David, Hugh, *The Fitzrovians* (Michael Joseph, 1988)
Davies, Aneirin Talfan, *Dylan: Druid of the Broken Body* (J. M. Dent, 1964)
Davies, James A., *Dylan Thomas's Places* (Christopher Davies, 1987)
Davies, Walford, *Dylan Thomas* (University of Wales Press, Cardiff, 1972)
Devas, Nicolette, *Two Flamboyant Fathers* (Collins, 1966)
Farson, Daniel, *Soho in the Fifties* (Michael Joseph, 1987)
Ferris, Paul, *Dylan Thomas* (Hodder and Stoughton, 1977)
FitzGibbon, Constantine, *The Life of Dylan Thomas* (J. M. Dent, 1965)
Gittins, Rob, *The Last Days of Dylan Thomas* (Macdonald, 1986)
Grigson, Geoffrey, *Recollections* (Chatto and Windus/Hogarth Press, 1984)
Hansford Johnson, Pamela, *Important to Me* (Macmillan, 1974)
Heath-Stubbs, John, *Hindsights* (Hodder and Stoughton, 1993)
Heppenstall, Rayner, *Four Absentees* (Barrie and Rockcliff, 1960)
Hewison, Robert, *Under Siege* (Weidenfeld & Nicolson, 1977)
Higham, David, *Literary Gent* (Jonathan Cape, 1978)
Holbrook, David, *Llareggub Revisited* (Bowes and Bowes, 1962)
Holroyd, Michael, *Augustus John* (Heinemann, 1974)
Jones, Daniel, *My Friend Dylan Thomas* (J. M. Dent, 1977)
Jones, Gwyn, *Background to Dylan Thomas* (Oxford University Press, Oxford, 1992)
Luke, Michael, *David Tennant and the Gargoyle Years* (Weidenfeld & Nicolson, 1991)
Maclaren-Ross, Julian, *Memoirs of the Forties* (Alan Ross, 1965)
Maud, Ralph, *Dylan Thomas in Print* (J. M. Dent, 1970)
Maud, Ralph, *Entrances to Dylan Thomas's Poetry* (Scorpion Press, 1963)
McKenna, Rollie, *Portrait of Dylan* (J. M. Dent, 1982)
Miller, Charles H., *Auden, an American Friendship* (Scribner, New York, 1983)
Norris, Leslie, (ed.), *Vernon Watkins 1906–1967* (Faber and Faber, 1970)
Norse, Harold, *Memoirs of a Bastard Angel* (Bloomsbury, 1990)
Pratt, Annis, *Dylan Thomas' Early Prose* (University of Pittsburgh Press, Pittsburgh, 1970)
Read, Bill and McKenna, Rollie, *The Days of Dylan Thomas* (Weidenfeld & Nicolson, 1965)
Sanesi, Roberto, *Dylan Thomas* (Lerici, Milan, 1960)
Sinclair, Andrew, *Dylan Thomas: Poet of His People* (Michael Joseph, 1975)
    War Like a Wasp (Hamish Hamilton, 1989)
Sitwell, Edith (ed. John Lehmann and Derek Parker), *Selected Letters* (Macmillan, 1970)
Stanford, Derek, *Dylan Thomas*, (Neville Spearman, 1954)
Taylor, A. J. P., *A Personal History* (Hamish Hamilton, 1983)
Tedlock, E. W. (ed.), *Dylan Thomas: The Legend and the Poet* (Heinemann, 1960)
Thomas, Caitlin, *Leftover Life to Kill* (Putnam, New York, 1957)
    Not Quite Posthumous Letter to My Daughter (Putnam, New York, 1963)
    (with George Tremlett), *Caitlin – Life with Dylan Thomas* (Secker and Warburg, 1986)
Treece, Henry, *Dylan Thomas: Dog among the Fairies* (Ernest Benn, 1949)
Tremlett, George, *Dylan Thomas* (Constable, 1991)
Watkins, Gwen, *Portrait of a Friend* (Gomer Press, 1983)

INDEX

271